Constitutional Law in Japan

AF703818

Constitutional Law in Japan

Second Edition

Hiroyuki Hata†

Go Nakagawa†

Takehisa Nakagawa

Hiromi Nishimura

Takayoshi Okada

This book was originally published as a monograph in the International Encyclopaedia of Laws/Constitutional Law.

Founding Editor: Roger Blanpain
General Editor: Frank Hendrickx
Volume Editors: André Alen & David Haljan

Wolters Kluwer

Published by:
Kluwer Law International B.V.
PO Box 316
2400 AH Alphen aan den Rijn
The Netherlands
E-mail: lrs-sales@wolterskluwer.com
Website: www.wolterskluwer.com/en/solutions/kluwerlawinternational

Sold and distributed by:
Wolters Kluwer Legal & Regulatory U.S.
920 Links Avenue
Landisville, PA 17538
United States of America
Email: customer.service@wolterskluwer.com

DISCLAIMER: The material in this volume is in the nature of general comment only. It is not offered as advice on any particular matter and should not be taken as such. The editor and the contributing authors expressly disclaim all liability to any person with regard to anything done or omitted to be done, and with respect to the consequences of anything done or omitted to be done wholly or partly in reliance upon the whole or any part of the contents of this volume. No reader should act or refrain from acting on the basis of any matter contained in this volume without first obtaining professional advice regarding the particular facts and circumstances at issue. Any and all opinions expressed herein are those of the particular author and are not necessarily those of the editor or publisher of this volume.

ISBN 978-94-035-4608-7

e-Book: ISBN 978-94-035-4618-6
web-PDF: ISBN 978-94-035-4628-5

© 2024 Kluwer Law International BV, The Netherlands

All rights reserved. No part of this publication may be reproduced, stored in a retrieval system, or transmitted in any form or by any means, electronic, mechanical, photocopying, recording, or otherwise, without the prior written permission of the publisher.

Permission to use this content must be obtained from the copyright owner. More information can be found at: www.wolterskluwer.com/en/solutions/legal-regulatory/permissions-reprints-and-licensing

The Authors

Originally by:

Professor Hiroyuki Hata† (born on January 18, 1930) is Professor Emeritus of Hiroshima University and Kinki University in Osaka, Japan. Professor Hata pursued his undergraduate (1950–1954) and graduate (1955–1960) legal studies at Kyoto University before being appointed to the Law Faculty of Hiroshima University in 1960. In 1961, he was promoted to the rank of Assistant Professor; in 1966 to Associate Professor, and in 1972 to full Professor. At Hiroshima University, he taught Comparative Constitutional Law as well as Japanese Constitutional Law. He was the head of the University's Research Institute for Higher Education (1985–1987) and served as Dean of the Faculty of Law from 1987 to 1991. Upon his retirement in 1994, he was appointed Professor Emeritus in recognition of his contribution to the University.

Professor Hata engaged in research at such foreign universities as Harvard University (1963–1964), Columbia University (1970–1971), the University of Hawaii (1986) and the University of Munich (1991), and taught U.S.-Japan Comparative Constitutional Law at the University of Hawaii (fall semester of 1993–1994). Professor Hata has won wide recognition for his work in Comparative Constitutional Law, particularly in regard to State Emergency Power, Judicial Review and Civil Rights. He has published many books on Constitutional Law, his most recent books are *American Government and the United States Supreme Court* (1992) and *Forum in Constitutional Law* (1994). On the international scene, he has presented papers at such prestigious conferences as the Higher Education seminar of OECDICERI (Boston, 1986), the International Conference on "Influence of the US Constitution on Pacific Nations" (Maui, Hawaii, 1987), World Congress of the International Association of Constitutional Law (Warsaw, 1991), among others.

Professor Hata served as Director or Councillor of various national scholarly associations, including the Japan Public Law Association, the Japanese-American Society for Legal Studies, the Japan Human Rights Law Association, etc.

In addition, he has served as head of administrative commissions and councils. In 1994, Kyoto University accorded Professor Hata an LLD degree. He taught Japanese

Constitutional Law at Kinki University, Osaka, Japan. He has served as the President (2004–2012) and the President Emeritus (2012–2016) of the same university.

Professor Hiroyuhiki Hata passed away in September 2023.

Professor Go Nakagawa† (born on February 24, 1934) was educated at the Faculty of Law, Kyoto University (1954–1957), and earned his LLM in Public Law (1959) and his LLD (1967) at the same University. He started teaching at the Osaka Prefectural University as a full-time Lecturer in 1962, joined the Law Faculty of Hiroshima University as an Associate Professor in 1967, and was promoted to full Professor in 1972. His teaching subjects covered administrative law, local government law and constitutional law. As a Visiting Scholar, he was affiliated with the University of Chicago, Stanford University, the University of California, Berkeley, the University of the Philippines, Thammasat University, the University of Hawaii and other universities. His highly acclaimed research covered many fields, especially comparative constitutional law, local government law and legal anthropology.

Professor Nakagawa published numerous books. Among them are *Fundamental Human Rights* (1991), *History of Local Government* (1990), *Japanese Legal Culture* (1989), *Philippino Psychology and Behavior* (1986), *Japanese Constitutional Law* (1985), *Chonaikai The Japanese Local Communities* (1983), *A Study of Executive Power* (1978) and *Comparative Constitutionalism* (1972). Though all of them are written in Japanese, *Chonaikai* has been quoted in foreign scholarly books. *Philippino Psychology and Behavior* has been deemed one of the best books about the Philippines for Japanese businesspeople stationed there. *Japanese Legal Culture* has been introduced on TV and remains one of his best-known books. He actively participated in international and domestic academic meetings, presenting papers on many occasions.

Joining the Educational Radio Program in Hiroshima, Professor Nakagawa gave a number of lectures on the radio. His serial radio lecture *Law and Culture* won him a prize in the nationwide contest of Educational Radio Programs (1988). He served as chair or vice-chair of such administrative commissions or committees as Hiroshima Prefecture's Land Expropriation Commission and Youth Education Committee, Hiroshima City's Steering Committee of Municipal Archives, etc. In the academic field, he also served as a director of the Japan Public Law Association and the Japan Finance Law Association. He was a visiting research fellow of the Foundation of Local Government Development in Manila and an executive member of EROPA in Japan. He served as a councillor of Hiroshima University (1991–1992) and director of the evening courses of Hiroshima University (1987–1989).

Uniquely among legal scholars, Professor Nakagawa was known as a fine prose writer in Japan, having published several novels and short stories and contributed a number of essays to various journals and magazines.

Professor Go Nakagawa passed away in February 1995.

Updated by:

Professor Takehisa Nakagawa (born on January 1, 1964), the eldest son of Professor Go Nakagawa, is a professor of law at the Graduate School/ Faculty of Law, Kobe University, Kobe, Japan. He received his BA (Law, 1986) and his LLM (1988) from the University of Tokyo, Tokyo, Japan, and earned an LLM (1990) from Harvard Law School in Cambridge, Massachusetts. He joined Kobe University Faculty of Law in 1993 as an Associate Professor and was promoted to Full Professor in 1999. From 1996 to 1998, he was a visiting scholar at Columbia University School of Law in New York City. He served as Dean of the School of Law/ Faculty of Law from 2015 to 2017.

His principal area of interest is public law, emphasizing administrative law, local government law, constitutional law, and the United States public law. He has written on a broad range of public law topics, including separation of powers, administrative litigation, governmental torts, governmental organizations, administrative procedures, and informal activities of administrative agencies (e.g., administrative guidance). His publications in Japanese include Gyosei-Tetsuzuki To Gyosei-Shido ("Administrative Procedure and Administrative Guidance: Comparative Law Analysis") (Yuhikaku Pub. Co., Tokyo, Japan 2000) and Hokaisyaku-no-Hohoron ("Legal Interpretation: Current Aspects and Future Prospects") (Yuhikaku Pub. Co., Tokyo, Japan 2021). His English publications include an article entitled "Administrative Informality in Japan: Governmental Activities Outside Statutory Authorization," in *Administrative Law Review*, Vol. 52 No. 1 pp. 175–211 (2000). He has done extensive research on comparative legal systems and has served on and provided assistance to various committees of both the Japanese government and local governments.

The Authors

Professor Hiromi Nishimura (born on May 1, 1951) is Professor Emeritus of Hiroshima University, Japan. He received a BA in political science (1975) from the Faculty of Political Science and Economics, Hiroshima University and earned an LLM (1978) from the Graduate School of Law of the same university. He started teaching at the Osaka Prefectural University as a full-time Lecturer in 1981 and was promoted to full Professor in 1992. Then he joined the Graduate School of Social Sciences of Hiroshima University as a Full Professor in 2004.

He engaged in research of American constitutional law at such universities as the University of California, Berkeley (1982–1983) and Duke University Law School (1983–1984) on the Social Science International Fellowship sponsored by the International House of Japan. He has taught Japanese constitutional law compared to American constitutional law. He also contributed to the mutual academic exchanges in research and education with foreign universities, especially French universities like Burgundy University and Tours University, by giving lectures on Japanese constitutional litigations, based on the agreements between them in 2012–2018.

He has published books like the following; Hanrei De Manabu Nihonkoku-Kenpo (Studying The Constitution of Japan Through Courts' Decisions, 3rd Edition) (Yushindo Pub. Co., Tokyo, Japan, 2024) and Rigaru-Maindo-Nyumon (The Introduction to Legal Mind, 2nd Edition) (Yushindo Pub. Co., Tokyo, Japan, 2019).

Professor Takayoshi Okada (born on December 17, 1977) is a Professor at the Prefectural University of Hiroshima, Hiroshima, Japan. He received a PhD from Osaka Prefectural University, Osaka, Japan, in 2006. He joined the Prefectural University of Hiroshima as a Lecturer in 2011 and was promoted to Associate Professor in 2017 and Full Professor in 2021.

Professor Okada specializes in constitutional law, with a particular interest in the problems faced by social minorities and vulnerable groups (e.g., the elderly, the sexual minorities, the disabled), and studies their legal remedies with reference to American law. In recent years, he has co-authored two books, Hanrei De Manabu Nihonkoku-Kenpo (Studying The Constitution of Japan Through Courts' Decisions 3rd Edition) (Yushindo Pub. Co., Tokyo, Japan, 2024) and Rigaru-Maindo-Nyumon (The Introduction to Legal Mind, 2nd Edition) (Yushindo Pub. Co., Tokyo, Japan, 2019), both edited by Professor Nishimura.

Table of Contents

List of Abbreviations

ACL Act	Administrative Case Litigation Act
AICRR	Act on Immigration Control and the Recognition of Refugees
ASMDP	Act on the Special Measures for Dowa Projects
Br.	Branch of a District Court (judgment of)
Dist. Ct.	District Court (judgment of)
DPJ	Democratic Party of Japan
G.B.	Grand Bench (Supreme Court Judgment)
GHQ	General Headquarters for the Allied Powers
High Ct.	High Court (judgment of)
ICCPR	International Covenant on Civil and Political Rights
ICESCR	International Covenant on Economic, Social and Cultural Rights
JSP	Japan Socialist Party
LDP	Liberal Democratic Party
PKO Cooperation Act	Act Concerning the Cooperation for United Nations Peace Keeping Operation
SAICTDJN	Special Act on Immigration Control of Those Divested of Japanese Nationality Based on the Conclusion of the Peace Treaty with Japan
SCAP	Supreme Commander for the Allied Powers
SDP	Social Democratic Party
Sup. Ct.	Supreme Court (judgment of)
Case Reporters	
Gyoshu	*Gyosei Saiban Reishu*
Kakeishu	*Saiko Saibansho Keiji Hanreishu*
Kaminshu	*Kakyu Saibansho Minji Saiban Reishu*
Keishu	*Saiko Saibansho Keiji Hanreishu*
Minshu	*Saiko Saibansho Minji Hanreishu*
Rominshu	*Rodo Kankei Minji Saiban Reishu*

List of Abbreviations

Shumin	*Saiko Saibansho Saibanshu Minji*
Periodicals	
Hanji	*Hanrei Jiho*
Hanta	*Hanrei Times*

General Introduction

by Prof. Go Nakagawa with updates by Prof. Takehisa Nakagawa

§1. A Brief History of the Japanese Constitutions

I. The Constitution of the Empire of Japan

1. Modern Japan has seen two constitutions outgrow the older regimes. The first Constitution of 1890, the so-called Meiji Constitution, was drafted after a thorough study of western constitutional laws by a group of Japanese scholars and government officials headed by Hirobumi Ito. The official title of the Meiji Constitution was "Constitution of the Empire of Japan." (In a traditional dating system unique to Japan, "eras" are associated with the individual names of Emperors. The term *Meiji* refers to one of such eras.) It was a product of the modernization movement of Japan, the Meiji Restoration, which began in 1868 and was strongly influenced by the Prussian Constitution.

2. The form of government stipulated by the Meiji Constitution was a constitutional monarchy. It was declared that the Empire of Japan was to be reigned over and governed by "an unbroken line of Emperors of the one and same dynasty" that had its beginnings in ancient times.

In political reality, however, Japanese Emperors, or *Tenno*, had long been ceremonial monarchs whose function was to preside at sacred rites and time-honored cultural events. Although the Meiji Constitution prescribed that the Emperor combined the whole sovereign power in himself, Japanese monarchs in modern times have exerted their powers only in a limited way. It is quite misleading to assume that Japan had long been governed by absolute monarchs like *Mikado* as portrayed in Gilbert and Sullivan's famous opera. The government and the throne were separated in Japanese political history as early as the thirteenth century.

This tradition of the political dualism of power and authority has been duly included in the various Japanese constitutional settings. Even during the pre-World War II period, which is often characterized as a time of totalitarianism, such dualism existed.

3. It is generally conceded that the Meiji Constitution was fatally vulnerable to the military abuse of governmental powers which, in turn, led to the fall of the Empire itself through World War II. Subsequent firm rejection of militarism is reflected in the current constitution.

II. The Constitution of Japan

4. Japan's second and current constitution was made during the occupation period after World War II. In the Potsdam Declaration (1945), the principal Allied powers, who were to determine the future of Japan after her unconditional surrender, declared:

> The Japanese government shall remove all obstacles to the revival and strengthening of democratic tendencies among the Japanese people. Freedom of speech, religion, and thought, as well as respect for fundamental human rights shall be established.
>
> The occupying forces of the Allies shall be withdrawn from Japan as soon as these objectives have been accomplished and there has been established in accordance with the freely expressed will of the Japanese people a peacefully inclined and responsible government.

It was clear that the Japanese people were expected to undertake their own governmental reforms. Though the Declaration was silent about the Meiji Constitution, it was generally assumed that the Constitution of the Empire needed substantial revision to adjust itself to the new international environment.

5. In 1945, General Douglas MacArthur, Supreme Commander for the Allied Powers (SCAP), suggested the amendment of the Meiji Constitution to Prime Minister Shidehara. Dr. Matsumoto, Minister of State at the time, headed a committee for drafting such an amendment. Unofficial drafting for revision was also undertaken by various political organizations and private groups.

The so-called Matsumoto draft, proposed by the Cabinet, was not welcomed by the General Headquarters (GHQ) for the Allied Powers. The draft was judged not to show an intention to democratize the older constitutional system sufficiently. Thus, MacArthur rejected the Matsumoto draft in 1946 and decided that the GHQ itself should prepare a draft constitution.

6. MacArthur left the draft preparation to Brigadier-General Whitney, Chief of Government Section of the GHQ, with the instruction that three major principles were to be incorporated in the draft. These principles have been called "MacArthur's Three Doctrines." They were as follows:

(1) The Emperor is the head of the State. His succession is dynastic. His duties and powers will be exercised in accordance with the Constitution and responsible to the basic will of the people as provided therein.

(2) War as a sovereign right of the nation is abolished. Japan renounces it as an instrumentality for settling its disputes and even for preserving its own security. It relies upon the higher ideals that are now stirring the world for its defense and its protection. No Japanese Army, Navy, or Air Force will ever be authorized and no rights of belligerency will ever be conferred upon any Japanese force.
(3) The feudal system of Japan will cease. No rights of peerage except those of the Imperial family will extend beyond the lives of those now existent. No patent of nobility will from this time forth embody within itself any National or Civic power of Government. Pattern budget after the British system.

The Government Section of the GHQ worked from February 4 to 10, 1946, and their draft was submitted to the Supreme Commander for his approval. Approved by MacArthur, the draft was handed to the representatives of the Japanese government. They were told that the Japanese government did not need to take further action in revising the Meiji Constitution. They understood this to be a directive rather than mere advice and hence were deeply embarrassed.

7. The Japanese government prepared a new draft of the constitution which was substantially similar to the one drafted by the GHQ. While Japanese people suspected that it had been written under the pressure of the GHQ, the new Cabinet draft received a favorable response from the people. Only the Communist Party was strongly opposed to the draft. The government submitted the draft to the Imperial Diet that consisted of the House of Representatives and the House of Peers formed under the Meiji Constitution. The Cabinet persisted in its efforts to get the Bill of Constitutional Amendment through the Diet. After approval by both Houses and the Privy Council attended by the Emperor, the new constitution was promulgated on November 3, 1946, which happened to be the anniversary of the birth of Emperor Meiji. It came into effect in 1947.

§2. Profile of the Government

I. Conversion of the Constitutional Principles

8. Mainly based upon Anglo-American ideas, the new Constitution of 1947 declares the following principles: the sovereignty of the people, inviolability of fundamental human rights, and supremacy of the Constitution. It also declares renunciation of war as a sovereign right of the nation. The maintenance of any armed forces is now banned. MacArthur's Three Doctrines were subtly transformed and incorporated into the present constitution. The sovereignty of the people, renunciation of war, and guarantee of fundamental human rights are not traceable to the Meiji Constitution.

The Emperor has become the symbol of the State and his functions are rigidly restricted. The bicameral Diet, which consists of elected members, has become "the highest organ of state power" (Article 44). Under the system of parliamentary government, the executive power is vested in the Cabinet headed by the Prime Minister, while the Emperor holds no governmental power. The judicial power is vested in the Supreme Court and lower courts, which also may exercise a newly created power of judicial review of the constitutionality of governmental actions, including statutes. Since the GHQ complained that the Matsumoto draft had contained no provision for local self-government, the new Constitution has established local autonomy as one of the major political principles.[1]

II. Sovereignty of the People

9. As a matter of procedure, the enactment of the Constitution of 1947 took the form of the amendment of the Constitution of the Empire of Japan (Meiji Constitution). In substance, however, it shifted the basic political doctrine of Japan from monarchical sovereignty to popular sovereignty. Article 1 of the 1947 Constitution declares, "The Emperor shall be the symbol of the State and the unity of the people, deriving his position from the will of the people with whom resides sovereign power." Incidentally, peerage and privileges accompanied by awards and honors were abolished and all the people were made equal under the law (Article 14).

In accordance with the democratization of the government and society, it was declared that family laws should be enacted from the standpoint of individual dignity and the essential equality of the two sexes (Article 24). Article 13 states, "All the people shall be respected as individuals." Many Japanese constitutional scholars generally understood this provision to be a manifesto of western type individualism.

10. At the outset of modern Japan, back in the mid-nineteenth century when the Meiji era started, establishing a powerful central government was inevitable. It was considered that the authority of the government had to be based on a firm ideological ground, which the Shogunate could not implement. *Tenno*, formerly a religious master whose authority could be traced back to the ancient myths, was agreed to be the only persona qualified as a national leader. Based on the *kokutai* (national polity) theory that evolved out of the study of Japanese classics, *Tenno*, designated as "Emperor" in the text of the Meiji Constitution, was assumed to be heavenly descended, divine, and sacred. At the same time, as a constitutional monarch, he was expected to pay due respect to the law.[2]

11. It was one of MacArthur's directives to his men that made sure that the Emperor system was preserved in the process of drafting the new Japanese constitution.

---

1. Supreme Commander for the Allied Powers, *Political Reorientation of Japan, September 1945 to September 1948*, Vol. I, 100 (Greenwood Press Publishers 1970).
2. H. Ito, *Commentaries on the Constitution of the Empire of Japan* 7 (Chuo-Daigaku 1909; reprinted University Publications of America, Inc. 1979).

Article 1 of the new Constitution of Japan provides that the Emperor shall be the symbol of the State and of the unity of the people. It further clarifies that sovereignty, the ultimate authority of the State, is vested in the people, from whose will the position of the Emperor derives. Also, based upon the theory of social contract, which produced the United States Constitution in 1787, the Preamble of the Constitution of Japan solemnly confirmed the sovereignty of the people.

12. However, there remains a problem of whether popular sovereignty is nominal or substantive: whether it is a synonym of a parliamentary government or that of the constituent power of the people. Although Article 41 declares that the Diet shall be the highest organ of the State power, such power is not concentrated in the Diet. Instead, it is shared by three major branches of government based on the principle of separation of powers. Most significantly, even the acts of the Diet may be declared void by the judiciary. Supremacy of the Diet prescribed in Article 41 is inconsistent with the actual constitutional system elaborated in other provisions of the Constitution. What the drafters really meant by Article 41 was, it may be assumed, not to establish impeccable popular sovereignty but rather to repeal monarchical sovereignty and to degrade the Emperor from the highest organ of the State. In any event, it is fairly probable that the drafters forgot to complete the picture of popular sovereignty and failed to flesh out parliamentary supremacy.

III. Renunciation of War

13. It is said that the Constitution places unusual emphasis on the peaceful cooperation of the Japanese people with other nations, the horror of war, and pacifism. These features are found in the preamble and Article 9 of the Constitution.

The unique and controversial war renunciation clause of Article 9 seems to be the offspring of MacArthur's Three Doctrines quoted above. However, MacArthur, at later dates, repeatedly insisted that it was Prime Minister Shidehara who first proposed the idea of the war renunciation clause. Given all the evidence available, Shidehara could not have made a proposal of that kind. When Shidehara visited MacArthur at his office, the Japanese government had already begun working on its draft of the constitutional amendment and the draft did not contain even a line of pacifist thinking.

It is inconceivable that the Prime Minister who was presiding over the Cabinet meetings substantially denounced his own government's draft of the Constitution. It is more reasonable to believe that MacArthur, who had originally wanted to disarm Japan forever but subsequently became disillusioned with the idea of peaceful coexistence with the communist countries in the face of the Korean War, tried to shuffle off upon Shidehara the responsibility for the inclusion of utopian pacifism in the Constitution. (To be accurate, however, the war renunciation clause of the Constitution may duly be characterized as more unilateral than utopian.)

14. Article 9 of the Constitution is unique in two ways. It declares the renunciation of all types of war. It was construed, at least during the occupation period, as abolishing even a war of self-defense and thus no war potential was allowed to Japan.

The full text of Article 9 runs as follows:

> Aspiring sincerely to an international peace based on justice and order, the Japanese people forever renounce war as a sovereign right of the nation and the threat or use of force as means of settling international disputes.
>
> In order to accomplish the aim of the preceding paragraph, land, sea, and air forces, as well as other war potential, will never be maintained. The right of belligerency of the State will not be recognized.

Consequently, emergency power is granted neither to the Cabinet nor to any other governmental organ. In a time of national emergency, the Cabinet is authorized only to convoke the House of Councillors in emergency sessions when the House of Representatives is dissolved (Article 54, paragraph 2). In order to root out all possibilities to abuse emergency power, the drafters of the Constitution seem to have gone so far as to expel emergency power from the text of the Constitution for fear of a revival of a militaristic government.[3]

15. Article 9 suggests that Japan renounces war even for defensive purposes and dispenses with armed forces to avoid any suspicion that she could again be a menace to world peace. Such had been the common understanding between MacArthur and the Japanese government. Subsequently, however, the international situation changed. MacArthur, on New Year's Day of 1950, expressed his newly developed view that the Constitution never denied the inalienable right of self-defense. The Japanese government then came to share his opinion, and with the purpose of legalization of modest rearmament started a new construction of the first phrase of the second paragraph of Article 9, which had been inserted by the Diet as a constitutional convention as suggested by an assembly member Ashida.

The first paragraph came to be construed that it denied only offensive war. Accordingly, the second paragraph, which starts with the phrase "in order to accomplish the aim of the first paragraph," was interpreted to prohibit the maintenance of forces and other war potentials exclusively for offensive purposes, while the maintenance of forces and other war potentials for defensive purposes was not prohibited.

16. The Supreme Court has cautiously refrained from deciding on the constitutionality of the Self-Defense Forces while accepting the constitutionality of the military bases of the United States Armed Forces in Japan under the Security Treaty between the two nations. The Supreme Court recognized the inherent right of self-defense of a sovereign State in the *Sunagawa* case (13 *Keishu* 3225, Sup. Ct., G.B.,

---

3. A.C. Oppler, *Legal Reform in Occupied Japan* 60 (Princeton University Press 1976).

December 16, 1959).[4] In the same case, it refused to consider the constitutionality of the Security Treaty because it held this to be a political question duly reserved for the political branches of the government.

The war renunciation clause remains a subject of grave political disputes. A lower court (District Court of Sapporo) once held the Self-Defense Forces unconstitutional in 1973. There was strong opposition from the leftist parties against the dispatch to the Persian Gulf area in 1991 of Self-Defense Forces' minesweepers.

IV. Guarantees of Fundamental Human Rights

17. Inspired by the idea of the social contract, the Constitution in Article 97 declares that fundamental human rights are eternal and inviolable rights conferred upon the people of present and future generations. Fundamental human rights are conceived of as "fruits of the age-old struggle of man to be free," and therefore, "to be held for all time inviolate." This idea of fundamental human rights was based on the same theory which underlies the Bill of Rights of the United States Constitution.

18. On the level of political ideology, fundamental human rights are equivalent to natural rights under natural law which is of Christian origin. Since natural law is another wording of the divine law, fundamental human rights are almost synonymous with natural rights, and thus, should be deemed as eternal and inviolable. As John Locke concluded, no human sanction can be good or valid against the fundamental law of Nature or the natural law.

Unfortunately, the Japanese people had not been acquainted with the idea of the natural law as defined by Locke. They could understand human rights only in their own governmental and social environments. For them, freedom was not much different from mere selfishness. Rousseauism was introduced to Japan back in 1882, and at that time, the natural rights were titled "heaven-sent" human rights. However, there was no idea of an Almighty God as the ultimate source of natural law and the natural rights thereof. Hence, Rousseau's theories were adjusted to the polytheistic religious climate of Japan. The idea of inherent human rights was viewed to have derived not from a Creator but from social justice which, in turn, referred to the elimination of social and economic inequalities among people.

Thus the Bill of Rights founded upon the idea of the social contract on the one hand and the social rights based on the idea of social justice on the other can be easily mixed in the Japanese legal mentality. Chapter 3 of the Constitution of Japan, which lists the "rights and duties" of the people, has been accepted as a catalog of heaven-sent civil liberties, while it also contains "government-wrought" human rights such as the right to a decent living, the right to work, workers' right to organize, and the right to educational opportunities.

---

4. Supreme Court of Japan, "Judgment upon the so-called *Sunagawa Case*," *Series of Prominent Judgments of the Supreme Court upon Questions of Constitutionality*, No. 4 (General Secretariat, Supreme Court of Japan, Tokyo 1960).

Therefore, strictly speaking, the rights and freedoms included in Chapter 3 of the Constitution do not necessarily correspond to the traditional notion of the Bill of Rights. Chapter 3 is a compilation of human rights and duties in man-made law and is rightly titled "Rights and Duties of the People."

19. The fundamental rights in the Constitution are classified into two groups: personal rights of liberty and social rights. The first group, which is based on a classical *laissez-faire* conception of civil liberty, is further divided into three categories: rights and freedoms for political, economic, and social activities; rights of claim to the government; and rights related to criminal justice. The second group of fundamental rights is the social rights emanating from social justice designed to promote the welfare of all the people through adequate governmental measures.

20. Regarding the first group of personal rights of liberty, its first category covers freedom from involuntary servitude except as punishment for a crime (Article 18); freedom of thought and conscience (Article 19); freedom of religion (Article 20); freedom of assembly and association as well as speech, press, and all other forms of expression (Article 21); freedom to choose one's residence and occupation (Article 22, paragraph 1); freedom to emigrate and to change nationality (Article 22, paragraph 2); academic freedom (Article 23); and the right to own property (Article 29, paragraph 1).

The second category relates to claims to the government and comprises the right to choose and dismiss public officials (Article 15, paragraph 1); the right of peaceful petition (Article 16); the right to sue the State or a public entity for damage resulting from the illegal act of any public official (Article 17); the right to claim just compensation for the taking of private property (Article 29, paragraph 3); and the right to criminal compensation in case acquitted (Article 40). The third category consists of rights which mostly concern protection from abuses of criminal prosecutions. These include the procedural right to be immune from criminal penalty except according to procedures established by law (Article 31); the right of access to the courts (Article 32); the right to be free from arrest except upon warrant issued by a competent judicial officer, excluding the case of a flagrant delict (Article 33); the right to be free from search and seizure except as provided by Article 33 (Article 35); the right to be informed of the charges and the right to counsel, when arrested (Article 34); the right to a speedy, public, and fair trial in all criminal cases and the right to secure or to be assigned a competent counsel when accused (Article 37); the privilege against self-incrimination (Article 38); and the immunity against double jeopardy (Article 39).

21. The idea of social rights has evolved since the Weimar Constitution of 1919. It may be said that the New Dealers assembled at the GHQ during the occupation period were aspiring to see their ideas realized in postwar Japan. Social rights clauses were easily accepted by the Japanese, a number of whom were close to starvation. As a matter of historical fact, the Japanese had long been conscious of the gravity of their worsening social problems. It was a happy concurrence of constitutional attitudes.

Such social rights in the Constitution consist of the right to maintain the minimum standards of wholesome and cultured living (Article 25); the right to receive an equal education corresponding to one's ability (Article 26); the right to work (Article 27); and the right of workers to organize, bargain, and act collectively (Article 28).

22. As a product of mass society, several "newly created human rights" have come into discussion. Among them are the right to know, the right to privacy, consumers' rights, and the right to a healthy environment.

These rights are assumed to be implicit in Article 13 and other articles of the Constitution. Since the Constitution of Japan has never been amended, a somewhat liberal interpretation has been deemed necessary to rank such new rights among the specifically listed constitutional rights. Though often referred to by the courts, these newly created rights are still in the process of legitimization.

§3. National Data and Symbols

I. Territory

23. Japan, or *Nippon* in Japanese, is located off the East coast of northern Asia, lying between longitude 156° 31 east and 124° west, and between latitude 24° 3 south and 45° 30 north. Japan has a total area of 377,819 km^2, including the so-called Northern Territories and Takeshima.

Though the national territory has never been specified in any of the Japanese constitutions, it consists of Hokkaido, which borders on Sakhalin and some other islands currently under Russian control; Honshu (meaning Mainland), which is the largest of all the islands and where the national capital Tokyo is located; Shikoku (which means four provinces); Kyushu (which means nine provinces), which faces the Korean Peninsula and the East China Sea; Okinawa, where several of the major United States military bases are established; and other numerous small islands.

For a long time, Japanese people have awaited the return of the Northern Territories, which are several of the Kurile Islands, namely, Kunashir, O. Iturup, Shikotan, and Habomai-Shoto. These islands have been continuously occupied since the end of World War II, first by the Soviet government and now by the Russian government. Takeshima, located in the Sea of Japan, is now claimed by Japan and South Korea.

II. People

24. As of October 1, 2020, Japan has a population of 126,146,000 (123,399,000 excluding foreigners). The number of households is placed at 55,705,000, and the average number of members in a household is 2.21. The population growth in the twentieth century has been accumulated in urban areas while the population of rural areas has been declining. The striking imbalance between the overpopulation in urban areas and the underpopulation in the countryside has posed serious problems to Japanese life. Examples of such problems include the extraordinarily high price of land in the expanding cities and the lack of youth, especially that of brides-to-be, in the rural areas. The simultaneous decline of both birth and death rates is another notable demographic feature after World War II. The average frequency of childbirth per woman was about 4.3 in the 1940s, which fell to 1.34 in 2020. It denotes the advancement of an aging society and a pressing shortage of labor power.

25. Japan's population has stopped growing after reaching 127,770,000 in 2011 and is now entering a decline phase, falling to 126,146,000 in 2020. It is estimated that by 2060 the total population will fall below 90 million and the aging rate will be close to 40%. The government of Japan is faced with the need to take active measures to cope with the declining birth rate and the aging population.

26. Ethnic Japanese are classified as a branch of the Mongoloid race and share many physical characteristics with other east Asian people. One of the ethnic minorities is the Ainu, usually classified as Proto-Caucasoid, who are concentrated mainly in Hokkaido. Full-blooded Ainus are very rare today. There are also large foreign communities consisting of Koreans and Chinese.

The geographical distribution of the Japanese language practically coincides with the territory of Japan. The Ainu language is almost extinct. The standard Japanese, mainly based on the Tokyo dialect, was established in the late nineteenth century and immediately spread through the education system, writings, and mass media. It is understood and used throughout the country while there are many local dialects spoken.

27. There is innate religious freedom in Japan. *Shinto* is an indigenous folk religion of Japan. It has neither dogma nor a strict moral code. It receives its foundation from the various myths that were partly recorded in *Kojiki* ("The Record of Ancient Matters," completed in 712) and *Nihon-Shoki* ("The Chronicle of Japan," written in 720). Like many other ancient folk religions, it is polytheistic. In Shinto, nature, ancestors, and eminent national figures are enshrined as gods, which are often intermingled with the Buddhist deities. In addition, even some of the Hindu gods and Chinese spirits have been introduced, then modified through Japanese thought, included in Shinto, and worshipped. In a typical Japanese home, both Shintoistic and Buddhist altars are found side by side, and both are prayed daily. Since Shinto, as the folk religion, is not exclusive by nature, a person or family may believe in Shintoistic gods and at the same time belong to a Buddhist or even a Christian sect. That is the main reason why there has been no religious war in Japan.

When the Tokugawa regime banned Christianity in 1612, it was not because of religious reasons but due to the maintenance of public order. The ban was lifted by the Meiji government in 1873. However, Shinto was subsidized by the Meiji government to provide for the upkeep of the main shrines. Subsequently, Shinto was abused by the government to preach ultranationalism until the end of World War II.

During the occupation period, the Supreme Commander demanded the separation of Shinto and the State. Ever since Shinto has been treated as a religious sect.[5]

III. Flag, Anthem, and Other National Symbols

28. The Constitution does not contain any provision regarding a national flag or an anthem. Prior to the year 1999, a national flag and anthem were used based on custom. On August 13, 1999, the Diet enacted a law entitled "Act on the National Flag and the National Anthem" approving and adopting the national flag and the national anthem (*see* paragraph 281).

The officially approved Japanese flag is designed as a red circle representing a rising sun with a white background. It is commonly called *Hinomaru*, or the rising sun flag.

The officially approved national anthem is *Kimigayo* which means "Wish your long life." Its author is unknown. The poem is a traditional one-stanza, thirty-one-syllable verse, from *Kokinshu*, an anthology compiled in the tenth century. Being simple and powerful, it was popularly sung at happy events. Though it was not dedicated to the Emperor, the meaning of the poem was tacitly changed to His Majesty's Reign after it was designated as the national anthem by the Ministry of Education in 1893. It was translated by Basil H. Chamberlain as follows:

> Thousands of years of happy reign be thine Rule on, my lord, till what are pebbles now By age united to mighty rocks shall grow Whose venerable sides the moss doth line.

The music was composed by Hiromori Hashi following the old style of imperial court music.

29. The Imperial crest is a conventionalized chrysanthemum flower with sixteen rays. It has no legal basis but has been accepted as a custom of long-standing. It is not only used as the chief insignia of the Japanese Imperial family but also as a symbol of the Japanese government and as such is now printed on the passport of Japanese nationals.

The years in Japan are numbered according to both the Gregorian system and its own era system. For example, 1996 falls in the eighth year of *Heisei*. The Japanese era system dates back to 645 A.D. when Japan started its first era of *Taika*. Each era is named by a combination of two characters representing a happy omen and is usually chosen from Chinese classics. In modern practice, that is, from the *Meiji* Era on, only one era name is given to each emperor's reign. Consequently, the duration of the era coincides with the emperor's reigning period.

Though not mandatory, the Japanese-era system is widely used among Japanese people and is usually required in official documents. The Era Act, which was enacted in 1979 with the implicit purpose of endorsing this time-honored tradition,

5. *Shinto* comprises two schools: traditional Shrine Shinto and newly founded sectarian Shinto dating from the nineteenth century. What is described here is Shrine Shinto.

provides that the era names shall be decided by cabinet order and that a new era starts only when a new emperor succeeds.

30. On May 1, 2019, the new era of *Reiwa* began due to the imperial transition from Emperor Akihito to Naruhito. The era name of *Riewa* comes from the *Man'yoshu* (Collection of Myriad Leaves), Japan's oldest anthology of poetry compiled in the eighth century.

Part I. Sources of Constitutional Law

Chapter 1. Treaties

by Prof. Go Nakagawa

§1. Directives of the SCAP

31. The Constitution of Japan was made after the Japanese government accepted the Potsdam Declaration on August 14, 1945, which set forth the terms of surrender. The Declaration provided that the occupying forces of the Allies should be withdrawn from Japan as soon as a peacefully inclined and responsible government had been established in accordance with the freely expressed will of the Japanese people.

Almost six years after Japan's surrender to the Allied Powers, the San Francisco Treaty of Peace, dated September 8, 1951, was concluded. With the effectuation of the treaty, the occupation ended and Japan regained her sovereignty.

32. It was considered that the SCAP was authorized by the Allied Powers to proceed with constitutional reform in Japan. This was because the Potsdam Declaration required the Japanese government to "remove all obstacles to the revival and strengthening of democratic tendencies among the Japanese people."

The directives of the Supreme Commander issued to enforce the Potsdam Declaration during the occupation period have been deemed valid irrespective of the constitutional provisions. The Supreme Court reviewed one of the directives by the Supreme Commander and declared that such directives were valid only when they were viewed as constitutional after the effectuation of the Peace Treaty. (7 *Keishu* 1562, Sup. Ct., G.B., July 22, 1953).[6]

6. Supreme Court of Japan, "Judgment upon Case of Validity of Cabinet Order No. 325 of 1950," *Series of Prominent Judgments of the Supreme Court upon Question of Constitutionality*, No. 1 (General Secretariat, Supreme Court of Japan, Tokyo 1954).

§2. TREATIES AND EXECUTIVE AGREEMENTS

33. The Cabinet concludes treaties (including executive agreements which are substantially equivalent to formal treaties) with prior or subsequent, depending on the circumstances, approval of the Diet (Article 73, No. 3).

It is generally agreed that treaties enjoy supremacy over other laws. Article 98, section 2 of the Japanese Constitution provides that the treaties concluded by Japan and established laws of nations shall be faithfully observed, while section 1 declares that the Constitution shall be the supreme law of the nation. Therefore, it is properly concluded that treaties are among the supreme laws of the nation. They are ranked above the statutes enacted by the Diet.

Though some treaties are self-executing and others are not, Article 98, paragraph 2 is construed as a legal ground for converting a treaty into an internal law without any further legislative action.

The Supreme Court refrained from reviewing the constitutionality of the Security Treaty between Japan and the United States on the ground that it was properly left to the discretion of the political branches of the government. In other words, it was political and not justiciable.

Chapter 2. Constitution

by Prof. Go Nakagawa with updates by Prof. Takehisa Nakagawa

§1. Classification

34. Constitutions may be classified as written or unwritten, evolved or enacted, and rigid or flexible. The Japanese Constitution is classified as a written, enacted, and rigid Constitution. It is a single document titled "The Constitution of Japan," which was adopted in 1946 as an amendment of—actually a whole revision of—the Imperial Constitution of Japan.

§2. Amendment of the Constitution

35. The Japanese Constitution may be amended, as Article 96 ordains, by the Diet initiative through a vote of two-thirds or more of all the members of each House, subject to popular ratification which requires the affirmative vote of a majority of all votes cast in a special referendum or in such election as the Diet specifies. When ratified, amendments shall immediately be promulgated by the Emperor in the name of the people as an integral part of the Constitution.

36. The substantive limits of the constitutional amendment have long been theoretically argued.

The majority view holds that duly prescribed limits on constitutional amendment do exist. Such limits are claimed regarding the major political principles vital to the Constitution, including renunciation of war, guarantee of fundamental human rights, and preservation of democratic government. It is argued that these limitations exist because of the declarations that the Japanese people "forever" renounce war, that fundamental human rights shall be conferred as "eternal and inviolable" rights and that representative government is based on "a universal principle of mankind." The minority view, however, argues that there can be no limits on the sovereign will to revise the Constitution.

The majority view has generally been connected with the political opinion unfavorable to the amendment of the Constitution while the minority has been connected with that favorable to the amendment. In political reality, Japanese people have been reluctant to amend the current Constitution for more than seventy years since its adoption, perhaps establishing a new world record for a never-revised Constitution.

37. Because of this political reality, there had been no statute establishing procedures for a Diet motion to amend the Constitution, or for a vote on its approval by the people (referendum). Finally, in 2007 the details of such procedures were enacted as the Act on Procedure for Amendment of the Constitution of Japan along with the 2007 amendment to the Diet Act.

The amended Diet Act details the procedure leading to a motion by the Diet. First, a draft constitutional amendment may be submitted either by a member of the Diet or by the Commissions on the Constitution set up in the House of Representatives and the House of Councillors. Submission by a Diet member requires the approval of at least one hundred members in the House of Representatives and at least fifty members in the House of Councillors. Second, the submitted draft goes to the Commission on the Constitution. They hold public hearings, hear experts' opinions, deliberate on the draft, and pass it if a majority of the participating members approve the draft. Third, if two-thirds of the total number of members of the House of Representatives and the House of Councillors respectively agree to the proposed amendment, a motion by the Diet to amend the Constitution is passed.

The Act on the Procedure for Amending the Constitution of Japan lays down the procedure for a referendum, including voting rights, the secrecy of the votes, counting the ballots, and judicial remedies for invalidation of the referendum.

In 2007, the Act on Procedures for Amendment of the Constitution of Japan was enacted, which introduced new provisions in the Diet Act. The Diet Act now provides that only the Diet members or the Constitutional Law Commissions ("*Kenpo-Shinsa-kai*") newly created in each House may introduce bills of Constitutional amendments. When a member of the House of Representatives introduces an amendment bill, he or she needs the support of more than one hundred members of the House, while a member of the House of Councillors needs the support of more than fifty colleagues of the House (section 68-2 to 68-6 and section 102-6 to 102-8). The Cabinet may not introduce such bills.

Chapter 3. Legislation

by Prof. Go Nakagawa

§1. Statutes Distinguished from the Constitution

38. A statute, as a written will of the legislature, is considered inferior in validity to the Constitution in the Japanese constitutional system. Article 81 of the Constitution explicitly provides that the constitutionality of any statute may be reviewed by the Supreme Court and the lower courts. Statutes are enacted and amended by a majority of both Houses, while the Constitution may be amended only through a much more demanding and supermajority process as mentioned above. The Constitution is definitely different from statutes in political importance.

§2. Statutes Auxiliary to the Constitution

39. While the Constitution states the general principles and framework of government, some statutes are enacted to implement the language of the Constitution and provide details of the constitutional subjects. Such acts include the Imperial House Act, the Public Offices Election Act, the Diet Act, the Rules of the House of Representatives, the Rules of the House of Councillors, the Cabinet Act, the Court Organization Act, and the Board of Audit Act. None of these statutes can claim the privilege of exemption from judicial review of constitutionality.

Chapter 4. Jurisprudence

by Prof. Go Nakagawa

§1. Case Law

40. The Japanese legal system in its modern times has generally been under the influence of the civil law tradition. Nevertheless, the system has become highly susceptible to Anglo-American influence since the end of World War II.

It has not been settled on the theoretical level whether judicial precedents have the same force as law. In constitutional cases, however, the decisions of the courts, especially those of the Supreme Court, are often invoked as sources of the Constitution. It may well be said that judicial decisions are widely deemed to be a source of constitutional law. Lower court decisions which do not conform to the Supreme Court's interpretation of the Constitution are still valid and only liable to be reversed in a final appeal.

§2. Legal Theories

41. It may be that constitutional theories in the academic world are slightly less important today than they used to be. However, such theories and academic views are often quite influential to the courts. This is particularly true when precedents on specific constitutional problems are not available or where earlier cases present divided views.

Chapter 5. Unwritten Law

by Prof. Go Nakagawa

§1. Customary Law

42. Customs are considered a supplementary source of law, but only when authorized as such by statutes. For example, section 238-6 of the Local Autonomy Act takes cognizance of old customs which may be applied in the use of public property. In the field of business, customary laws are entertained by courts. However, there is no room for customary criminal law which can be enforced by the courts. The reason for this is that, as is declared in Article 31 of the Constitution, criminal penalties may only be imposed in accordance with procedures established by law.

It is generally considered that there is no room for the application of customary laws on the level of constitutional interpretations since custom is not mentioned in the text of the Constitution.

§2. Reason

43. Where there is no definite legal source available, the reason for the law, or the spirit of the Constitution as inferred from the text thereof, may be invoked and applied to the case for the purpose of resolving constitutional problems. Constitutional provisions are usually stated in general words, statutes and judicial precedents are not always sufficient to provide answers to constitutional disputes.

Constitutional provisions themselves may provide the reason for an interpretation of a statute. For example, an employment agreement that resulted in sexual discrimination against female workers was held invalid on the ground that it violated the "public order and good morals" clause in the Civil Code (35 *Minshu* 300, Sup. Ct., March 24, 1981). Section 90 of the Civil Code provides that any legal acts which contravene "public order and good morals" shall be null and void. Although, on general principle, the Supreme Court has rejected the direct application of constitutional provisions to civil cases between private entities, it may be said that in the above case, the Civil Code provision was interpreted to carry out the purpose and principle prescribed in Article 14, paragraph 1 of the Constitution. Article 14, paragraph 1, which prohibited discrimination because of race, creed, sex, social status, or family origin, was thus indirectly applied to this civil case through the interpretation of the Civil Code.

Chapter 6. Subordinate Rules and Regulations

by Prof. Go Nakagawa

§1. Orders, Rules, and Regulations: National Government

44. It is laid down in Article 73, No. 6 of the Constitution that the Cabinet shall "Enact cabinet orders in order to execute the provisions of the Constitution and of the law." The Article continues to provide that penal provisions may not be included in cabinet orders "unless authorized by such law."

In addition to the Cabinet itself, each Ministry (e.g., Cabinet Office, Ministry of Finance, and Ministry of Economy, Trade and Industry) and each Agency (e.g., Financial Services Agency and Consumer Affairs Agency) may enact orders pursuant to statutory delegation. Independent commissions, such as the Fair Trade Commission and the Central Labor Relations Board, may make regulations on the subjects within their jurisdiction. The Board of Audit provided for in Article 90 of the Constitution and established by the Board of Audit Act, and the National Personnel Authority, established by the National Civil Service Act, are also authorized to enact rules within their jurisdictions, both of which also enjoy independence from the Cabinet.

Delegation of authority by statutes is the source of legislative authority exercised by administrative organs. While such delegated administrative legislation arises from an evident necessity of practical government, the Supreme Court has imposed certain limitations on such delegation, observing the general principle that legislative grants by the Diet to administrative organs should be definite and particular (6 *Keishu* 1346, Sup. Ct., G.B., December 24, 1952). Nonetheless, the Supreme Court has rarely invalidated what appears to be an excessively broad delegation of the legislative power to administrative organs, even when such delegation seems quite close to a *carte blanche* to the administrative organ.

§2. Local Ordinances and Regulations: Local Governments

45. It is provided in Article 94 of the Constitution that local public entities, namely, prefectures and municipalities, "shall have the right ... to enact their own regulations within law."

Although the Constitution is silent as to which organs of the local public entities are authorized to issue such regulations, the Local Autonomy Act specifies that local assemblies may issue *Jorei* (local ordinances). The scope of ordinance-making power of local public entities is not as limited as that of administrative agencies. This is because the former is elective while the latter is appointive. According to the Supreme Court opinion, delegation of power to establish punitive provisions within ordinances of local assemblies under the Local Autonomy Act is permissible as far as the extent of delegation is limited to a considerable degree (16 *Keishu* 577, Sup. Ct., G.B., May 30, 1962). This is because activities of local assemblies can be analogized to those of the Diet in the sense that both are elected political bodies.

When a statute specifically delegates to local public entities the power to create relevant ordinances, the standards provided for in such statute are rather broad and general (*see* paragraph 185).

46. *Kisoku* (local regulations) are authorized to be issued, under the Local Autonomy Act and other relevant statutes, by the chief executive (e.g., governors of prefectures, mayors of cities, and heads of towns and villages) and the commissions (e.g., boards of education, expropriation commissions, election commissions, and prefectural public safety commissions).

Chapter 7. Hierarchy of Legal Rules

by Prof. Go Nakagawa

§1. Priority

47. The Constitution is the fundamental law of the land and has the authority of the highest order against which no other legal rules can prevail. According to the popular view among constitutional theorists in Japan, both statutes and treaties, which are enforceable by the courts, should conform to the Constitution. In case of conflict between a statute and a treaty, the latter is given priority over the former.

Administrative rules and regulations issued by administrative organs of the national government (cabinet orders, ministerial orders, etc.) on one hand and local ordinances and regulations promulgated by the local public entities on the other are both subordinate to the statutes and the Constitution. While the two categories are on the same level of authority under the Constitution, the Local Autonomy Act provides that in case of conflict, national administrative rules and regulations are to control.

§2. Interpretation

48. Though judicial precedents are neither codified nor specified by any written law as legal sources, interpretations of the Constitution by the courts are always preferred over interpretations by any other governmental organ.

To fill in the details of the legal system, interpretations of the Constitution by administrative organs play an important role in the actual workings of the government. Where there is no other authoritative interpretation of the Constitution, administrative interpretations of the Constitution are deemed to have de facto authority. Corresponding to the increase of discretionary powers of administrative organs, administrative interpretations of the Constitution have come to carry increased weight in the governmental process.

When a constitutional provision is self-executing and not implemented by a statute, interpretations by governmental organs may be the practical equivalent of legislation unless an act of the legislature supersedes them.

49. Examples of non-self-executing provisions of the Constitution, which remain dormant unless activated by legislative implementation, are found in its Bill of Rights chapter. Article 25, paragraph 1 provides that all people "have the right to maintain the minimum standards of wholesome and cultured living." The establishment of such standards is left to the legislative branch.

It has generally been considered that the Constitution only provides a programmatic declaration that obligates the government to seek as a goal the right of each citizen to live a decent life. This program can only be implemented through statutory enactment (the "Programmatic Declaration Theory," *see* paragraph 363 *infra*). According to this theory, which has been supported by the Supreme Court (*Staple*

Food Control Act case, 2 *Keishu* 1235, G.B., September 29, 1948), the right to live embodied in Article 25, paragraph 1 is not self-executing and creates no legally enforceable right.

The Supreme Court has held that the right to live should be viewed as having come into being as a result of the enactment of the Livelihood Protection Act (21 *Minshu* 1043, Sup. Ct., G.B., May 24, 1967).[7] This opinion has been severely criticized by legal scholars and public opinion.

However, the Supreme Court suggested that even where there is no statutory provision to provide for compensation for taking private property, compensation is nonetheless to be claimed directly based on Article 29, paragraph 3 of the Constitution which reads, "Private property may be taken for public use upon just compensation therefor" (22 *Keishu* 1402, Sup. Ct., G.B., November 27, 1968).

7. Supreme Court of Japan, "Judgment in the so-called *Asahi Case*," *Series of Prominent Judgments of the Supreme Court upon Question of Constitutionality*, No. 10 (General Secretariat, Supreme Court of Japan, Tokyo 1968).

Part II. Form of Government

Chapter 1. General Introduction

by Prof. Go Nakagawa with updates by Prof. Takehisa Nakagawa

§1. Overview of the National Government

I. Separation of Powers

50. The national government of Japan is formed according to the doctrine of separation of powers which is also found in other constitutions including that of the United States.

The Constitution of Japan lists three categories of governmental power: legislative, executive, and judicial power. Each power is vested in separate organs, namely, the Diet, the Cabinet, the Supreme Court and other courts. Article 41 provides that the Diet shall be the sole lawmaking organ of the State, while Article 65 states that executive power shall be vested in the Cabinet. It is laid down in Article 76 that the whole judicial power is vested in the Supreme Court and inferior courts established by law.

51. Such three branches are rather interrelated in the actual working of their functions. Each branch is not limited to such peculiar power as would be defined under a "pure" doctrine of separation of powers.[8] Overlap of governmental powers is to some extent unavoidable, which leads to a "practical" doctrine of separation of powers.

52. For example, the Diet is declared to be the highest lawmaking organ of the State. In addition to legislation, it exercises various powers including but not limited to the nomination of the Prime Minister, approval of treaties, decisions on national financial policies, and proposals for amendment to the Constitution.

The Cabinet is the highest executive or administrative organ of the national government.[9] It may enact cabinet orders to execute the provisions of the Constitution

---

8. M.J. Vile, *Constitutionalism and the Separation of Powers* 13 (Clarendon Press 1967).
9. The terms executive power and administrative power may be used interchangeably because in many countries adopting the cabinet government system the Cabinet has come to combine the executive power and the administrative power.

and laws and may also conclude treaties subject to subsequent approval by the Diet. The Constitution does not prohibit judicial power to be exercised by organs of the executive branch, but judicial decisions by an executive organ are not to be final.

In addition to judicial power, the Supreme Court is vested with limited rulemaking power: it establishes the rules of practice and procedure for matters relating to attorneys, the internal discipline of the courts, and the administration of judicial affairs. The power to make rules for inferior courts may be delegated by the Supreme Court to such courts. The Supreme Court also exercises certain administrative power, including the nomination of judges for inferior courts. Such nominated inferior court judges need to be appointed by the Cabinet as provided by the Constitution.

II. Parliamentary Government

53. The "pure" doctrinal separation of powers is usually softened through the rules and practice of checks and balances. The principle of checks and balances is usually applied among the legislative, executive, and judicial branches and between the two Houses of the legislature.

The Constitution of Japan contains parliamentary government and judicial review as ingredients of checks and balances. While this might be an unusual combination of the British and American prototypes, there have been no serious political deadlocks between the legislative and judicial branches so far. Under the parliamentary system, the Cabinet may hold office as long as it is given confidence by the House of Representatives, which is the Lower House of the Diet. Different from the American-type presidential government, the Japanese Prime Minister must be a member of the Diet and a majority of the Ministers of State must be members of the Diet (Articles 67 and 68).

54. The text of the Meiji Constitution provided that the Ministers were appointed solely by the Emperor and were individually responsible only to the Emperor. Nevertheless, even under the old Constitution, the parliamentary system had evolved as a "regular constitutional course," as part of sound political practice during the period prior to the national emergency which led to World War II. Influenced by the ideas of constitutional monarchy and party government, Cabinet members, though appointed by the Emperor, were considered to be jointly responsible to the Parliament.

55. Under the present Constitution, it has generally been regarded that the cabinet system has shifted to the British model. Now the Cabinet is collectively responsible to the Lower House (the House of Representatives) for the general conduct of affairs and is concerned with political matters but not legal matters.[10] The offices of the individual Ministers are not impeachable. The political responsibility of the Cabinet consists in its being obliged to resign *en masse* when it loses the confidence of the Lower House. Article 69 of the Constitution provides that, in case the House

10. H. Kelsen, *General Theory of Law and State* 300 et seq. (Harvard University Press 1949).

of Representatives passes a nonconfidence resolution or rejects a confidence resolution, all the Cabinet members must resign unless the House is dissolved within ten days. If the House is dissolved, a new election must take place within forty days of the dissolution.

The House of Representatives may be dissolved at any time by the Emperor with the advice and approval of the Cabinet as stated in Article 7. The power of the Lower House to show nonconfidence in the Cabinet is thus balanced with the power of the Cabinet to dissolve the House of Representatives at its will.

III. Judicial Review

56. Another device for checks and balances is a judicial review based on the American model. This system was introduced to the Japanese constitutional history through the drafting of the Constitution of Japan by the GHQ. Judicial review is the power of courts to declare acts of the legislative or executive branches unconstitutional. Though the United States Constitution is notoriously silent on such judicial review, it was established by the Supreme Court in *Marbury v. Madison*, 1 Cr. 137 (U.S. 1803) and has since functioned as one of the most valued examples of constitutional heritage of American jurisprudence.

Judicial review is based upon the idea that the Constitution is the supreme law of the land, that governmental acts contrary to the Constitution are void, and that the judiciary is the final arbiter of the meaning of the Constitution and determiner of constitutional cases.[11]

57. Several provisions of the Constitution express the idea mentioned above. First, Article 98 of the Constitution declares that the Constitution shall be the supreme law of the land and no law, order, or other governmental act contrary to its provisions shall be valid. Second, Article 81 provides that the Supreme Court is the court of last resort and is vested with the power to determine the constitutionality of any law, order, regulation, or official act. Finally, the supremacy of the Constitution and the exemption of no governmental act from review of constitutionality are both confirmed by Article 99 which provides that all public officials including the Emperor, members of the Diet, Ministers of State, and judges have the obligation to respect and uphold the Constitution.

58. Since constitutional cases are prone to political arguments, the Supreme Court of Japan has used self-restraint in exercising its power of judicial review over constitutional matters, and it has been branded as conservative. However, as a matter of fact, it has not been monolithic, often being split between the conservative majority and the liberal minority. It might be safe to generalize that the Supreme Court of Japan has continued its judicial self-restraint in fear of judicial usurpation of the power of the political branches to establish and control public policy.

11. J.C. Plano & M. Greenberg, *The American Political Dictionary* 213 (Holt, Rinehart and Winston, Inc. 2d ed. 1962).

Considerable criticism has been made, especially from the academic world, that the Supreme Court has served as a rubber stamp for governmental actions. Perhaps because the idea of judicial review is a bit too radical for the Japanese version of democracy, and because it cannot be traced to the traditional political values of the Japanese, the Supreme Court has rarely nullified or reversed governmental actions as unconstitutional. However, judges of lower courts are sometimes active in dealing with the constitutionality of governmental actions. Constitutional decisions often-times provoke public controversies which appear on the front pages of newspapers.

§2. Political Parties

I. Liberal Democratic Party

59. In a parliamentary democracy, political parties as associations of people sharing common political opinions, rather than individual members of the Parliament, are the most powerful and effective vehicles for molding political platforms into public will. Individuals join or support the party that best promotes their views of economic and social interests. To carry out such demands and expectations, political parties are always struggling to win government power.

The Japanese Constitution, like the United States Constitution, is silent on political parties. Nonetheless, it is undeniable that political parties are expected to play a decisive role in the governmental processes. Japan has never adopted a one-party system and no political party is legally excluded from competing for power in the political arena. The right to organize political parties is guaranteed by Article 21 as part of the freedom of association.

60. Since the ruling party or the dominant coalition of parties in the two Houses of the Diet can nominate the Prime Minister by majority rule, the leading party has advantages in controlling both the lawmaking and administrative processes. As for the selection of the Prime Minister, Article 67 of the Constitution provides that in case the House of Representatives (Lower House) and the House of Councillors (Upper House) disagree, and if no agreement can be reached through a joint committee of both Houses, or if the House of Councillors fails to reach a decision within ten days, the decision of the House of Representatives as to who shall be the Prime Minister shall be that of the whole Diet. It indicates not only the supremacy of the Lower House over the Upper House but also the crucial political importance of securing a majority in the Lower House.

If no single party commands an absolute majority, a coalition Cabinet which consists of two or more parties may be formed, sacrificing uniformity of the Cabinet and consequent political instability.

61. Conservative parties, substantially the same as the current Liberal Democratic Party (*Jiyuminshuto*) (LDP), have dominated the postwar political scene.

There existed minimal likelihood that their control of government would be seriously challenged[12] until the LDP lost its majority in the Lower House in 1993. Unlike the Japan Socialist Party (JSP) (*Shakaito*) (now renamed as the Social Democratic Party (*Syakaiminnshuto*) (SDP) in 1996) or the Japan Communist Party (*Kyosanto*),[13] the LDP and other conservative parties have no ideological conformity because they are not necessarily organized on a particular ideology. Rather, they simply share the idea of democracy (interpreted in the Japanese way) and due respect for traditional values. The conservative parties, not bound by any fixed ideological values, have cleverly adjusted themselves to the changing international environment and economic crises.

62. Between 1955 and 1993 saw an enduring so-called 1955 political regime with ideological rivalry between the LDP as the government party and the JSP as the biggest opposition party.

The LDP-JSP rivalry was most acute on constitutional amendment and the Japan-US Security Agreement. The LDP called for constitutional reform "by the Japanese people" and the renewal of the Japan-US Security Treaty. The JSP well represented the political camp against any constitutional revision and the security arrangement between Japan and the United States.

The 1955 political regime finally collapsed with the 1993 Lower House election. The LDP and other smaller parties then started to form coalition governments, with only two brief exceptions. Those were the 1993–1994 period when some newly created parties became the ruling parties and the 2009–2012 period when the Democratic Party of Japan (DPJ) took power.

After a long absence of a shadow Cabinet, the JSP finally formed such a Cabinet in 1991. It even coalesced with other parties to form a coalition Cabinet in 1993. However, the popularity of the party had markedly dwindled by this time.

In the 1993 election, when the LDP lost its majority in the Lower House, new parties gained support, including the Japan New Party (*Nihonshinto*) which had been formed in 1992 by reformist conservatives under the leadership of Morihiro Hosokawa, and the *Shinsei* Party (*Shinseito*) and the New Party "Initiatives" (*Shinto-Sakigake*) (NPI), both of which were established just before the 1993 election by reform-oriented former LDP members who had left the party. Thus, in 1993, the House of Representatives named Morihiro Hosokawa as Prime Minister, and his Cabinet was formed upon a coalition of "non-LDP and noncommunist parties." For the first time in its history, the LDP became an opposition party while the *Shinsei* Party, one of the "new parties," provided the core personnel of the Hosokawa Cabinet.

Since then, the Cabinet has been formed upon a coalition of several parties. Meanwhile, the LDP and the JSP for the first time tried to share many of their political platforms and activities, including criticism of the *Shinsei* Party. In 1994, the two long-established parties, along with the NPI, formed a coalition (the LDP-JSP-NPI

---

12. W.M. Tsuneishi, *Japanese Political Style: An Introduction to the Government and Politics of Modern Japan* 125 (Harper & Row 1966).
13. They are deemed as the core parties of "renovationist" or "reformist" (not revolutionary) parties.

coalition) and successfully had Tomiichi Murayama, President of the JSP, nominated as a new Prime Minister. The LDP returned as the ruling party after Murayama's resignation in 1996 when Ryutaro Hashimoto was named Prime Minister. Hashimoto was the first LDP Prime Minister since 1993. In 1995, the JSP changed its name to the SDP partly because of the change made in its platform to form the LDP-JSP (now SDP)-NPI coalition and also to stop its steady decline in popularity.

During most of the period of the LDP-SDP-NPI coalition government (1994–1998), the largest opposition party was the *Shinsei* Party. In an effort to integrate the influence of the opposition parties, the *Shinsei* Party decided in 1994 to dissolve itself into a "new, new party." Some other opposition parties, including the Clean Governance Party (*Komeito,* established in 1964) and the Japan New Party, immediately joined this plan. With the dissolution of these parties, a "new, new party" was established in late 1994 with the name of the New Frontier Party (*Shinshinto*). The New Frontier Party was originally thought to be a formidable threat to the LDP-SDP-NPI coalition government. However, due to internal struggle, the New Frontier Party gradually lost many of its eminent members. In 1997, the New Frontier Party split itself into several parties. Many of its former Clean Governance Party members regrouped to form the New Clean Governance Party (*Shin-Komeito*). The platform of the New Frontier Party was adopted by a newly established party led by Ichiro Ozawa, which was called the Liberal Party (*Jiyuto*).

While the New Frontier Party was in struggle, another new party was separately formed in 1996. It was called the Democratic Party (*Minshuto*), and since the 1997 dissolution of the New Frontier Party, it has become the largest opposition party. The Democratic Party includes, among others, former NPI members and former SDP members. In 1998, the Democratic Party became even larger by merging with some small parties.

The LDP-SDP-NPI coalition collapsed when the SDP and NPI left the coalition just before the 1998 election for the House of Councillors. The election turned out to be a disastrous defeat for all three parties. This result was considered to represent a nationwide criticism of the economic policies of the Hashimoto Cabinet, and Hashimoto resigned. The LDP supported Keizo Obuchi who had been a Minister of Foreign Affairs in the Hashimoto Cabinet to be the next Prime Minister. The Obuchi Cabinet started in 1998 under a new coalition between the LDP and the Liberal Party. For the second Obuchi Cabinet, the coalition was joined by the New Clean Governance Party in 1999. In 2000, the Liberal Party, under the leadership of Ichiro Ozawa, left the coalition. Those members of the Liberal Party who wanted to stay in the government stepped out of the Liberal Party to form a new party called the New Conservative Party (*Hoshuto*). Thus, the next Cabinet under the premiership of Yoshiro Mori, who became Prime Minister after the sudden death of Obuchi, was supported by a newer coalition between the LDP, the New Clean Governance Party, and the New Conservative Party.

63. The political parties in the 2010s were as follows:

> Prime Minister Mori agreed to hold early elections for the LDP President to improve his party's chances in crucial July 2001 Upper House elections. On

April 24, 2001, riding a wave of grassroots desire for change, maverick politician Junichiro Koizumi was elected as the new LDP leader with his platform of economic and political reforms. Koizumi became Japan's 56th Prime Minister on April 26, 2001.

Under the slogan "No economic recovery without structural reform," he served as Prime Minister for about five and a half years, until September 26, 2006. His proposals for large-scale reform, including privatization of the Japan Post, Japan's state-owned postal monopoly and one of the world's largest financial institutions with nearly JPY 331 trillion of assets, were rejected by the LDP, Koizumi's party, and other parties in the Diet. On August 8, 2005, Koizumi called for a snap election to the Lower House. The election was scheduled for September 11, 2005, with the LDP achieving a landslide victory under Koizumi's leadership. The Diet of 2005 then approved his Japan Post reform proposals.

In 2006, the Diet nominated the new LDP President Shinzō Abe to succeed Junichiro Koizumi as Prime Minister. He was Japan's youngest post-World War II prime minister and the first one born after the war. On September 12, 2007, Abe surprised Japan by announcing his abrupt resignation from office. Yasuo Fukuda, a veteran LDP member, replaced Abe.

In 2008, Prime Minister Fukuda introduced a bill allowing ships to continue the Self-Defense Forces' refueling mission in the Indian Ocean to support the U.S.-led operations in Afghanistan. He used the LDP's overwhelming majority in the Lower House to ignore the opinion of the Upper House controlled by the opposition parties. Fukuda resigned suddenly on September 1, 2008, just a few weeks after reshuffling his cabinet. Tarō Asō became the new LDP President, and on September 24, 2008, he was appointed as 92nd Prime Minister.

In 2009, Prime Minister Asō dissolved the Lower House. In the ensuing election, the opposition party DPJ led by Yukio Hatoyama won a majority. On September 16, 2009, the president of DPJ, Hatoyama, was elected as the 93rd Prime Minister of Japan. It was the beginning of the DJP Cabinet period which lasted three years.

64. The second decade of the twenty-first century started with three DJP Cabinets, followed then by the revival of the LDP government.

The Hatoyama-led DJP cabinet initially started with a high approval rating of over 70%, but public distrust soon peaked. On June 2, 2010, he resigned, and the newly elected DPJ's president Naoto Kan became Prime Minister.

Kan soon suffered a setback in the 2010 Upper House election. On March 11, 2011, the Great East Japan Earthquake struck. His government had to deal with increasing work to reconstruct life and industry after the disaster, including the management of the Fukushima nuclear accident. Criticism of Naoto Kan's way of dealing with the situation grew, and demands for his resignation began to emerge—even from his own party. In light of this, he announced his intention to step down.

The Diet chose Yoshihiko Noda as the 95th Prime Minister on August 30, 2011. Although the Noda Cabinet succeeded in getting the bill for the integrated reform of the social security and tax systems passed by the Diet in 2012, it lost momentum and support concerning the consumption tax and other issues. Albeit undesired, Noda had no choice but to dissolve the Lower House on November 16, 2012.

The results of the ensuing election of December 16 were in favor of the LDP, which won an absolute majority with the leadership of former Prime Minister Shinzō Abe. The Diet chose him as the 96th Prime Minister of Japan. "Abenomics," the ambitiously self-titled fiscal policy, attracted Japanese voters, and his Cabinet remained in power from December 26, 2012 to September 16, 2020.

Shinzo Abe was Prime Minister for 2,822 consecutive days. This is the longest in Japan's constitutional history. Including his first cabinet (2006–2007), Abe's tenure as Prime Minister totaled 3,188 days, also the longest in Japan's constitutional history.

The Abe Cabinet focused on "Abenomics," consisting of the three arrows of monetary easing, fiscal stimulus, and growth strategy; exercised initiative to amend laws to raise the consumption tax twice, and brought about the enactment of a series of security-related laws in 2015 that allow the Government of Japan limited exercise of collective self-defense.

Along with Abenomics, the signature of the Abe Cabinet was aggressive diplomacy. It launched a free and open Indo-Pacific strategy. It also made possible a visit to Hiroshima by former U.S. President Barack Obama and further strengthened the Japan-U.S. alliance with former President Donald Trump.

The Cabinet was also eager to promote negotiations for the Trans-Pacific Partnership (TPP), which was a proposed free trade agreement between twelve Pacific Rim economies. After the United States' withdrawal, the other eleven countries confirmed that negotiations would continue, in part because the Abe Cabinet reportedly took an active role. The eleven countries signed the Comprehensive and Progressive Agreement on Trans-Pacific Partnership (CPTPP) in 2018.

The Abe Cabinet resigned in 2020, and a new Cabinet was formed by Yoshihide Kan, the LDP president and a member of the House of Representatives. He served as Prime Minister from September 16, 2020, to October 4, 2021. His Cabinet was instrumental in the COVID-19 measures and established the Digital Agency. His refusal to appoint several members of the Science Council of Japan caused various controversies. The Tokyo 2020 Olympic Games were held one year later (July–August 2021) due to the expansion of the COVID-19 crisis.

After the resignation of the Kan Cabinet, Fumio Kishida, a member of the House of Representatives who was also the LDP president, has served as the Prime Minister since October 4, 2021.

On July 8, 2022, Shinzo Abe was shot and killed during a campaign speech in Nara, Japan. The gunman reportedly had a grudge against the former Unification Church, a religious organization, leading him to shoot Abe with a gun of his own making because he believed Abe had ties to the organization. The suspect was criminally indicted in January 2023. Abe was given a state funeral in September 2022. This is the first state funeral for a former prime minister since Shigeru Yoshida died in 1967, and the second since the end of World War II. It now became widely known that the defendant had a grudge against the former Unification Church and shot Abe, who he thought was politically friendly with that religious group.

II. Factions and *Zoku* Diet Members

65. Virtually every political party in Japan breaks into several factions formed by personal ties (*jinmyaku*). The factional organization is marked by strong patron-client relationships among members whose relationships are strengthened by the faction leader. In the case of the LDP which had long been the single government party, faction leaders, in return for the faction members' votes in a party-presidential election to be held every two years, distribute not only political funds provided by interest groups and individuals but also ministerial and other governmental positions won by negotiation with other factions.

A presidential election of a government party bears definite political importance because the person elected is most likely to be designated as the new Prime Minister and his faction might generally enjoy a predominant position over other factions.

Faction politics is not the monopoly of government parties. Opposition parties also consist of factions that struggle for the position of party leaders. In summary, the political parties of Japan are federations consisting of several factions. As a result, party loyalty is shown by the support for policies of the party, consistent with factional interests, rather than for support of ideology.[14]

66. Political parties are always trying to attract as many channels of raising political funds as possible both to carry on election campaigns and to finance day-to-day political activities. Generally speaking, the main contributors to the conservative parties are among big businesses; those to the Socialist Party (now SDP) are the Federation of Labor Unions (*Rengo*); the Communist Party relies on subscribers of the *Red Flag*, a daily newspaper issued by the party. Discussion of political financing would be best treated in books dealing with political science.[15]

67. The party in power, which holds a majority of seats in the Lower House, usually does not act as a steamroller in connection with legislative activities. In standing committees of the Diet, members from opposition parties most often speak up to try to make the government concede in major policy making. The government and the government parties try to reach a compromise with the opposition parties utilizing various concessions. This is the main reason why some government bills, backed by the government parties, often fail to pass the Diet.

68. Those Diet members of the government parties who have sufficient expertise and influence on policy-making and other decision-making of a particular ministry of the national government are commonly called *zoku*, such as Commerce-*zoku*, Education-*zoku*, and Defense-*zoku*. The term *zoku* means tribe, which connotes groups of individuals with special expertise in and influence on specific administrative areas.

---

14. For the organization of the LDP based on faction politics, *see* G.L. Curtis, *The Japanese Way of Politics* 80 et seq. (Columbia University Press 1988).
15. On political financing and fund-raising, *see* G.L. Curtis, *The Japanese Way of Politics* 176 et seq. (Columbia University Press 1988).

They might be viewed as a kind of pressure group. However, with their expertise and personal connections, they act as effective political channels to particular ministries (or divisions thereof) which are responsible for narrower areas than the issues that interest groups typically deal with.[16] The existence of *zoku* is a good example of legislative participation in administrative processes in Japanese politics.

16. For details of *zoku* Diet members, *see* G.L. Curtis, *The Japanese Way of Politics* 114 et seq. (Columbia University Press 1988).

Chapter 2. Head of State

by Prof. Go Nakagawa with updates by Prof. Takehisa Nakagawa

§1. Making the Emperor the Symbol of the State

I. Political Stability and the Monarchy

69. In modern Japan, the monarchy has played a crucial role in securing political stability. The throne has been transmitted through a single line of a continuous dynasty, the foundation of which goes back to the mythical age. As early as ancient times, the office of *Tenno* had become more cultural than military. In most of the history after the start of the Shogunate government (early in the twelfth century), *Tenno* has had minimal involvement with political and military affairs. Except for the fanatic Tennism in the 1930s and 1940s which drove the Japanese people to extremes and abuses in the name of the Emperor, the tradition of "passive emperor" has generally been kept undisturbed and remains so today.[17] Nonetheless, even in the 1930s and 1940s, the Emperor used self-restraint in exercising his constitutional powers and as a genuine constitutional monarch refrained from taking leadership in political and military affairs. One of the principal defects of the Meiji Constitution was its vulnerability to the usurpation of prerogative powers of the Emperor by the military.

70. To carry out the Potsdam Declaration, to make the Emperor a safer monarch, and to democratize the Japanese government, the constitutional change from monarchical sovereignty to popular sovereignty was inevitable.

The imperial system of Japan, if it sticks to its traditional form, might be seen as neither inconsistent with nor menacing to the principles of popular sovereignty and democracy embodied in the present Constitution. There are other views that, based on, for example, the materialistic view of left-wing theorists (which legitimatized the Russian Revolution against czarism), the imperial system must be deemed as a remainder of, and a possible restorer of, an undemocratic, authoritarian regime.

Under the new constitutional system, the Japanese Emperor is obliged to uphold the Constitution. The Imperial Family's current role is much closer to the political tradition of Japan.

II. The Locus of Sovereignty

71. General MacArthur wanted to preserve the imperial institution with the intent peacefully to control occupied Japan. According to his autobiography entitled *Reminiscences*, it appears that he was deeply impressed by Emperor Hirohito as the

17. J.W. Hall, *A Monarch for Modern Japan, in Political Development in Modern Japan* 41 (R.E. Ward ed., Princeton University Press 1968).

"First Gentleman in Japan." However, he had already hung Japanese enemy generals in Manila without a trace of mercy and understanding. It remains to be answered whether MacArthur's policy to preserve the imperial institution in post-war Japan was motivated primarily by his personal experience or other motives.

72. MacArthur's notes to the Government Section of the GHQ (the Three Doctrines quoted above in paragraph 6) stated that the Emperor was the head of the State. Furthermore, the Emperor was supposed to be responsible for the basic will of the people. The American officers in charge of constitutional revision paraphrased these notes and added their own devices.

First, they wanted to make the Emperor a mere symbol of the State. For this purpose, they introduced popular sovereignty and tried to set legal limits on the imperial powers through "advice and consent of the Cabinet." Article 1 of the draft of the Constitution made the Emperor the symbol of the State "deriving his position from the sovereign will of the People, and from no other source." In the translation of the draft, however, the Japanese government chose the Japanese word *kokumin* which could be interpreted to include the Emperor in the "People."[18]

Second, the American officers wanted the Emperor's acts to be checked by the Cabinet. Though the Japanese government was not happy with the American wording of "advice and consent" of the Cabinet, it accepted the idea, eventually substituting a slightly more modest word, "approval," for the word "consent."

73. The outline of the system is as follows:

(3) *Article 1.* The Emperor shall be the symbol of the State and of the unity of the people, deriving his position from the will of the people with whom resides sovereign power.

Article 3. The advice and approval of the Cabinet shall be required for all acts of the Emperor in matters of state, and the Cabinet shall be responsible therefor.

§2. Status of the Emperor

I. Political Status

74. There still exists a theoretical divergence of opinions about the head of the country because no mention is made in the Constitution of the head of the State or the sovereign. It may be concluded that the status of the Emperor corresponds to that of the head of the State notwithstanding that his role is strictly limited to the sphere of ceremony. His major political contribution is to preserve political stability and to provide a sense of national unity as a public figure responsible for the national cultural heritage.

---

18. *See* K. Inoue, *MacArthur's Japanese Constitution: A Linguistic and Cultural Study of Its Making* 220 (The University of Chicago Press 1991).

75. As a governmental organ, the Emperor is dependent on the Cabinet and the Diet. His office belongs to the administrative branch and his acts are under the control of the Cabinet by means of the advice and approval clause. Article 4 spells out that he shall have no power related to the government.

76. The imperial throne is dynastic but its succession is stipulated by the Imperial House Act passed by the Diet in accordance with Article 2 of the Constitution. The giving to or receiving of property or gifts by the Imperial House is prohibited by Article 8 unless there is authorization by the Diet. The Imperial institution retains adequate traditional features, but its administration has been drastically democratized under the Constitution. In addition to the business enumerated in the Constitution, the Emperor can do what is appropriate to his status as the national symbol, such as making goodwill visits to foreign countries and social welfare facilities.

II. Legal Status

77. Since the Meiji Constitution assumed that the Emperor was sacred and inviolable, offenses against the Imperial House were aggravated offenses according to the old Penal Code. According to the de facto official commentaries on the Meiji Constitution, "Not only shall there be no irreverence for the Emperor's person, but also shall He neither be made a topic of derogatory comment nor one of discussion."[19]

The disavowal of the divinity of the Emperor by the Emperor himself immediately after World War II was followed by the new Constitution that implicitly denied the sacredness of the Emperor. Incidentally, this resulted in the repeal of lese-majesty in the old Penal Code. Though the Supreme Court bypassed an opportunity to review the constitutionality of offenses against the Imperial House, a minority opinion expressed the idea that such offenses had substantially been abolished even before the enforcement of the new Constitution and the amendment of the Penal Code (2 *Keishu* 529, Sup. Ct., G.B., May 26, 1948).

78. In a case of libel against the Emperor, the Prime Minister is to file a suit in a court on the Emperor's behalf. Punitive sanctions arising from the forgery of an Imperial edict are aggravated as compared with those arising from the forgery of other official documents (section 154 of the Penal Code).

It is generally accepted that the Emperor may not be made responsible for penal offenses since such responsibilities are incompatible with his status as the symbol of the State. Although in theory, the Emperor is not exempt from civil liabilities, the Supreme Court has declared that the Emperor should not be taken to court in either a criminal or civil case (43 *Minshu* 1160, Sup. Ct., November 20, 1989). If this is so, who can be sued? Theoretically, the State should be the appropriate party to a civil suit for damages arising out of an act of the Emperor, and the Cabinet, which,

19. H. Ito, *Commentaries on the Constitution of the Empire of Japan* 7 (Chuo-Daigaku 1909; reprinted University Publications of America, Inc. 1979).

according to the Constitution is responsible for the Emperor's acts, should be designated as the only appropriate organ to handle such a suit as well as other royal legal problems.

79. The Constitution and the Imperial Household Act are silent on whether the Emperor may abdicate of his own accord. Under the Meiji and current Constitutions, the succession of Emperors occurred only upon death. However, Emperor Akihito had secretly expressed his wish to abdicate, fearing that his advanced age would make it difficult for him to continue to act as Emperor.

80. After due consideration by the government of the Emperor's wish and other circumstances, it decided to introduce new legislation. On June 9, 2017, the Diet passed the Act on Special Provisions of the Imperial Household Law Concerning the Abdication of the Emperor. Based on this special one-time act, the 125th Emperor Akihito was able to abdicate. His elder son, Naruhito, ascended to the throne as the 126th Emperor of Japan on May 1, 2019.

§3. Competence

I. Acts in Matters of State

81. The advice and approval of the Cabinet are required for all acts of the Emperor and the Cabinet is responsible for all such acts. The imperial prerogatives must be strictly limited to the sphere of ceremony. The Emperor may delegate the performance of his acts in matters of state to the Regent designated in accordance with the Imperial House Act. The Regent shall perform his acts in the name of the Emperor.

The acts of the Emperor in matters of state are enumerated in Articles 6 and 7 of the Constitution. The Emperor and the Regent have the obligation to respect and uphold the Constitution (Article 99).

82. Article 6 of the Constitution provides that the Emperor appoints both the Prime Minister (who is nominated by the Diet) and the Chief Justice of the Supreme Court (who is designated by the Cabinet). The Imperial appointment is interpreted to be made with the advice and approval of the Cabinet.

83. Article 7 sets forth a list of ten acts in matters of state which are to be performed by the Emperor with the advice and approval of the Cabinet, as follows:

(1) Promulgation of amendments to the Constitution, laws, cabinet orders and treaties.
(2) Convocation of the Diet.
(3) Dissolution of the House of Representatives.
(4) Proclamation of the general election of members of the Diet.

(5) Attestation of the appointment and dismissal of Ministers of State and other officials as provided for by law, and of full powers and credentials of Ambassadors and Ministers.
(6) Attestation of general and special amnesty, commutation of punishment, reprieve, and restoration of rights.
(7) Awarding of honors.
(8) Attestation of instruments of ratification and other diplomatic documents as provided for by law.
(9) Receiving foreign ambassadors and ministers.
(10) Performance of ceremonial functions.

II. Dissolution of the House of Representatives

84. Among these acts (*see* paragraph 83), the dissolution of the Lower House has created political and legal controversies. The prevailing academic view supports the constitutionality of dissolution based on Article 7, which, as a practical matter, gives a free hand to the Cabinet to determine when to dissolve the House.

85. On August 28, 1952, the House of Representatives was dissolved by the Cabinet headed by Prime Minister Shigeru Yoshida. This "Surprise Dissolution" became the target of criticism by the opposition parties.

A politician who lost his seat in the House in the ensuing election filed a suit against the State claiming that the dissolution of the House under Article 7 of the Constitution was unconstitutional. It was contended by the plaintiff that the power of dissolution could only be used when the House of Representatives either passed a nonconfidence resolution or rejected a confidence resolution and when the Cabinet did not resign *en bloc* as provided in Article 69. Thus, the plaintiff continued, the House was not to be dissolved at liberty by the Cabinet invoking Article 7 of the Constitution.

The majority opinion of the Supreme Court refused to entertain the suit and ruled that certain governmental acts which are categorized as political questions are, even if they constitute a case, not reviewable by the judiciary because of the inherent limitations resulting from the principle of separation of powers and the nonpolitical nature of the judicial power. Dissolution of Parliament by the Cabinet was found to be such a political question. According to the minority opinion, the constitutionality of the dissolution of the House was reviewable by the judiciary. Nonetheless, the minority opinions upheld the constitutionality of the dissolution saying that dissolution based solely on Article 7 was constitutional (14 *Minshu* 1206, Sup. Ct., G.B., June 8, 1960).

Chapter 3. The Legislature

by Prof. Go Nakagawa with updates by Prof. Takehisa Nakagawa

§1. The National Diet

I. Bicameral System

86. "A truly representative legislative body," remarked the Government Section of the GHQ rather idealistically in the document entitled Political Reorientation of Japan, "based upon universal adult suffrage, responsible to the electorate, free of domination by the executive, and having full legislative powers, including control over the raising and spending of all public money, is a primary requisite of any blueprint for democracy under a representative form of government."[20] It is fair to say that the constitutional reform of the Imperial Diet was made along this line, but no mention of the composition of the legislature was made.

87. The draft of the Constitution of Japan written by the Government Section of the GHQ adopted unicameralism, stating: "The Diet shall consist of one House of elected representatives" with a membership between 300 and 500. This provision was revised by the Imperial Diet to provide for two Houses and was divided into two articles, to separate the structure of the Diet from the elective representative nature of its membership. In addition, a new article highlighting the separateness of each House from the other was added, by way of caution, in the ratified Constitution:

> (10)*Article 42.* The Diet shall consist of two Houses, namely the House of Representatives and the House of Councillors.
>
> *Article 43.* Both Houses shall consist of elected members, representative of all the people. The number of the members of each House shall be fixed by law.
>
> *Article 48.* No person shall be permitted to be a member of both Houses simultaneously.

The American drafters could not find any reasonable explanation for a bicameral system in a unitary state, though they did not insist on a one-House system. The Japanese government adhered to the bicameral system, not in the hope of preserving a typical parliamentary system of constitutional monarchy, but for fear of the possible emergence of a leftist-dominated House. Such fear turned out to be imaginary in succeeding years.

---

20. *Political Reorientation of Japan, September 1945 to September 1948*, Vol. I, p. 145. This text lists the following reforms as the most significant: (a) Popular sovereignty replaces the sovereignty of the Emperor. (b) The Diet is the highest organ of state power. (c) An elected House of Councillors replaces the House of Peers. (d) The Cabinet is responsible to the Diet. (e) The Diet law supersedes the repealed imperial law of the Houses. (f) The people are legally delivered from the last vestiges of feudal heritage. (g) The "invisible government" of crown agencies is abolished.

88. As ordained by the Constitution, both Houses of the Diet consist of members elected by the people. Bicameralism is consistent with the principle of checks and balances, but each House should be based on different types of representation. Otherwise, each would be a useless duplicate of the other.[21] Representation in the two-House legislature responds to various political interests, such as population, geographic area, or other considerations to assure that political units which have popular voting strength are appropriately represented.

Before the 1995 amendment of the Public Offices Election Act, representation in the House of Representatives was based on population, while in the House of Councillors, it is based evenly on geographic area and the strength of political parties, thus bringing together the concepts of territorial representation and proportional representation. The 1995 amendment introduced proportional representation as well into the House of Representatives election (*see* paragraph 92).

II. Composition and Electoral System

89. The Constitution establishes the basic principles regarding the qualifications of members of both Houses and the electoral system. In the interest of flexibility, the Constitution provides that the details are to be determined by statutory laws such as the Diet Act and the Public Offices Election Act.[22]

The basic principle regarding the qualifications of members of both Houses and their electors is set forth in Article 44 which stipulates, "[T]here shall be no discrimination because of race, creed, sex, social status, family origin, education, property or income." Under the old Constitution, the Upper House of the Imperial Diet was called the House of Peers. Its membership consisted of the aristocracy, prominent citizens appointed by the Emperor, and the wealthy chosen from among higher taxpayers. With the adoption of the present Constitution, the House of Peers was replaced with the House of Councillors.

While the "class-based" nature of the Upper House was abolished, some differences in the qualifications of members of the two Houses are found in the relevant statutes. One of the most visible differences might be that a candidate for the House of Councillors must be at least 30 years of age while a candidate for the House of Representatives must be at least 25. The voting franchise for all public offices is extended to all Japanese nationals at least 18 years of age[23] excluding those who

---

21. H. Kelsen, *General Theory of Law and State* 298 (Harvard University Press 1949).
22. There are Standing Committees and Special Committees in each House. Article 41 of the Diet Act stipulates that Standing Committees examine the bills, petitions, and other items which come under their respective spheres of work, and lists twenty Committees of the House of Representatives and seventeen Committees of the House of Councillors. As stated in Art. 45, Special Committees examine specially designated matters which do not come within the jurisdiction of any Standing Committee. Article 46 stipulates, "Membership of Standing Committees and Special Committees shall be allotted in proportion to the numeral strength of political parties or groups in the respective Houses."
23. The voting age was lowered from 20 to 18 by the 2015 amendment to the Public Offices Election Act, effective as of Jun. 19, 2016.

have been sentenced to penal servitude or confinement and whose terms of punishment have not been completed (excluding suspension of sentence), or who have been sentenced to penal servitude or confinement charged with offenses in relation to election to public office, voting, or popular referendum of the Supreme Court Justices but whose sentence is suspended (sections 9–11 of the Public Offices Election Act).

90. The Constitution provides that the term of office of the members of the House of Representatives is four years unless terminated earlier in case of dissolution (Article 45), while that of the members of the House of Councillors is six years with the election for half the members taking place every three years (Article 46). Thus, the House of Councillors, which is not subject to dissolution, may (if called into session by the Cabinet in times of national emergency) function as the National Diet while the House of Representatives is dissolved. Its determinations, however, when so functioning are provisional and become void unless ratified by the newly constituted House of Representatives.

91. Electoral districts, voting methods, and other matters about the election of members of both Houses are set out in the Public Offices Election Act.

The House of Representatives consists of a fixed number of members, which is set at 465 as of 2021 (section 4, paragraph 1 of the Public Offices Election Act). Though Japan had adopted the mid-size electoral district for seventy years since 1925, under which a voter casts a vote and three to five candidates are elected from an electoral district, in 1995 it introduced a new system for the House of Representatives election, under which a voter has two votes, namely, one for an individual candidate and the other for the list of candidates submitted by a political party. In 1999, the number of members of the House of Representatives was reduced from 500 to 480. Out of the 480 seats, 300 are filled from small, single-member electoral districts, and 180 are assigned to proportional representation. As of 2021, the 465 seats are divided into 289 for single-member electoral districts and 176 for proportional representation.

The House of Councillors consists of a fixed number of 248 as of 2021 (section 4, paragraph 2 of the Public Offices Election Act), of which 148 are to be elected from electoral districts corresponding to each prefecture and the Tokyo Metropolis to each of which several seats in the House are assigned as specified in the Act. The remaining one hundred are to be distributed to the political parties which are required to predetermine the hierarchical preference among their candidates to be elected.

92. The number of Councillors and Representatives of the Diet is supposed to be apportioned to each electoral district in proportion to the number of qualified electors. This is implicit in Article 14 of the Constitution as a part of the guarantee of equal protection under the law. However, the legislature has generally been reluctant to act on matters of reapportionment, thus infringing upon the equality of voting value, to the disadvantage of those electors who reside in rapidly swelling districts.

93. When malapportionment of the House of Representatives was first challenged and brought before the Supreme Court, the Court refused to review constitutionality on the ground that the apportionment problem was not a matter for the judicial branch but instead belonged to the field of legislative policy. When later litigation came before the Court, the disparity between the most populous vis-à-vis the least populous district was 1 to 4.99. This time the Court intervened and declared the said inequality of voting rights unconstitutional (30 *Minshu* 223, Sup. Ct., G.B., April 14, 1976).[24]

94. As to the House of Councillors, the Court denied the claim of unconstitutionality based on a disparity of 1 to 5.26 because representation in the House of Councillors was not exclusively based on the population (37 *Minshu* 345, Sup. Ct., G.B., April 27, 1983).[25] In later decisions, the Court seemed to have difficulty in drawing a definite line between constitutional and unconstitutional voting disparity, to say nothing of attempting to reach a one person-one vote ideal.

Unequal voting value as high as 1 to 3.18 was found to be inadmissible but not unconstitutional while a disparity of 1 to 2.92 was held constitutional by the Court. The question may be raised as to whether the line of demarcation (supposedly 1 to 3) is rational, or whether the Court has already lost its way in a political dilemma. (For more Supreme Court decisions *see* paragraphs 159 and 386.).

95. Finally, each House may independently judge disputes related to the qualifications of its members. But to deny a seat to any member, it is necessary to pass a resolution by a special majority of two-thirds or more of the members present (Article 55).

§2. Position

I. The Highest and the Sole Lawmaking Organ of the State

96. The Diet is unquestionably the highest lawmaking organ of the State as far as the Constitution is concerned. The Constitution stipulates, "The Diet shall be the highest organ of State power and shall be the sole law-making organ of the State" (Article 41).

97. However, at the same time, the Constitution gives legislating powers to national government organs other than the Diet. Article 73 gives the Cabinet the

24. Supreme Court of Japan, "Judgment upon Case of Constitutionality of the Provisions of the Public Offices Election Act on Election Districts and the Apportionment of Seats," *Series of Prominent Judgments of the Supreme Court upon Questions of Constitutionality*, No. 17 (General Secretariat, Supreme Court of Japan, Tokyo 1981).
25. Supreme Court of Japan, "Judgment upon Case of Constitutionality of the Provisions on the Apportionment of Seats of Members of the House of Councillors," *Series of Prominent Judgments of the Supreme Court upon Questions of Constitutionality*, No. 19 (General Secretariat, Supreme Court of Japan, Tokyo 1984).

authority to enact executive orders, and the Supreme Court may make rules of practice and procedure and may regulate matters relating to attorneys, the internal discipline of the courts and the administration of judicial affairs as provided in Article 77. Furthermore, each House may determine the rules of meetings, proceedings, and internal discipline as provided in Article 58. Simply stated, the legislating power of the State is by no means monopolized by the Diet.

What then does the Constitution mean by the phrase "the sole lawmaking organ of the State"? It is presumed that the drafters unconsciously planned to alienate the Emperor from the legislating power of the State by positioning the Diet as the only legitimate legislative organ of the national government.

98. The same may be said about the declaration of the "highest organ of the State power." The Diet is not necessarily the highest organ of the State given judicial power to invalidate legislation enacted by the Diet. What is made supreme by the Constitution is not the will of the Diet but the Constitution itself.

Why then was the Diet declared as the highest organ of the State? Does this idea not run against the principle of separation of powers or sound too classical in the context of the undeniable political reality of the administrative State? It may well be conjectured that the drafters of the Constitution felt the need to legally contradict the idea of Imperial sovereignty memorialized in the old Constitution. It must have been their primary purpose to deny to the Emperor any source of the sovereign power of the State, including legislative power, by ranking the Diet as the highest and the sole lawmaking organ of the State.

II. Legal Status

99. Even though the highest organ of the State is a eulogistic name of the Diet, its members are provided with fairly comfortable privileges and immunities as constituents of the highest legislature of the State. Based on the modern political tradition, members of both Houses may "not be held liable outside the House for speeches, debates or votes cast inside the House" (Article 51), and, except in a case of "in flagrant delict" outside the House as provided by the Diet Act, they are "exempt from apprehension while the Diet is in session, and any members apprehended before the opening of the session shall be freed during the term of the session upon demand of the House" (Article 50).

100. For the purpose of enabling members of both Houses to concentrate on State business, they are entitled to "appropriate annual payment from the national treasury in accordance with law" (Article 49). The Diet Act states concretely: "an annual allowance should be no less in amount than the highest pay for government officials in general," that is, not less than that for vice ministers. Moreover, a retirement allowance is provided for members at the end of their Diet service. They also have the franking privilege as provided by the Diet Act. For the convenience of the members and for the benefit of financing both Houses, "expenditures of each House shall be appropriated independently in the national budget," as provided in section 32 of the Diet Act.

§3. COMPETENCE AND WORKING

I. Superiority of the House of Representatives

101. With the enactment of the Constitution, the old Upper House, the House of Peers, not only changed its name and composition but also lost its previous exalted position over the House of Representatives. In addition, several provisions of the Constitution placed the House of Councillors, the new Upper House, in a subordinate position.[26]

102. As a rule, a bill passed by both Houses becomes law as provided in Article 59. Even if the House of Councillors makes an objection to a bill passed by the House of Representatives, the latter may pass the bill a second time by a two-thirds majority of the members present. If such a supermajority is obtained, the bill becomes law. Also, if the House of Councillors objects to a bill, the House of Representatives may call for a meeting of a joint committee of both Houses to see if a compromise may be reached. If no compromise is reached, the House of Representatives may by a two-thirds vote, override the Councillors' objection. When the House of Councillors fails to take final action within sixty days after receipt of a bill passed by the House of Representatives, the House of Representatives may deem the bill as rejected by the other House except in time of recess.

103. It is likewise required that a budget be passed by both Houses. It must first be submitted to the House of Representatives as provided in Article 60. When the House of Councillors objects to a budget passed by the House of Representatives and no agreement can be reached (even through a joint committee of both Houses), or the House of Councillors fails to take final action within thirty days (excluding any period of recess) after the receipt of the budget passed by the House of Representatives, the decision of the Lower House becomes that of the Diet. The same formula is applied to the Diet approval required for the conclusion of a treaty (Article 61).

104. A slightly modified formula is applied to the process of nominating the Prime Minister. As a general rule, the Prime Minister is nominated from among the Diet's members by a resolution of the Diet as provided in Article 67. When the two Houses cannot agree on their selection or the House of Councillors fails to make a nomination within ten days, excluding the period of recess, after one has been made by the House of Representatives, the decision of the latter becomes that of the Diet.

105. Furthermore, when the House of Representatives is dissolved, the House of Councillors shall be closed at the same time unless called into session by the Cabinet in time of national emergency. Any measures taken by the House of Councillors in an emergency session, are regarded as provisional and become void unless ratified by the House of Representatives within ten days after the opening of the next session of the Diet (Article 54, paragraphs 2 and 3).

---

26. For details, *see Political Reorientation of Japan, September 1945 to September 1948*, p. 184.

106. Thus, under the Constitution, the Lower House occupies a superior position over the Upper House. This is in sharp contrast to the relationship established in the older Constitution. Yet, the political importance of the House of Councillors in the actual legislative process should not be underestimated. As a matter of practice, the failure of the government party to hold the majority over the opposition in the Upper House has resulted in a serious hindrance to its policy-making ability.

II. Meeting of the Diet

107. It is the Emperor who convokes the Diet, dissolves the House of Representatives and proclaims the general election for members of the Diet. But he may only act with the advice and approval of the Cabinet. His role in government is strictly limited as the fount of honor and is practically similar to that of an honorary president who is outside the political arena.[27] To convoke the Diet, an Imperial rescript is to be promulgated. At the beginning of each session, members of the Diet hear the speech from the throne, which ceremoniously announces the opening of the Diet.

An ordinary session of the Diet is to be convoked once a year (Article 52), sometime in December, while special sessions of the Diet may be called by the Cabinet at its will or under demand from a quarter or more of the total members of either House (Article 53). The term of an ordinary session lasts 150 days unless the term of members expires before the end of said period. As previously mentioned, when the members of the House of Representatives are newly elected after dissolution, the Diet must be convoked within thirty days from the date of the election.

108. As mentioned earlier, each House may select its president and other officials (Article 58), determine the rules of its proceedings, and punish members for disorderly conduct. The elective officers of each House, as listed in the Diet Act, are President (i.e., Speaker), Vice President, President *pro tem*, standing committee chairs, and Secretary-General. The President of each House is in charge of maintaining order in the House, adjusting its proceedings, supervising its business and representing the House.

Business is not allowed to be transacted in either House unless one-third or more of its total membership is present (Article 56). All actions of each House must be decided by a majority of those present. In case of a tie, the presiding officer (i.e., President of the House) may decide the issue (Article 56).

Deliberation in each House shall be public, but a secret meeting may be held where two-thirds or more of those members present pass a resolution for a secret meeting (Article 57). Each House must keep a record of proceedings for publication and general circulation, excepting such parts of proceedings of a secret session as may be deemed to require secrecy (Article 57). One-fifth or more of the members present in each House can demand votes of the members to be recorded in the minutes.

27. R.M. MacIver, *The Web of Government* 155 (MacMillan Co. 1947). The Japanese monarchy is so limited that it is well woven into the democratic governmental system.

III. Interpellations and Impeachment

109. It is prescribed in Article 63 of the Constitution that the Prime Minister and other Ministers of State must appear in either House when their presence is required to answer interpellations, while they may at any time appear to speak on bills. Ministers need not hold seats in a House to answer or explain or speak on a bill.

110. The Diet Act has several complementary provisions to the Constitution. The Cabinet may, for instance, appoint representatives of the government to assist Ministers in the Diet with the approval of the President of each House. These representatives of the government consist of high-ranking officials. The President of each House transmits to the Cabinet a concise statement of an interpellation presented by a member of each House and approved by the President (or by either House, in case the President disapproves and a House disagrees with him). The Cabinet must make a reply within seven days of receipt of the statements. A committee in either House may request the presence of a Minister or a representative of the government at its meeting. Also, a committee may request the presence of, and explanation by, the President of the Board of Audit and auditors at its meeting. However, the Chief Justice of the Supreme Court or a deputy designated by him, may, with the consent of a committee, attend committee meetings to give explanations.

111. Judges are guaranteed their independence in performing their official duties (Article 76) and may be removed only by public impeachment except for judicially declared mental or physical incompetence to perform official duties (Article 78). An impeachment court is set up from among the members of both Houses to try those judges against whom removal proceedings have been instituted (Article 64). The Impeachment of Judges Act was enacted to carry into execution this constitutional provision. The Act specifies impeachable offenses as follows: (i) conduct in grave contravention of official duties or grave neglect of official duties, and (ii) other misconduct seriously affecting the integrity of a judge. The Impeachment Committee consists of ten members (plus five reserve members) from each House, while the Court of Impeachment consists of seven members (plus four reserve members) from each House. Both the members of the Impeachment Committee and the judges of the Impeachment Court are guaranteed that they can exercise their official power independently. A resolution of the Impeachment Committee and a judgment of the Court of Impeachment are determined by a majority of members or judges present, but to pass a resolution to proceed with impeachment and to render a judgment of removal, a two-thirds majority of each is needed.

IV. Investigations and Petitions

112. Each House is empowered to perform investigations in relation to government affairs and to demand the presence and testimony of witnesses and the production of records (Article 62). According to the Act for Oath and Testimony of

Witness in the Diet, a House may request any person to appear as a witness or to produce papers in connection with an investigation concerning national administration.

This has given rise to a confrontation among varying constitutional theories. The majority view holds the power of investigation of each House to be auxiliary to the legislative power while the minority views it as an independent power. Although the auxiliary power theory was previously the most popular one, a third theory, which views power as a device for carrying out the people's right to know, has arisen and has gained some popularity.

113. The power of investigation of each House has posed a sensitive problem to the independence of judicial officers and the separation of powers in relation to the judiciary. The threat has been more imaginary than real because it is a widely accepted idea that the Houses should not abuse the investigatory power, still less they should substantially usurp the functions of the courts. This view could prevent each House from investigating matters relevant to past or future litigation and could prevent inquiries into matters pertinent to litigation pending in the courts.[28] Furthermore, a lower court once contended that, while an investigation may be concurrently conducted by either of the Houses and by the public prosecutors, such legislative investigation must not be permitted as to constitute political pressure on, or a hindrance to, prosecutorial judgments.

114. The right of peaceful petition for the enactment, repeal, or amendment of laws and for other purposes is guaranteed by Article 16 of the Constitution. Though the Constitution does not specify where to petition, section 3 of the Petition Act stipulates, "The petition shall be filed in the governmental or public office which has the jurisdiction for petition matters." In accordance with the Petition Act, section 79 of the Diet Act provides that a written petition must be presented to either House through its members. Each House receives and disposes of petitions independently.

28. L.H. Tribe, *American Constitutional Law* 376 (Foundation Press 2d ed. 1988).

Chapter 4. The Executive

by Prof. Go Nakagawa with updates by Prof. Takehisa Nakagawa

§1. The Cabinet

I. General Principles

115. Based on the doctrine of separation of powers, it is ordained that executive power is vested in the Cabinet (Article 65). The distinction between executive power and administrative power has no substantial significance. These terms are used interchangeably in Japanese legal texts. The powers of the executive organs are, as a general matter, derived from statutes though some of the important policy-making powers, formerly conceived of as prerogative powers of the Emperor, are given to the Cabinet directly by the Constitution.

In the present stage of the administrative state, the constitutional principle of the supremacy of the Diet is becoming shaky as the administrative needs of the people are ever-expanding and the government is constantly required to respond to the demands of the people.

116. Administrative functions of the national government are not monopolized by the Cabinet and administrative agencies thereunder. The Board of Audit exercises its auditing power as an organ independent of the Cabinet as provided by the Board of Audit Act and the Constitution. The Diet has certain administrative authority, such as the power to nominate the Prime Minister while the Supreme Court may nominate the judges of inferior courts. The Emperor may perform some administrative functions that are without any political implications.

II. Composition and Qualifications

117. The Cabinet consists of the Prime Minister, who is its head, and other Ministers of State (Article 66). The Prime Minister is designated from among the members of the Diet as has been described above. The Prime Minister may appoint Ministers of State, half of whom must be chosen from among the members of the Diet, and may remove a Minister of State at will (Article 68). As of 2021, the number of Ministers of State, other than the Prime Minister, is limited to not more than fourteen under the Cabinet Act, section 2, paragraph 2. The provision also provides, "if required by special circumstances, the number may be increased by not more than three, to make the total not more than seventeen." In order to assist the work of the Cabinet, the Cabinet Secretariat is set up under the Cabinet Act. It is in charge of preparing the agenda of Cabinet meetings and other miscellaneous affairs of the Cabinet. The Cabinet Secretary-General shall be a Minister of State.

118. As a matter of political reality, the Prime Minister is bound by the power relationships among the political factions of his party or coalition partners. For

Cabinet stability and because the Prime Minister is either chosen from among factions of the majority party or by a coalition of parties, the positions of Ministers of State are usually apportioned according to the size of and political affinity of each faction or party. In other words, being a political product of a coalition of competing factions, the Prime Minister cannot exercise a true discretionary power of removal over Ministers of State.

119. Neither the Constitution nor laws stipulate any qualifications for a Minister except that the Prime Minister and other Ministers of State must be civilians (Article 66, paragraph 2). This civilian clause was inserted into the Constitution at the request of the GHQ due to pressure from a Member State of the Far Eastern Commission. Echoing grave concern about the fatal weakness in civilian control over the military in Japan before and during World War II and corresponding to the renunciation of war declared in Article 9, the Constitution ordained that military personnel be disqualified from the office of Ministers of State.

§2. Legal Status of the Cabinet Members

I. Privileges

120. Because members of the Diet are granted the privilege to be free from arrest during the term of the session (Article 50), a Cabinet member who is concurrently a member of either House is exempt from apprehension while the Diet is in session. In addition, Ministers of State may not be subject to legal action (criminal action) during their tenure of office without the consent of the Prime Minister; provided, however, that no right of action shall be impaired by this privilege (Article 75). It is considered that this provision includes exemption from arrest and detention as well.

121. It is widely agreed that the Prime Minister is deemed as one of the Ministers of State although some theorists exclude the Prime Minister from this category.

The proviso that no right of legal action is impaired means the proscription of public prosecution is to be temporarily suspended during the period of privilege.

II. Collective Responsibility

122. Even though Ministers of State may be individually charged by the Diet with negligence or failure to perform their official duties or with personal fault or misdeed, they are responsible to the Diet for the general conduct of affairs not as individuals but as a body. The third paragraph of Article 66 states, "The Cabinet, in the exercise of executive power, shall be collectively responsible to the Diet." The joint responsibility of the Ministers is based on the convention that except when a Minister of State personally resigns, every member of the Cabinet is responsible for all matters that pass the Cabinet, without reservation.[29] This rule is the foundation of a British-type parliamentary government because it assures the unity of the Cabinet in a practical sense.

Whenever a vacancy occurs in the post of Prime Minister, or upon the first convocation of the Diet after an election of the House of Representatives, the Cabinet must resign *en masse* (Article 70). Until a new Prime Minister is appointed, the existing Cabinet is to continue to perform its duties (Article 71).

§3. Competence of the Prime Minister

I. Political Hindrance to the Office

123. The Prime Minister is the chief executive officer of the government and is deemed to be the leader of the dominant political party though such political leadership is often nominal. It is generally expected that the Prime Minister negotiates with all the faction leaders of his party as well as coalition partners, and, whenever necessary, even with opposition party leaders on policy matters relating to policy making. Because the bond among faction members is usually stronger than the goal of party solidarity, it is not unusual for a Prime Minister to have difficulty managing relations both with opposition parties as well as with intra-opposition groups. Because of factional politics, generally speaking, the Prime Minister can never be a strong executive organ in the government. Even though Cabinet members shall be appointed or removed at the Prime Minister's will, the reality is that the Cabinet is organized through negotiation among the representatives of the factions and coalition parties. Therefore, even the Prime Minister himself may be in danger of being removed from office when serious factional or coalition disputes occur or when major factional leaders agree to appoint a new Prime Minister.

Despite the lack of strong political leadership in the executive branch, efficient bureaucracy has played a steady and positive role in national policy-making decisions. Local governments have also increased their administrative functions to respond to the administrative needs of the people.

124. In postwar Japan, the tenure of office for prime ministers has generally been short and not very stable. There were a few notable exceptions, such as the cabinets of Shigeru Yoshida (1948–1953), Hayato Ikeda (1960–1964), Eisaku Sato (1964–1972), Yasuhiro Nakasone (1982–1987), Junichiro Koizumi (2001–2006), and Shinzo Abe (2012–2020).

In the late 1990s, concerns came to be shared that unstable Cabinets, with weak leadership from the Prime Minister, would hinder the government's swift and bold decision-making. One of the results was the 1999 amendment to the Cabinet Act which, aiming for more decisive leadership from the Prime Minister, has included

29. Based on the description of E.C.S. Wade & G. Godfrey Phillips, *Constitutional Law* 66 (Longmans, Green and Co. 1931).

several provisions to the effect that the Cabinet does not only coordinate among each Ministry and Agency but also makes its policies (section 4, paragraph 2 and section 12, paragraph 2).

In recent years, the relationship between politics and bureaucracy has changed dramatically to strengthen the leadership of the Prime Minister. It is not clear whether this change is a product of the amendment of the Cabinet Act or not.

II. Chief Executive of the Government

125. The head of the State and the chief executive are deliberately separated in Japan. The Emperor is the ceremonial head of the State while the Prime Minister and the Cabinet are to lead the government and formulate its policies.

Outlining the powers of the chief executive, Article 72 of the Constitution states, "The Prime Minister, representing the Cabinet, submits bills, reports on general national affairs and foreign relations to the Diet and exercises control and supervision over various administrative branches."

126. While the abovementioned provision (paragraph 125) makes the Prime Minister's office superior to those of other Ministers of State, its actual powers are under the control of the Cabinet meeting over which the Prime Minister presides. Only when agreed by the Cabinet, may the Prime Minister submit bills, budgets and other proposals, and report national affairs and foreign relations to the Diet. Control and supervision over various administrative organs by the Prime Minister may be exercised only in accordance with policies decided at Cabinet meetings. It is not expected that direction and supervision be done at the Prime Minister's will. Even when the Prime Minister adjudicates conflicts relating to jurisdiction between the competent Ministers, as the Cabinet Act stipulates it, consultation at Cabinet meetings must be followed.

The weak Prime Ministership, which has been maintained since the pre-World War II period, is derived from the traditionally negative attitude of the Japanese people against iron-willed executive leadership.

127. Most of the legislative proposals are made in the form of government bills, which are drawn up by officials of a department of the executive branch and introduced by the Cabinet. Other legislative proposals are drafted by members of the Diet, members of pressure groups, or interested citizens, to be introduced by individual members of the Diet. Article 72 suggests that bills may include proposals for constitutional amendments (as to whether the Cabinet may propose a constitutional amendment in the form of a regular bill, *see* paragraph 37).

128. Administrative commissions, such as the Fair Trade Commission, National Public Safety Commission, Central Labor Relations Board, and other independent administrative authorities, such as the Board of Audit and National Personnel Authority, are not under the control or supervision of the Prime Minister in performing their functions.

§4. Competence of the Cabinet

I. Discretionary Powers

129. The majority of the constitutional powers of the Cabinet are susceptible to statutory limitations, though some of them, due to their executive and discretionary nature, are not so limited. Metaphorically speaking, such discretionary powers of the Cabinet may be viewed as transformed Royal prerogatives of the older Constitution that came to be provided for in the new Constitution as the powers of the Cabinet. They are listed in Article 73 of the Constitution as follows:

- Manage foreign affairs.
- Conclude treaties with the prior or subsequent, depending on circumstances, approval of the Diet.
- Decide on general amnesty, special amnesty, commutation of punishment, reprieve, and restoration of rights.

The Cabinet may exercise its discretion in these areas. Discretionary powers of the Cabinet can be challenged on such grounds as excess or irregularity. However, such a challenge can only be made to the Diet, a political branch, and not to the court because they are considered political questions and hence not justiciable.

130. Treaties are considered to include attached executive agreements as well as other forms of international agreements signed by the Japanese government.[30] In the treaty-making process, it is the Cabinet that negotiates, signs, and ratifies, while it is the Diet that gives or withholds approval for ratification of a treaty. The Diet has no legal power to modify treaties during the process of approval but it can, as a practical matter, modify treaties by informing the Cabinet of what kind of treaty it is willing to support.

Even a treaty that has failed to be approved by the Diet after ratification by the Cabinet is generally considered valid between the concerned countries. As a result, the Cabinet is under an obligation to abolish the treaty. However, it has been contended by some theorists that questions as to the validity of treaties should be left to the general principles of international law.

The procedure for pardons granted by the Cabinet and then attested to by the Emperor is set out in the Act of Grace.

II. Administrative Powers

131. Aside from the discretionary powers of the Cabinet which are historically derived from Royal prerogatives, the Cabinet is responsible for administrative

30. In the *Sunagawa* case of 1959, the Supreme Court held the executive agreement as a delegated legislation based on the Treaty of the Mutual Security Act between Japan and the United States (1951). *See* para. 16. Nevertheless, the agreement under s. 6 of the Treaty of Mutual Cooperation and Security between Japan and the United States (1960) was submitted to the Diet for its approval.

functions created under the laws. In addition to other general administrative functions, Article 73 of the Constitution specifies certain administrative powers as follows:

- Administer the law faithfully; conduct affairs of state.
- Administer the civil service, in accordance with standards established by law.
- Prepare the budget and present it to the Diet.
- Enact cabinet orders in order to execute the provisions of this Constitution and of the law. However, it cannot include penal provisions in such cabinet orders unless authorized by such law.

132. The responsibility of the Cabinet to "administer the law faithfully" corresponds to Article II, section 2, paragraph 3 of the Constitution of the United States which states: "he (the President) shall take care that the laws be faithfully executed."

However, this type of provision does not have much significance in a cabinet government of the British type.

133. In the Meiji Constitution, it was provided that the Emperor exercised the power to appoint and dismiss officials as part of his sovereign power. Not only has the appointing and dismissing power been moved to the Cabinet but it has also been limited by statutes. Standards of the civil service are set out in the National Civil Service Act.[31] The National Personnel Authority, an independent administrative organ, which combines quasi-legislative and quasi-judicial powers as well as administrative power, is in charge of enforcing the Act.

134. According to the prevailing academic view, the budget, a fiscal program for the next ensuing year, is deemed to be a law that should pass the Diet. Little doubt may exist of its being a kind of law because the Constitution requires consideration and decision by the Diet as provided in Article 86. However, as a budget is effective only for a year and is not directly concerned with the rights and duties of the people, some constitutional scholars contend that the budget should be considered special legislation which is different from ordinary statutes in its effect.

135. The drafters must have modeled the cabinet order after the executive order of the President of the United States which is implicit in the United States Constitution. It poses two major constitutional problems. The first is whether a cabinet order can enforce provisions of the Constitution when no statute is available. The majority view is opposed to such power, although the text of Article 73 may be read as supporting the power.

The second problem involves delegated legislation. The Cabinet Act restates the cabinet order clause of the Constitution by providing that no provision imposing

---

31. Section 2 of the National Civil Service Act provides that the national civil service is divided into regular government service and special government service. The regular government service comprises all positions in the national civil service other than those in special government service. The special government service comprises the Ministers of State, members of the Diet, judges, ambassadors, and several others.

obligations or restricting rights may be included in cabinet orders unless authorized by law (section 11 of the Cabinet Act). It is a worldwide, general tendency to increase the delegation of legislative power to administrative agencies. This results from the fact that the legislatures in modern democracies are overloaded with the duties of making numerous and highly technical laws. There being no legal objection to the delegated legislative power itself, the question is, however, to what extent the Constitution allows the delegation of legislative power to the Cabinet and other administrative agencies.

136. The Supreme Court has said that delegation should be particular and definite. But a question remains as to how to establish a clear and indisputable distinction between constitutional and unconstitutional delegation. At present, there is little possibility that the Court will declare a specific delegation unconstitutional.

For example, section 102 of the National Civil Service Act imposes restrictions on the political activities of regular government officials by providing, "No person in the service shall solicit, receive, or be in any manner concerned in soliciting or receiving any subscription or other benefit for any political party or political purpose" (paragraph 1). Rule 14-7 issued by the National Personnel Authority regulates the details of the prohibited political activities of regular government officials. The Supreme Court upheld the constitutionality of such legislative delegation of details to the National Personnel Authority (12 *Keishu* 1272, Sup. Ct., May 1, 1958). Many constitutional law scholars disagree with the Supreme Court, arguing that the delegation by the National Service Act was virtually a *carte blanche*.

Re-delegation of delegated power without authorization for such re-delegation in the statute was held constitutional by the Supreme Court on the ground that the original delegation of power was adequately defined in the legislation (12 *Keishu* 2407, Sup. Ct., July 9, 1958).

137. As part of the continuous efforts for administrative reform by the government, "Central Government Reform" has been pursued from 1999 to 2000. The leadership of the Prime Minister has legally been strengthened by revising the Cabinet Act (*see* paragraphs 123–126). As of January 2001, the national administrative organs under the Cabinet were reorganized, several departments being merged, split up, or renamed. A new agency named "Cabinet Office" was created to support directly the Cabinet, which office was to be ranked superior to the other Ministries and Agencies under the Cabinet. (The reshuffle did not include independent agencies, such as the Fair Trade Commission. *See* the list below.)

Before January 1, 2001	*Since January 1, 2001*
Prime Minister's Office General Affairs Agency Economic Planning Agency Science and Technology Agency National Land Agency Okinawa Development Agency	Cabinet Office

Before January 1, 2001	*Since January 1, 2001*
General Affairs Agency Ministry of Home Affairs Ministry of Posts and Telecommunications	Ministry of General Affairs
Ministry of Justice	Ministry of Justice
Ministry of Foreign Affairs	Ministry of Foreign Affairs
Ministry of Treasury	Ministry of Finance Financial Services Agency
Ministry of Education Science and Technology Agency	Ministry of Education and Science
Ministry of Labor Ministry of Health and Welfare	Ministry of Welfare and Labor
Ministry of Agriculture, Forestry, and Fisheries	Ministry of Agriculture, Forestry, and Fisheries
Ministry of International Trade and Industry (MITI)	Ministry of Economy, Trade, and Industry (METI)
Ministry of Construction Ministry of Transportation National Land Agency Hokkaido Development Agency	Ministry of National Land and Transport
Environmental Agency	Ministry of Environment
Defense Agency	Defense Agency (Ministry of Defense since January 9, 2007)

The new governmental instrumentality of "independent administrative corporations" was introduced by statute in 1999 and new fifty-seven corporations were established in 2001. All the national universities, which used to be part of the Ministry of Education, were reestablished as "national university corporations" in 2004.

Chapter 5. The Judiciary

by Prof. Hiroyuki Hata with updates by Prof. Hiromi Nishimura and Prof. Takayoshi Okada

§1. Judicial Organization

I. General Introduction

A. *Unitary Judicial Organization: Ordinary Law Courts Decide All Legal Cases Including Administrative Cases*

138. Under the Meiji Constitution (1889), the courts of law exercised judicial power in accordance with the law in the name of the Emperor (Article 57). These courts, however, were not empowered to accept administrative suits, namely, suits challenging the legality of governmental actions. These suits had to be referred to the separate Administrative Court established under the Administrative Adjudication Act and located in Tokyo. In other words, the Meiji Constitution (which was modeled on the Prussian Constitution of 1850) distinguished between the courts of law and the Administrative Court. Courts of law did not have the power to decide administrative cases.

It must also be noted that the Administrative Adjudication Act limited the Administrative Court's authority to a certain category of administrative cases. In particular, the Administrative Court could not accept a suit seeking damages resulting from governmental wrongdoing.

139. Unlike the Meiji Constitution, the Constitution of Japan (which was enacted during the American occupation) was strongly influenced by the Anglo-American legal system. Accordingly, the term "judicial power" used in Article 76 of the Constitution is to be interpreted as having the same meaning as in Anglo-American law. Paragraph 1 of Article 76, using language similar to that contained in the United States Constitution, Article III, section 1, stipulates, "the whole judicial power is vested in a Supreme Court and in such inferior courts as are established by law." Paragraph 2 of the same article provides, "No extraordinary tribunal shall be established, nor shall any organ or agency of the Executive be given final judicial power." These provisions explicitly show that there is no room in the Constitution of Japan for such an organ as the Administrative Court which existed under the Meiji Constitution. However, this does not mean that nonjudicial organs cannot perform functions of a judicial nature. In fact, many independent administrative bodies, such as the Fair Trade Commission, civil service commissions, election commissions, labor relations boards, and boards of education perform judicial-type functions in settling disputes. Decisions given by these agencies are not final (Article 76, paragraph 2), and can be referred to the ordinary law courts for final adjudication should either party to the dispute so desire.

140. In order to ask a court of law for a legal remedy, a person must (except in such cases as specially laid down by law) have standing to sue. Namely, a plaintiff must prove that he, she or any entity has had his, her or its own legal rights or legally protected interests impaired.

At the moment, there are two categories of cases in which a plaintiff is not required to establish standing before filing a suit with the court. One category covers cases involving a challenge to the legality of an election by a voter (sections 203, 204, 207 and 208 of the Public Offices Election Act), and the other deals with cases involving a demand for the return of public funds illegally spent by heads of local governments (section 242-2 of the Local Autonomy Act) (*infra* paragraph 289). It follows from the nature of the ordinary law courts that they, unlike the Constitutional Courts of Germany, Italy and Austria, are not empowered to review legal disputes in the abstract (*infra* paragraph 155).

B. *Categories of the Courts of Law*

141. The inferior courts of law established by law (Article 76, paragraph 2) include High Courts, District Courts, Family Courts and Summary Courts (section 2, paragraph 1 of the Judiciary Act). At present, there are 8 High Courts (with 6 branch courts and an Intellectual Property High Court), 50 District Courts (with 203 branch courts), 50 Family Courts (with 203 branch courts and 77 branch offices) and 438 Summary Courts throughout the nation. The Supreme Court, the highest court of law, is established by the Constitution. The following is a brief explanation of the role of the Supreme Court and the abovementioned inferior courts.

1. Summary Court

142. The Summary Court exercises both civil and criminal jurisdiction. It has original jurisdiction over civil cases involving minor claims not exceeding JPY 600,000 and original jurisdiction over criminal cases involving petty offenses (section 33, paragraph 1 of the Judiciary Act). Although it cannot, as a general matter, impose imprisonment or heavier punishment, it is authorized to pass a sentence of imprisonment at forced labor for a period not to exceed three years in certain cases specifically enumerated by law (section 33, paragraph 2 of the Judiciary Act). Cases that the court considers deserve heavier punishment must be transferred to the District Court (section 33, paragraph 3 of the Judiciary Act).

Both civil and criminal cases brought before the Summary Court are decided by a single judge.

2. Family Court

143. The Family Court disposes of disputes within a family, such as those related to marriage, inheritance of an estate, custody of a child and other family matters. Such matters are handled by way of conciliation or adjudication. In addition, the Family Court has jurisdiction over juvenile delinquency cases (section 31-3, paragraph 1, Nos. 1 and 2 of the Judiciary Act). Conciliation is conducted by a judge and family court-appointed conciliators working together, while adjudication is handled by a single judge acting alone.

3. District Court

144. The District Court has general original jurisdiction over all civil and criminal cases except those specifically stipulated by law to fall under the jurisdiction of other courts (section 24, Nos. 1 and 2 of the Judiciary Act). Though basically a first-instance court, it also exercises appellate jurisdiction over appeals lodged against Summary Court decisions in civil cases (section 24, Nos. 3 and 4 of the Judiciary Act). In the District Court, most cases are handled by a single judge. However, serious cases, appellate cases and certain other cases specified by law are handled by a panel of three judges (section 26 of the Judiciary Act).

4. High Court

145. The High Court is a court of intermediate appeals exercising appellate jurisdiction over appeals filed against judgments rendered in the first instance by the District Court and the Family Court in civil and criminal cases, and the Summary Court in criminal cases (section 16, Nos. 1–3 of the Judiciary Act). It has original jurisdiction in cases specifically enumerated in the Judiciary Act or other laws (section 17 of the Judiciary Act). Among cases that are referred to the High Court in the first instance are cases related to insurrection (sections 77–79 of the Penal Code), and cases filed by a voter to contest the legality of an election (sections 203, 204, 207 and 208 of the Public Offices Election Act), habeas corpus cases (section 4 of the Habeas Corpus Act). In the High Court, cases are handled by a panel of three judges, except for cases in which the law specifically stipulates otherwise. There are two kinds of cases that are dealt with by a panel of five judges. These are cases concerning insurrection (section 18, paragraph 2 of the Judiciary Act) and cases related to a decision on fair trade matters by the Tokyo District Court (section 18, paragraph 1 of the Judiciary Act; section 87 of the Anti-Trust Act).

5. Supreme Court

146. The Supreme Court exercises appellate jurisdiction over all cases as the court of last resort. It also has original and final jurisdiction in impeachment proceedings against commissioners of the National Personnel Authority (section 9, paragraph 1 of the National Civil Service Act). Cases brought before the Supreme Court are heard and decided either by the Grand Bench consisting of all Justices, namely, the Chief Justice and fourteen Associate Justices, or by any of the three Petty Benches which are composed of three or more (usually five) Justices (section

9, paragraphs 1 and 2 of the Judiciary Act). Though the Supreme Court has discretion over whether to refer a case to the Grand Bench or the Petty Bench, the latter is neither empowered to declare any law, order, regulation or official act unconstitutional nor to change the Supreme Court's previous interpretation of the Constitution, law or order (section 10 of the Judiciary Act). Such matters are relegated solely to the Grand Bench. In addition, to further guarantee the independence of the judiciary the Supreme Court is vested with the power to make rules concerning court procedure, attorneys, the internal discipline of the courts and the administration of judicial affairs (Article 77, paragraph 1 of the Judiciary Act). Furthermore, it has the power to nominate candidates for inferior court judgeships (Article 80, paragraph 1 of the Judiciary Act). The most notable of the powers given to the Supreme Court is the power to determine the constitutionality of legislation (Article 81 of the Judiciary Act) (*infra* paragraph 155).

147. In addition to the law courts mentioned above, there is a governmental organ named the Judges' Impeachment Court (hereinafter referred to as the Impeachment Court) which has the authority to try impeachment cases against judges who have grossly neglected their duties (Article 64 of the Constitution; section 2 of the Judges' Impeachment Act). It is composed of fourteen members: seven members from each of the House of Representatives and the House of Councillors (section 16 of the Judges' Impeachment Act). It decides cases seeking the removal of grossly derelict judges upon indictment by the Judges Indictment Committee which consists of twenty members: ten members from each House (section 5 of the Judges' Impeachment Act). Though the Impeachment Court is a type of "extraordinary tribunal" generally prohibited by the Constitution (Article 76, paragraph 2), it is recognized as a constitutional exception (Article 64).

II. Structure of Courts of Law

148. The judicial system under the Constitution of Japan is composed of three tiers of courts. The Supreme Court, which is the top tier, is the court of last resort exercising appellate jurisdiction over appeals lodged against judgments rendered in first- or second-instance cases by a High Court. A High Court, which is a middle-tier court, has jurisdiction to hear appeals against judgments rendered by courts on the bottom tier such as a District Court, Family Court or Summary Court.

149. In civil and administrative cases, a judgment given in the first instance by a Summary Court can be appealed to a District Court, and then on to a High Court. Only if there exists a constitutional question can such cases be further appealed to the Supreme Court (section 327 of the Code of Civil Procedure). However, a first-instance judgment of a District Court can be appealed to a High Court and then to the Supreme Court, though the latter only accepts appeals involving constitutional questions or questions of law material to the judgment appealed from (sections 302 and 303 of the Code of Civil Procedure). Finding of facts is limited to the courts of first and second instance. The court of final instance deals only with questions of law.

150. In criminal cases, the finding of facts is in principle limited to the first-instance court, while the second and third-instance courts handle questions of law. The third instance court, namely, the Supreme Court, accepts only appeals involving a constitutional question or a conflict with judicial precedents (section 405 of the Code of Criminal Procedure).

151. As a general rule, Japan has adopted a three-instance court system. However, there are some exceptions to the three-instance system. For example, there are a few cases in which a judgment rendered by the first-instance court can only be appealed directly to the Supreme Court (section 21 of the Habeas Corpus Act and section 25 of the Public Offices Election Act). There are also cases in which an appeal from a judgment given in the first instance by a bottom-tier court can be made directly to the Supreme Court "over the second-instance court" (section 281, paragraph 1 and section 311, paragraph 2 of the Code of Civil Procedure; section 406 of the Code of Criminal Procedure; section 254 of the Rule of Criminal Procedure). This is commonly known as a "jumping decision." Also, needless to say, cases that originate in a High Court cannot be appealed more than once (section 311, paragraph 1 of the Code of Civil Procedure; section 405 of the Code of Criminal Procedure).

III. Constitutional and Legal Status of the Judges

152. Article 79 provides, "The Supreme Court shall consist of a Chief Justice and such number of Justices as may be determined by law." The number of Justices other than a Chief Justice is fixed at fourteen (section 5, paragraph 3 of the Judiciary Act). The Chief Justice is appointed by the Emperor upon the designation of the Diet (Article 6, paragraph 2), while other Justices of the Supreme Court are appointed by the Cabinet and attested to by the Emperor (Article 80, paragraph 1). Only the Justices of the Supreme Court are subject to a popular referendum. Article 79, paragraph 2 provides that:

> The appointment of the Justices of the Supreme Court shall be reviewed by the people at the first general election of members of the House of Representatives following their appointment, and shall be reviewed again at the first general election of members of the House of Representatives after a lapse of 10 years and in the same manner thereafter.

Paragraph 3 of the same article further states, "In cases mentioned in the foregoing paragraph, when the majority of the voters favors the dismissal of a judge, he shall be dismissed."

153. The Justices of the Supreme Court are required to retire upon attainment of age 70 (Article 79, paragraph 5, section 50 of the Judiciary Act), while lower court judges, except for judges of Summary Courts, must retire upon attainment of age 65 (Article 80, paragraph 1, section 50 of the Judiciary Act).

The mandatory retirement age of Summary Court judges is set at 70 (the same provisions).

All lower court judges are appointed for a term of ten years with the privilege of reappointment (Article 80, paragraph 1). Those judges who seek reappointment are usually renominated by the Supreme Court and reappointed by the Cabinet. However, there have been a few cases in which judges were refused renomination or reappointment.

154. Under the Constitution of Japan, judges are guaranteed complete independence in performing their duties. Article 76, paragraph 3 of the Constitution stipulates, "All judges shall be independent in the exercise of their conscience and shall be bound only by this Constitution and the laws."

Article 78 additionally provides that:

> Judges shall not be removed except by public impeachment unless judicially declared mentally or physically incompetent to perform official duties. No disciplinary action against judges shall be administered by any executive organ or agency.

Referring to the impeachment stipulated in the provision, judges who have grossly violated or neglected official duties or have committed such a misdeed as to seriously injure the prestige of the judges can be dismissed by the Impeachment Court established by the Diet (Article 64). The Impeachment Court, composed of fourteen judges who are evenly chosen from among the members of the House of Representatives and the House of Councillors (*supra* paragraph 147), is independent in the exercise of its powers (sections 2 and 16 of the Judges' Impeachment Act).

155. Unlike the Meiji Constitution (1890), the present Constitution has expressly vested the judicial courts with the power to review the constitutionality of laws enacted by the Diet. Article 98 stipulates that:

> This Constitution shall be the supreme law of the nation and no law, ordinance, imperial rescript or other act of government, or part thereof, contrary to the provisions hereof, shall have legal force or validity.

In order to guarantee the supremacy of the Constitution, Article 81 states, "The Supreme Court is the court of last resort with power to determine the constitutionality of any law, order, regulation or official act."

At the time of the adoption of the Constitution of Japan, scholarly opinion on whether the judicial courts had the power to determine the constitutionality of legislation was sharply divided. Some influential constitutional lawyers were of the opinion that the Supreme Court of Japan was comparable to the Constitutional Courts of Germany, Italy, etc., with the power to review legislation in the abstract. When the Korean War broke out in June 1950, and the Japanese government, in accordance with the directive issued by Gen. Douglas MacArthur, then SCAP, established a 75,000-man Police Reserve (renamed as Security Forces and Self-Defense Forces as it grew in scale), an opposition party head filed a petition with the Supreme Court asking that all laws and executive acts creating the Police Reserve be declared null and void on the ground that the Reserve violated Article 9, paragraph 2 which prohibits Japan from maintaining an armed force. The Supreme Court rejected the petition on the ground that the plaintiff had no standing to sue, declaring that the Supreme Court was a judicial court that could review legislation only in relation to concrete legal disputes (*Police Reserve* case, 6 *Minshu* 783, Sup. Ct., G.B., October 8, 1952).

156. There are only twelve cases, including two malapportionment cases, in which the Supreme Court declared statutory provisions unconstitutional, though it has frequently invalidated acts of government, or narrowed the meaning of statutes, on constitutional grounds. These twelve cases are as follows.

157. The Patricide case of 1973. Patricide had been made a crime punishable by death or life imprisonment under section 200 of the Penal Code. Though a court had the discretion to reduce the penalty by half (in the case of the death penalty, to a minimum of ten years in prison, and in the case of life imprisonment, to a minimum of seven years in prison), the Supreme Court declared the law unconstitutional because it violated Article 14 which prohibits discrimination on irrational grounds (27 *Keishu* 265, Sup. Ct., G.B., April 4, 1973). (*See also* paragraphs 254, 255.).

158. The Drug Store case of 1975. Section 6, paragraph 2 of the Pharmaceutical Business Act had stipulated that no license should be issued to a drug store unless the distance between the planned location and an existing drug store was more than that determined by a prefectural ordinance. A druggist who had been denied a license to open a drug store because the planned site was too close to an existing drug store challenged the constitutionality of the Act and Hiroshima Prefecture's ordinance which had provided for zoning of new drug stores on the ground that they infringed on his right to choose and pursue his own occupation as guaranteed by Article 22, paragraph 1 of the Constitution. Though the government argued that a concentration of drug stores within a narrow area may lead to a futile competition among their owners thereby causing a supply of defective medicine and thus the law and ordinance served the best interest of the general public, the Supreme Court declared the law and ordinance in question unconstitutional (29 *Minshu* 572, Sup. Ct., G.B., April 30, 1975).

159. The Malapportionment cases of 1976 and 1985. On April 14, 1976, the Supreme Court declared that the rules of apportionment for members of the House of Representatives prescribed in Schedule 1 of the Public Offices Election Act, under which the maximum relative difference between electoral districts in the ratio of the voting population per Representative was 1 to 4.99 at the time of the 1972 election, violated Articles 14, 15 and 44 of the Constitution, which requires electoral equality. However, the Court held that although the election at issue was based on an unconstitutional apportionment and therefore invalid, the petition for invalidation of the election could not be granted based on the general principle of law implied in section 31 of the Administrative Case Litigation Act (ACL Act) which authorized the Court to preserve defective administrative acts rather than annul them if it found that great harm to the public interest would result if the acts were invalidated (*Chiba Prefecture Election Commission*, 30 *Minshu* 223, Sup. Ct., G.B., April 14, 1976). Such a decision is called a "circumstance decision."

Though revised after the *Chiba* case decision, the imbalance between electoral districts in the value of a vote had again widened to an intolerable extent. Therefore, voters in various areas filed suits challenging the constitutionality of the apportionment rules for Representatives. On July 17, 1985, the Supreme Court declared the rules of apportionment for the 1983 election unconstitutional. The maximum relative difference in the ratio of the voters per Representative at the time of the 1983 election had reached 1 to 4.40, a degree that violated the constitutional requirement of electoral equality. As in the previous malapportionment case, the Court again vacated the petition to nullify the election on the basis of the spirit of section 31 of the ACL Act (*Hiroshima Prefecture Election Commission*, 39 *Minshu* 1100, Sup. Ct., G.B., July 17, 1985).

160. The Forestry Act case of 1987. Section 186 of the Forestry Act, contrary to the provisions of section 256, paragraph 1 of the Civil Code, prohibited a minor co-owner from asking for a division of the ownership of a forest because such a division might cause the forest to be fractionalized and eventually ruined. The Supreme Court held that the Diet's judgment in regulating the minor co-owner's property right for the public welfare had exceeded its discretionary power and that the legislation in question violated Article 29, paragraph 2 of the Constitution and was therefore invalid (41 *Minshu* 408, Sup. Ct., G.B., April 22, 1987).

161. The Postal Act case of 2002. Section 68 of the former Postal Act provided that, for the mail handled by the State, the State shall pay damages up to a certain amount of money only when all or part of registered mail is lost or damaged, cash on delivery mail was delivered but without collecting cash, or all or part of parcel mail is lost or damaged. In addition, section 73 of the former Postal Act limited claimants of damages to the sender of the mail or the recipient with the sender's consent. However, Article 17 of the Constitution stipulates, "Every person may sue for redress as provided by law from the State or a public entity, in case he has suffered damage through illegal act of any public official." The Supreme Court ruled that the immunity provision in the Postal Act was unconstitutional and invalid, holding the following: (1) There is a legitimate legislative purpose in limiting the scope and subject matter of damages in view of the nature of the postal service, which is to process a large volume of mail fairly and evenly throughout the country at low rates under constrained resources. (2) However, it is difficult to recognize the rationality of a provision that allows exemption or limitation of liability even in exceptional cases where tort liability is caused by postal workers' intentional acts or gross negligence. (3) Therefore, sections 68 and 73 of the (former) Postal Act are invalid because they deviate from the scope of discretion granted to the legislature by Article 17 of the Constitution (56 *Minshu* 1439, Sup. Ct., G.B., September 11, 2002).

162. The Overseas Vote case of 2005. In this case, the constitutionality of denying the right to vote to Japanese nationals residing abroad was challenged. The main points of the Supreme Court's decision are as follows: (1) With regard to legislative discretion regarding restrictions on the right to vote or the exercise of the right to vote, it is not permissible in principle to restrict the right to vote or the exercise of the right to vote of citizens, except for certain restrictions on the right to vote of persons who themselves have committed acts that are detrimental to the fairness of elections. (2) In order to restrict a citizen's right to vote or the exercise of that right, there must be compelling reasons, such as the fact that, in the absence of such restrictions, it would be virtually impossible or extremely difficult to ensure fairness in elections. (3) Restricting the exercise of the right to vote without such reasons violates Article 15, paragraphs 1 and 3, Article 43, paragraph 1, and the proviso to Article 44 of the Constitution. (4) The legislative measure limiting the participation of overseas citizens in national elections to the election of members elected by proportional representation in both houses of the Diet cannot be deemed to have such compelling reasons. Therefore, the restriction will be unconstitutional at the time of the first general election of the House of Representatives or regular election of the House of Councillors to be held after the handing down of the judgment (59 *Minshu* 2087, Sup. Ct., G.B., September 14, 2005).

This is a landmark decision, for it ruled that legislative inaction, i.e., the Diet's failure to amend properly the Public Offices Election Act from the perspective of guaranteeing the voting rights of overseas citizens, was illegal and allowed the plaintiffs to claim damages under the State Compensation Act (JPY 5,000 per plaintiff). Until now, whether or not the Diet enacts, amends, or repeals a certain statute has been a matter of the Diet's broad discretion or left to its political judgment. It had been thought that political responsibility could be held through elections and that, except in exceptional cases (when the Diet dares to enact laws that clearly violate the Constitution), no legal responsibility would be obtained.

However, this judgment is based on the principle that (1) "it is obvious that the content of the legislation or the legislative inaction illegally infringes the rights guaranteed to the people under the Constitution," or (2) "where it is essential to take necessary legislative measures to ensure that the people have the opportunity to exercise their rights guaranteed by the Constitution, and the Diet fails to do so for a long period of time without justifiable reasons," the court can exceptionally hold that the legislative acts or legislative inactions of Diet members are evaluated as illegal in the application of the State Compensation Act. In this case, it was judged that the fact that no legislative action was taken for more than ten years until the election in question, after the amendment bill that had been submitted but scrapped, constituted an exceptional case under (2).

In response to this ruling, the Diet amended the Public Offices Election Act in 2006 to allow overseas citizens to vote at diplomatic missions or by mail in all national elections if they are registered on the Overseas Electoral Register through an overseas diplomatic mission. The impact of this Supreme Court decision was influential. For example, the Tokyo District Court ruled that the provision of the Public Offices Election Act (section 11, paragraph 1, Item 1), which stipulates that a person who has had a guardian appointed to manage his or her property under an adult guardianship system does not have the right to vote, cannot be considered an "unavoidable" restriction on the right to vote and is unconstitutional (2178 *Hanji* 3, Tokyo Dist. Ct., March 14, 2013). After this ruling, though the defendant State appealed to the Tokyo High Court, the Diet took swift action to repeal the provision. This is a rare case in which a ruling of the first court led to an immediate amendment of the statute. However, the Osaka High Court ruled that section 11, paragraph 1, Item 2 of the Public Offices Election Act, which does not allow prisoners (those sentenced to imprisonment or more until the end of its enforcement) to exercise their right to vote, is unconstitutional because it cannot be said that there are "unavoidable reasons" for the restriction of the right to vote for prisoners (Osaka High Court decisions, September 27, 2013). So far, there has been no movement to amend the Act, the response of the Diet here standing in sharp contrast.

163. The Nationality Act case of 2008. This was a case concerning the nationality of a child born to a Japanese father and a foreign mother. According to the Nationality Act, if a Japanese father acknowledges his child before the child's birth, even without marriage, the child acquires Japanese nationality (section 2, paragraph 1 of the Nationality Act). However, after the birth of the child, Japanese nationality cannot be acquired unless the parents marry, even if there is an acknowledgment (the system of legitimatization of illegitimate children or quasi-legitimacy: section 3, paragraph 1 of the Nationality Act). Therefore, people who could not acquire Japanese nationality due to this provision of the Nationality Act filed a lawsuit claiming violation of Article 14 of the Constitution. The main points of the Supreme Court decision are as follows: (1) According to the Nationality Act, section 3, paragraph 1, the acquisition of Japanese nationality is not recognized simply because the father, who is a Japanese citizen, acknowledges the child after birth, where the mother is not a Japanese citizen. The Act provides for the acquisition of Japanese nationality only in cases of quasi-legitimacy. This is the reason for the distinction in this case. (2) Even if the biological father is a Japanese citizen, if the child does not acquire Japanese nationality by birth, there is a possibility that the child will have close ties to the foreign country of the mother's nationality throughout his or her life. Therefore, it is understood that section 3, paragraph 1 of the Nationality Act, while based on the principle of lineage, establishes certain requirements that are indicators of close ties with Japan, in addition to the existence of a legal parent-child relationship with a Japanese citizen, and allows acquisition of Japanese nationality after birth only when these requirements are met. (3) Such legislative purpose itself has a rational basis. However, in light of the changes in the domestic and international social environment surrounding Japan, it is now difficult to find a rational connection between the legislative purpose and the requirement of quasi-legitimacy for the acquisition of Japanese nationality after birth. (4) The provision of section 3, paragraph 1 of the Nationality Act violates Article 14, paragraph 1 of the Constitution (62 *Minshu* 1367, Sup. Ct., G.B., June 4, 2008).

164. The Inheritance Discrimination case of 2013. In a case where the constitutionality of the proviso to section 900, paragraph 4 of the Civil Code, which provides that a child born out of wedlock shall receive one-half of the legal share of inheritance of a child born in wedlock, was questioned, the Supreme Court held this to be unconstitutional: (1) Even though the institution of legal marriage itself is well-established in Japan, due to changes in public awareness, the international environment, and the recognition of respect for the individual in the family community, it is not permissible to disadvantage a child because the parents were not married, a matter that the child has no room to choose or modify. (2) The provision of the proviso to section 900, paragraph 4 of the Civil Code has lost its rational basis today and violates Article 14 of the Constitution (67 *Minshu* 1320, Sup. Ct., G.B., September 4, 2013).

165. The Restriction on Remarriage for Women case of 2015. The Supreme Court ruled that the provision of section 733, paragraph 1 of the Civil Code, which prohibits remarriage for six months (180 days) after divorce only for women, is unconstitutional and invalid, finding as follows. The legislative purpose of section 733, paragraph 1 of the Civil Code is to clarify the relationship between father and child, which is reasonable. However, in light of the presumption of legitimacy in section 772 of the Civil Code, a ban on remarriage for one hundred days is sufficient. The number of people marrying later in life is increasing, while the number of people who remarry is increasing, and there is a growing demand to reduce restrictions on remarriage as much as possible. Therefore, the portion exceeding one hundred days is an excessive restriction on the freedom of marriage that lacks rationality and violates the principle of equality under Article 14 of the Constitution and the essential equality of both sexes under Article 24 of the Constitution (69 *Minshu* 2427, Sup. Ct., G.B., December 16, 2015).

166. The National Review for Judges of the Supreme Court case of 2022. The appointment of the judges of the Supreme Court shall be reviewed by the people at the first general election of members of the House of Representatives following their appointment. In this case, when the majority of the voters favor the dismissal of a judge, he shall be dismissed (Article 79, paragraphs 2 and 3). This is the national review of judges of the Supreme Court. The Constitution stipulates that the people have the inalienable right to choose their public officials and to dismiss them (Article 15, paragraph 1). However, Japanese citizens who reside outside Japan and do not have a domicile within a municipality of Japan were not allowed to exercise this right of national review. The system of national elections has been revised over the past twenty years, and today citizens outside of Japan can cast their votes. However, the national review of the Supreme Court judges has continued to be unavailable to those who live outside of Japan. The Supreme Court ruled this to be unconstitutional. The Court held as follows. Restrictions on the right of national review or its exercise are not permissible in principle, and there must be compelling reasons for such restrictions. However, it is not understood that it is virtually impossible or extremely difficult to take legislative measures to enable the exercise of the right of review by overseas nationals while ensuring the fairness of the national review. In this way, even if there are issues to be considered in establishing a system to allow overseas nationals to exercise the right of review, it cannot be considered that there is any compelling reason for the fact that no legislative measures have been taken. Therefore, the fact that the Act on National Review for Judges of the Supreme Court does not allow overseas nationals to exercise the right of review at all violates Article 15, paragraph 1 and Article 79, paragraphs 2 and 3 of the Constitution (76 *Minshu* 711, Sup. Ct., G.B., May 25, 2022).

167. The Surgical Requirements in Gender Change case of 2023 In recent years, constitutional suits concerning the human rights of sexual minorities have attracted much attention. Important judgments were issued on the constitutional issues regarding transgender people. In one case, in dispute was the issue of whether or not the provision of the "Act on Special Cases in Handling Gender Status for Persons with Gender Identity Disorder" (section 3, paragraph 1, Item 4 of the Act), which requires surgery to remove the reproductive function when changing the gender status on the family register, is in violation of the Constitution. Regarding this case, in January 2019, the Supreme Court ruled that it was constitutional. The judgment is as follows. (a) Under this provision, a person may be forced to undergo unwanted surgery for gender change. Therefore, it is undeniable that this provision restricts the "freedom not to be subjected to physical invasion," which is guaranteed by Article 13 of the Constitution. (b) However, it is understood that this provision is based on the consideration that if a child is born with reproductive functions based on the gender before the change, it may cause problems in the parent-child relationship and disrupt society, and consideration must be given to avoid a sudden change in the long-standing distinction between men and women in terms of biological gender. (c) Whether such consideration is appropriate or not will evolve with changes in social conditions. The constitutionality of this provision should be subject to constant review. However, in light of current social conditions, it cannot be said that this provision violates the Constitution at this time (261 *Shumin* 1, Sup. Ct., January 23, 2019). While the Supreme Court acknowledged the suspicion that the provision was unconstitutional, it ultimately ruled that it was constitutional at that time.

In 2023, a similar case was decided to be heard again by the Grand Bench of the Supreme Court, which ruled it unconstitutional on October 25 of the same year. A summary of the Supreme Court's judgment is as follows:

(1) The purpose of this provision is understood to be as stated in (b) above. However, transgender persons are a small minority in society as a whole. A significant number of those seeking gender change undergo reproductive loss surgery in order to resolve their discomfort with the physical characteristics of their biological gender. Furthermore, it is believed that there are many people who are not comfortable with having a child with their natural reproductive function. Even if this provision did not exist, it would be extremely rare for a person who has undergone a gender change ruling without undergoing reproductive loss surgery to have a child, which would cause problems related to the parent-child relationship.
(2) The social situation has also changed. Approximately nineteen years have passed since the Act went into effect in 2004, and more than 10,000 people have changed their gender. Since 2004, the Ministry of Justice has been conducting human rights awareness activities with the goal of eliminating prejudice and other forms of discrimination on the basis of gender identity disorder.

Since 2010, the Ministry of Education, Culture, Sports, Science and Technology (MEXT) has issued a notice requesting boards of education and other organizations to give due consideration to the feelings of students with gender identity disorder in school education and has prepared and distributed manuals for teachers and staff. In 2016, the Ministry of Health, Labor, and Welfare also asked employers not to exclude sexual minorities in their hiring selection criteria when recruiting workers. In June 2023, the Law for the Promotion of LGBT Understanding was enacted to contribute to the realization of a society tolerant of diversity in sexual orientation and gender identity. At the time of enactment of the Act (2004), the majority of countries that had gender change procedures required the loss of reproductive functions. However, the World Health Organization and other organizations subsequently issued a joint statement in 2014 opposing the requirement of reproductive incapacity. In addition, the European Court of Human Rights ruled in 2017 that it violates the European Convention on Human Rights, and now an increasing number of countries—a significant number of them and mainly Western countries—do not require the loss of reproductive functions.

(3) Advances in medical knowledge are also important. At the time of the enactment of the Act, gender reassignment surgery, including the loss of reproductive function, was positioned as the final stage of treatment in a step-by-step treatment. The imposition of a requirement that the person have undergone reproductive loss surgery was medically reasonably related to the fact that the person had undergone the necessary treatment for gender identity disorder. However, after the enactment of the Act, the concept of step-by-step treatment was no longer adopted due to the generalized awareness of the symptoms of gender identity disorder and the diversity of treatment approaches. It was assumed that what kind of physical treatment was needed depended on the patient. Whether or not a person has received the necessary treatment is no longer determined by whether or not the person has undergone gender reassignment surgery, and imposing a requirement of loss of reproductive functions lacks rational relevance from a medical standpoint. With the development of medical knowledge, this provision has forced transgender persons who do not require reproductive loss surgery as a treatment to make a harsh choice between two options. The choice is whether to give up the freedom not to be subjected to physical invasion and thus undergo a severe physical invasion (namely, the surgery for loss of reproductive function), or whether to give up the important legal benefit of being treated in accordance with one's gender identity under the law and thus renounce gender change. The restrictions on freedom from bodily invasion under this provision are excessive, and the degree of restriction should be significant.

(4) The restriction of freedom from bodily invasion by this provision cannot be considered necessary and reasonable, given that the necessity for such restriction has now been reduced and the degree of the restriction has become serious. This provision violates Article 13 of the Constitution and is invalid (77 *Minshu* 1792, Sup. Ct., G.B., October 25, 2023).

Chapter 6. Independent Agencies

by Prof. Hiroyuki Hata with updates by Prof. Takehisa Nakagawa

§1. Board of Audit

I. General

168. Article 90 of the Constitution stipulates, "Final accounts of the expenditures and revenues of the State shall be audited annually by a Board of Audit and submitted to the Diet, together with the statement of audit during the fiscal year immediately following the period" (paragraph 1) and "The organization and competency of the Board of Audit shall be determined by law" (paragraph 2). All modern democracies, either constitutionally or by statute, have set up an independent body to ensure the proper operation of the finances of their respective governments.

The Meiji Constitution also provided for an independent organ named the Board of Audit which was established to audit the expenditures and revenues of the State (Article 72). According to section 23 of the old Board of Audit Act, however, expenses concerning matters involving governmental secrecy were not subject to examination by the Board of Audit. Such an exception is not recognized under the present Board of Audit Act.

II. Organization

169. The Board of Audit is legally independent of the Cabinet (section 1 of the Board of Audit Act). It is composed of a Council of three Auditors and a secretariat (section 2). An Auditor is appointed for a term of seven years (renewable for one more term only) by the Cabinet with the consent of both Houses of the Diet and attested to by the Emperor (section 4 and section 5, paragraph 1). A Chief Auditor is elected from among the Auditors themselves and appointed by the Cabinet (section 3).

In order to guarantee the Board's independence from interference from the Cabinet, the Auditors are assured of the right to remain in office until they reach the retirement age of 65 (section 5, paragraph 3), except for cases in which they have either been judged as mentally or physically incompetent to perform official duties or have been found to be neglectful of their duties as determined by the decision of two other members of the Board (subject to the approval of the both Houses of the Diet) (section 6). They may also be removed where they have been sentenced to imprisonment or have been subjected to more severe criminal penalties (section 7). In order to secure the independence of the Board of Audit, it is accorded special privileges with respect to its budget. One such privilege is that the Cabinet cannot make a written estimate of the expenses of the Board of Audit without hearing the opinion of the President of the Board (section 18, paragraph 2 of the Public Finance Act). Another is that when the Cabinet reduces the estimated sum of expenditures for the Board of Audit it must affix to the budget the details of the estimated expenditures submitted by the Board and at the same time must specify a source of revenue which the Diet needs in justification for amending the amount of expenditures of the Board (section 19).

III. Competence

170. Final accounts of the expenditures and revenues of the State are examined by the Board of Audit and submitted to the Diet along with the statement of audit which the Board has made (Article 90 of the Constitution). As the Meiji Constitution had not stipulated the time of submission, such accounts were usually submitted to the Diet two years after the period was audited. Unlike its predecessor, the Constitution of Japan expressly orders that accounts be submitted "during the fiscal year immediately following the period covered." The Public Finance Act further provides that the accounts be usually submitted to the Diet during the ordinary session to be convened during the fiscal year following the year audited (section 40).

171. The Board of Audit examines and decides on the legality and propriety of the accounting of State organs, organs of public entities, etc., as stipulated by various statutes, as well as of the final account of expenditures and revenues of the State itself (section 20 of the Board of Audit Act). In conducting the audit, the Board may demand the production of books, papers and reports necessary for it to perform its functions and may require the presence and testimony of those concerned with expenditures (section 26). The Board may also ask State organs, organs of public entities, etc., to produce materials or give expert opinions whenever necessary (section 28). Though its finding of illegality or impropriety in the accounts does not legally bring about the annulment of expenditures and revenues by State organs, organs of public entities, etc., the Board is empowered to demand that heads of those organs or related persons correct errors (section 34). In addition, the Board may ask the administering authorities or the persons in charge to improve laws and ordinances, systems, and ways of administration that are considered to have caused errors (section 36). If as a result of the audit, the Board has found that officials who engage in the accounting of State funds have inflicted serious damage on the State by a willful or grossly negligent act, the Board may ask heads of agencies or other persons who supervise such officials to take disciplinary actions (section 31, paragraph 1). Also, the Board must report to the public prosecutor's office any finding that officials who engage in the accounting business of the State have committed a crime with respect to their official duties (section 33).

§2. Independent Administrative Commissions or Board

I. General

172. One of the most characteristic administrative reforms carried out in postwar Japan was the adoption of administrative commissions or boards in many fields of administration. Needless to say, administrative commissions were originated and developed in late nineteenth century and early twentieth century America where existing national, state and local legislatures (as representatives of the people) and judicial courts (as guardians of the rights and freedoms of the people) had become incapable of directly responding to popular needs. The commission scheme proliferated as the expanding role of government was bringing about highly specialized and complex administrative activities. Features of administrative commissions or boards are:

(1) that they have a plural membership of three, five or a larger number;
(2) that they are independent of the heads of the executive branch in the exercise of their functions; and
(3) that they are usually vested with quasi-legislative and quasi-judicial powers.

Administrative organs of such a nature were not known in prewar Japan which was traditionally under a strong centralized bureaucratic government. Such organs were introduced into Japan as part of the postwar administrative reforms enforced under the strong influence of the American occupation forces which sought to democratize the governmental system of Japan. Therefore, many of such agencies were abolished as the occupation of Japan ended.

173. Critical views voiced against administrative commissions or boards, when they were introduced, were mainly based on the views:

(1) that the location of responsibility is unclear as the Board has plural membership;
(2) that it is inefficient for the same reason;
(3) that the adoption of administrative commissions enlarges the administrative structure and makes administration more costly; and
(4) that it is difficult to find able persons to head or serve as members of commissions.

In addition, there was opposition to the adoption of administrative commissions based on the following two constitutional grounds: First, that the Cabinet cannot be responsible to the Diet in the exercise of executive power as required by the Constitution of Japan (Article 66, paragraph 3) if commissions perform their duties independently of the Cabinet. Article 66, paragraph 3 stipulates, “The Cabinet, in the exercise of executive power, shall be collectively responsible to the Diet.” Second, the exercise of quasi-legislative and quasi-judicial power by administrative commissions violates the constitutional requirement of separation of powers.

As to the former, the great majority of legal scholars, lawyers and administrators are of the opinion that, though administrative commissions perform their duties independently, the Cabinet, so long as it has the power to appoint members of commissions and to establish commission budgets, can assume the responsibility to the Diet for the exercise of executive power, as required by section 65, paragraph 3 of the Constitution. As to the latter, it is also generally agreed that the exercise of quasi-judicial power and quasi-legislative power by administrative commissions does not invade the spheres of the Diet and the judicial courts, provided that decisions made by commissions can eventually be appealed to the courts and that the appointment of both presidents and members of commissions is subject to the approval of the Diet, as provided for by laws enacted by the Diet.

174. There is also a scholarly opinion that supports the constitutionality of administrative commissions from a different point of view. According to this theory, Article 65, paragraph 2 is a provision intended to place the exercise of executive power under the control of the Diet, which is constitutionally the highest organ of State power (Article 41). Therefore, so long as the Diet can control administrative commissions through the power to impeach their members (e.g., section 1 of the Act Concerning the Impeachment of Members of the National Personnel Authority) or through the power of the Cabinet to appoint and the Diet to consent to the appointment of their members, the establishment of commissions does not violate the Constitution even if the Cabinet cannot directly control them.

On the theory that there exist certain categories of administration action which from the nature of things must be handled without interference from the Cabinet, administrative commissions established to deal with such matters must be and have been sustained as constitutional under the abovementioned conditions.

II. Categories of Administrative Commissions or Boards

175. Administrative commissions or boards are established for various purposes and can be summarized as falling into the following categories depending on the nature of their purposes.

A. Politically Independent Commissions

176. This type of commission includes the National Public Safety Commission (section 4 of the Police Act), prefectural public safety commissions (section 38, paragraph 1 of the Police Act), National Personnel Authority (section 3, paragraph 1 of the National Civil Service Act), prefectural and local personnel boards (section 7, paragraphs 1 and 2 of the Local Civil Service Act), Fair Trade Commission (section 27 of the Anti-Monopoly Act), Central Election Commission (section 5, paragraph 1 of the Public Offices Election Act), prefectural and local election boards (section 5, paragraph 1 of the Public Offices Election Act), prefectural and municipal boards of education (section 2 of the Act Concerning the Structure and Management of Local Administration of Education), etc.

B. Commissions Requiring Expert Knowledge or Experience

177. The Commission on the Adjustment of Environmental Disputes (section 3 of the Act on the Settlement of Environmental Pollution Disputes), Bar Examination Commission (section 12 of the Bar Examination Act), etc., fall within this category of commissions. The Fair Trade Commission (section 27 of the Anti-Monopoly Act) and prefectural and municipal boards of education, mentioned in A, can also be placed in this category.

C. Commissions Designed to Perform Quasi-Judicial Functions

178. These include the Public Security Examination Commission (sections 1–2 of the Act for Establishment of the Public Security Examination Commission), prefectural expropriation commissions (section 51 of the Land Expropriation Act), prefectural labor relations boards (section 19-12, paragraph 1 of the Labor Union Act), and property tax appraisal boards (section 423, paragraph 1 of the Local Tax Act). Also, such administrative bodies as the National Personnel Authority and the prefectural and local personnel boards concurrently perform quasi-judicial functions.

179. The Fair Trade Commission had long performed a quasi-judicial function before its quasi-judicial procedure was abolished in the 2013 amendment to the Anti-monopoly Act after somewhat confusing debates on making the Commission act fairly. The amendment took effect on April 1, 2015. The Commission now issues cease and desist orders and monetary civil penalties without conducting quasi-judicial procedures. Those seeking to appeal or review the Commission's orders must bring an action against the Commission in the District Court of Tokyo for judicial relief.

D. Arbitral Commissions

180. Included in this category are the Central Labor Relations Board (section 19-2 of the Labor Union Act), prefectural labor relations boards (section 19-12, paragraph I of the Labor Union Act), agriculture boards (section 3, paragraph 1 of the Act Concerning the Agriculture Boards), prefectural sea area fishery adjustment boards (section 136 of the Fishery Act).

181. One of the recent additions to the list is the Committee on Dispute Resolution between the National and Local governments (section 250-7 of the Local Autonomy Act) established in 2000. Upon complaints by local governments, the Commission is to review the legality of the involvement of national agencies in the affairs of local public entities.

Part III. The State and Its Subdivisions

Chapter 1. Local Self-Government

by Prof. Go Nakagawa with updates by Prof. Takehisa Nakagawa

§1. Devices for Democratic Decentralization

I. Principle of Local Autonomy

182. Since Japan is a unitary state, it has had no component states. However, it has created and maintained local governments.

The pre-World War II local government system in Japan was modeled after the continental European system, especially the German type. In contrast to this prewar centralized system, the newly established local government system under the Constitution of 1947 is oriented toward decentralization and contains American-influenced devices for direct democracy.

183. In drafting the Constitution, the GHQ for the Allied Powers was eager to remake the Japanese local government according to the American model though it did not go as far as transplanting the theory of States' Rights into Japan.[32] The GHQ's basic aim seems to have been to introduce direct election of local public officials and to provide for such local home rule as is accorded to municipalities under the constitutions and statutes in the United States. Firm adherence to the American type of local government is evident in the original draft of Chapter 8 of the Constitution:

> *Article LXXXVI.* The governors of prefectures, the mayors of cities and towns and the chief executive officers of all other subordinate bodies politic and corporate having tax power, the members of prefectural and local legislative assemblies, and such other prefectural and local officials as the Diet may determine, shall be elected by direct popular vote within their several communities.
>
> *Article LXXXVII.* The inhabitants of metropolitan areas, cities and towns shall be secure in their right to manage their property, affairs and government and to frame their own characters within such laws as the Diet may enact.

32. *Political Reorientation of Japan, September 1945 to September 1948*, Vol. I, p. 260.

> *Article LXXXVIII.* The Diet shall pass no local or special act applicable to a metropolitan area, city or town where a general act can be made applicable unless it be made subject to the acceptance of a majority of the electorate of such community.

All these provisions were derived from the experience of American local governments. Articles 93–95 in Chapter 8 of the ratified Constitution, each of which corresponds to the above provisions respectively, were mostly adapted to the Japanese legal system and political reality. An exception is Article 95 which incidentally is the least important when it comes to the actual working of the Japanese local government (*see* paragraph 196).

184. Furthermore, at the beginning of Chapter 8, a newly created provision focusing on the ruling principle of local self-government was added:

> *Article 92.* Regulations concerning organization and operation of local public entities shall be fixed by law in accordance with the basic principle of local autonomy.

As the Constitution gives no definition of "the principle of local autonomy," there have been disputes over what this principle means. The Supreme Court held that the 1954 amendment to the Police Act, which transferred from cities or other municipalities to prefectures the responsibility for the maintenance of the police forces, did not violate the principle of local autonomy ordained by the Constitution (16 *Minshu* 445, Sup. Ct., March 7, 1962). The Supreme Court has never invalidated a single piece of legislation on the ground that it violates "the basic principle of local autonomy." There is also little prospect that the Court will behave differently in the future.

II. Scope and Validity of Local Ordinances

185. The first paragraph of Article 93 states: "The local public entities shall establish assemblies as their deliberative organs in accordance with the law," while Article 94 states: "Local public entities shall have the right to manage their property, affairs and administration and to enact their own regulations within the law."

The Constitution being not clear whether it designates the local assembly as a legislative organ, the Local Autonomy Act provides in section 96 that the assembly of an ordinary local public body may enact ordinances.[33] Thus, "regulations" of Article

33. Section 96 of the Local Autonomy Act specifies the powers of a local assembly as follows:

1. Enact, amend or abolish ordinances;
2. Fix the budget;
3. Authorize the settlements of accounts;
4. Fix the levy or collection of local taxes or the collection of assessments, charges, admission dues of fees, except as provided for by laws or by cabinet orders duly authorized by laws;

94 of the Constitution include ordinances enacted by the local assemblies as well as regulations issued by local chief executives, both of which are stipulated in the Local Autonomy Act.

186. As implied in Article 94 of the Constitution, which states, "Local public entities shall have the right to manage their property, affairs and administration and to enact their own regulations within law,"[34] criminal penalty may be provided for in ordinances. The Local Autonomy Act expressly authorizes the local assembly to impose criminal penalties by enacting ordinances, such as imprisonment not exceeding two years, fines not exceeding JPY 1,000,000, detention, minor fines, and criminal confiscation. It also authorizes the local assembly to establish administrative money penalties not exceeding JPY 50,000 (section 14, paragraph 3). Prosecution of criminal offenders is under the jurisdiction of the national courts.

187. Ordinances may be enacted for any function of local government insofar as they are not in conflict with national laws: the Constitution, statutes, cabinet orders, ministerial regulations, and other delegated rules. The question then arises as to what extent local ordinances should be allowed to regulate matters that can also be subject to national laws. The Supreme Court has had several opportunities to review the question and has upheld the legality of the ordinances in many cases.

---

5. Authorize such contracts as may come under the scope prescribed by ordinance pursuant to the standards established by cabinet order with respect to the purpose and the amount of money involved;
6. Authorize the barter, investment or offer as a means of payment, or cession or lease without compensation of the public property, except in cases provided by ordinance;
7. Trust properties;
8. Authorize the procurement or disposition of such public properties as may come under the scope prescribed by ordinances pursuant to the standards established by the cabinet order with respect to the category and the value, except as provided above;
9. Accept encumbered contributions or donations;
10. Renounce any right, except in cases provided by laws or Cabinet orders duly authorized by laws or by ordinance;
11. Confer the exclusive right in the use of important public facilities specified by ordinance for a period longer than prescribed by ordinance;
12. Authorize the presentation of complaint (appeal for review, etc.), lawsuit, offer for settlement, submission to mediation, conciliation or arbitration in a case where the ordinary local public body is a party;
13. Fix the indemnity legally due thereto;
14. Exercise overall adjustment of the activities of various public organizations within the area; and
15. Perform otherwise such affairs as may come under the powers thereof by laws or by cabinet orders duly authorized by laws.

Paragraph 2 of s. 96 adds: "In addition to those enumerated above, the ordinary local public body may by ordinance specify the affairs thereof that shall be performed upon resolution of the assembly."

34. There is a group of ordinances which are called "administrative affairs ordinances." They are defined as those which impose restrictions on the liberties and rights of the people for the maintenance of social order, safety, and a good environment of the communities. The constitutional ground for administrative affairs ordinances lies in the "right to manage administration" of local public entities in Art. 94 of the Constitution.

In the case of an Osaka City ordinance which provided a criminal penalty for matters not having been regulated by national laws yet, the Supreme Court reasoned that because a local assembly was comparable to the Diet in terms of popular representation, ordinances could be analogized to statutes (16 *Keishu* 577, Sup. Ct., G.B., May 30, 1962). The Court later pointed out that, as long as they are consistent with the statute, ordinances may be made by individual local circumstances (29 *Keishu* 489, Sup. Ct., G.B., September 10, 1975). This case involved a Tokushima City ordinance that provided for criminal penalties for acts that were also subject to national laws.

§2. Political Rights of Residents

I. Voting

188. The second paragraph of Article 93 of the Constitution stipulates, "The chief executive officers of all local public entities, the members of their assemblies, and such other local officials as may be determined by law shall be elected by direct popular vote within their several communities." The popular election clause puts all the offices of the governor, mayor, and other municipal heads under the principles of representative government. This is regarded as one of the most fundamental changes from the pre-World War II local government system in which governors of prefectures, Hokkaido, and the Tokyo Metropolis were appointed as national officials of the Ministry of Internal Affairs.

Though the Constitution anticipates that other local officials than the chief executive officers be elected as well, no local government officials except governors, mayors, and heads of towns and villages presently hold elective office under the Local Autonomy Act.

II. Direct Demand and Resident's Suit

189. Based on the principle of direct democracy, the Local Autonomy Act sets up institutions for popular control over the administration of public affairs of the local government. The direct demand and the resident's suits are two important examples of the procedures for popular control in the local government system.

190. Chapter 5 of the Local Autonomy Act provides for four kinds of direct demands:

(1) demand for enactment, amendment or abolition of ordinances;
(2) demand for audit;
(3) demand for dissolution of the assembly; and
(4) demand for removal of members of the assembly, the chief executive and other high-ranking officials.

To initiate a direct demand, support from a certain specified number of persons with voting rights for their local assembly members and chief executive is required. The Local Autonomy Act requires a fiftieth of such persons for the demands (1) and (2) above and one-third for (3) and (4). Such concurrence must be shown in the form of lists of signatures of supporting residents.

191. Chapter 9, subchapter 10 of the Local Autonomy Act provides for administrative and judicial proceedings for auditing financial matters of the local governments on the residents' initiative. Each resident has the right to make a request for an audit of alleged illegal or otherwise improper expenditures. Such request must be made to the auditors of each prefecture and municipality and must be accompanied by documents showing the allegation.

When not satisfied with the results of the audit made by the auditors or with other specified matters in the Local Autonomy Act, the complaining resident may file a resident's suit in court. Different from the so-called taxpayer's suit, any resident who has voting rights may be a complainant. Such a suit has increasingly been utilized for the purpose of obtaining popular control over local government administration.

Chapter 2. Forms of Local Government

by Prof. Go Nakagawa with updates by Prof. Takehisa Nakagawa

§1. Legal Status of Local Public Entities

I. Prefectures and Municipalities

192. The Constitution is silent about what constitutes "local public entities" mentioned in Article 93. It seems that the framers took it for granted that local governments in Japan should consist of prefectures and municipalities that had already existed as local governmental units when the Constitution was drafted. Thus, the local public entities mentioned in the Constitution have been interpreted to be the same as already existing prefectures and municipalities.

However, the Local Autonomy Act classifies local public entities into two categories: sections 1–3 of the Act classifies local public entities into "ordinary" and "extraordinary" local public entities.

"Ordinary" local public entities consist of prefectures and municipalities. There are forty-seven prefectures which consist of *To* (Tokyo-*to*), *Do* (Hokkai*do*), *Fu* (Kyoto-*fu* and Osaka-*fu*), and *Ken* (all other prefectures) as well as some 1,700 municipalities as of 2021 (reduced from 3,200 as of 2000) which are classified into cities (*Shi*), towns (*Cho*), and villages (*Son*). Prefectures are regional local governmental units embracing municipalities.

"Extraordinary" local public entities shall include special wards, associations of local public entities, property wards, and local development corporations.

193. While the structures and functions of *Do*, *Fu*, and *Ken* are uniform, Tokyo-*to* is somewhat different in its structure and functions from other local units. Only Tokyo-*to* has special wards (*Ku*), which are classified as "extraordinary" local public entities, in addition to ordinary municipalities such as cities, towns and villages. The boundary of the old City of Tokyo is divided into twenty-three special wards (*Ku*) while the rest of the Tokyo-*to* area is divided into ordinary municipalities. Special wards are legally equivalent to cities according to the Local Autonomy Act.

As to their constitutional status, the Supreme Court ruled that the special wards of Tokyo-*to* do not correspond to "the local public entities" provided for in paragraph 2 of Article 93 of the Constitution, and thus local officials of such special wards need not be directly elected (17 *Keishu* 121, Sup. Ct., G.B., March 27, 1963). However, under the current Public Offices Election Act, heads of the special wards are now popularly elected.

194. Municipalities are often referred to as basic units of local government in Japan because they are closer to the residents than prefectures.

Despite the difference in the titles, there is no substantial legal difference between towns and villages in terms of their functions. Cities are required to be urbanized and to have 50,000 or more population (section 8 of the Local Autonomy Act). They are entrusted with more urban functions than towns and villages.

A city with a population of more than 500,000 is qualified to become a "designated city" through cabinet order (section 252-19 of the Local Autonomy Act). Such designated cities take over important functions from the prefectural government and are guaranteed more independence than ordinary cities. The first designated cities were Kyoto, Osaka, Kobe, Nagoya, and Yokohama in 1956, there are now twenty cities (as of 2024), including Kitakyushu, Sapporo, Kawasaki, Fukuoka, Hiroshima, Sendai, and Chiba. The Local Autonomy Act provides for other types of major cities, such as "kernel city" and "special city" (section 252-22 and 252-26).

II. Central-Local Relations

195. The Constitution uses few words to describe the relationship between the national and local governments: it provides that the system of local government is to be fixed through statutes by the Diet "in accordance with the principle of local autonomy" (Article 92).

Structures and functions of local governments are not defined by each locality's charter: rather, they are provided for in statutes, such as the Local Autonomy Act (enacted in 1947), Local Civil Service Act (1950), Local Finance Act (1948), and Local Tax Act (1950). This is one of the main reasons why the structure and function of local governments in Japan are almost uniform throughout the country.

196. Before the major amendment of 1999 to the Local Autonomy Act, which took effect in April 2000, many national functions were implemented by the hand of local executive organs under the supervision of national governmental agencies: national agencies "depute" some of their functions to the chief executives or other executive organs of local governments for local implementation (*see* paragraph 201). The functions "deputed" this way were to be administered by local executive organs as if they were organs of the national government and thus were not subject to regulation by ordinances enacted by local assemblies.[35] As a result, local governments, although not always compelled to conform to the policies of the national government, were usually highly responsive to such policies.

To prevent excessive use of the "deputing" of functions, the Local Autonomy Act provided that functions be deputed to local chief executives only through statutes or cabinet orders.

197. In 1995, the Promotion of Decentralization Act was enacted, under which the Committee for Promotion of Decentralization was set up. The Committee issued several reports in 1996 and 1997 which vigorously recommended steps to be taken towards substantial decentralization of the central-local relations. Based on these recommendations, the government drafted comprehensive plans for decentralization in 1998. The plans were eventually put into a number of bills, including a major amendment to the Local Autonomy Act itself, which were introduced to the Diet and enacted in 1999. The new Local Autonomy Act, along with other amendments to

35. However, the 1991 amendment to the Local Autonomy Act made such "deputed" functions subject to inspections by the assembly as well as by auditors.

various statutes, took effect in April 2000. As part of this reform, the "deputed" functions of executive chiefs of local governments (paragraph 201) were abolished.

This 1995–1999 movement is regarded as the third wave of local government reform in Japan following those made during the Meiji Restoration and the early postwar years.

198. The "special law" referred to in Article 95 of the Constitution is the one that applied only to specific local public entities. It may only be enacted by the Diet with the consent of the majority of the voters of such local public entities. The special law provision, however, does not have much significance in the Japanese local governmental system because its system is highly standardized through statutes of nationwide applicability.

As a practical matter, there is little possibility that the Diet would abuse its legislative power to cause a disadvantage to a specific local public entity. Several special laws have been enacted so far, but they have always been to the advantage of the local governments concerned. Thus, the referendum proceeding was merely ceremonial with no substantial negative votes. The earliest examples of special laws based on Article 95 include the Hiroshima Peace Memorial City Construction Act of 1949.

§2. Internal Structure of Local Government

I. Legislative Branch

199. The framers of the Constitution adopted the British-type parliamentary system for the national government and the American-type presidential system for local governments. The powers and responsibilities of local governments are shared by their chief executives and assemblies in accordance with the principle of separation of powers.

The local assembly consists of one house whose members are elected by direct popular vote for a four-year term of office as provided in the Local Autonomy Act (sections 17 and 93). Membership in a local assembly is incompatible with membership in the Diet, any other local assembly, or full-time employment in any local government. The number of members of the assembly of a local government is stipulated in the Local Autonomy Act and is based on the population (sections 90 and 91). If special circumstances exist, the number may be reduced or increased by enacting an ordinance.

A chairperson and a vice-chairperson are elected in each local assembly. Standing committees and special committees may be created by ordinances. The maximum number of standing committees is prescribed in the Local Autonomy Act.

200. The most important powers of the local assembly are those to enact ordinances and to fix the budget. If the chief executive has an objection to an affirmative resolution of the assembly regarding either the budget or the enactment, amendment or abolition of an ordinance, the so-called general veto power may be exercised by the chief executive. With this veto, such proposals are to be returned to the assembly for reconsideration. To override the veto, the concurrence of more than two-thirds of the assembly members present is required.

The chief executive is given the so-called special veto power. If the chief executive considers that any resolution of the assembly or any election held by the assembly is either *ultra vires* or contrary to law or rules of procedure, such resolution may be returned to the assembly for reconsideration or reelection may be ordered.

If the chief executive considers that any resolution involving either revenue or expenditure is impossible to execute, such resolution must be returned for reconsideration. Furthermore, if the assembly passes a resolution to strike out or reduce the obligatory expenses under law, the expenses duly charged by competent government agencies under law, or other obligatory expenses of an ordinary local public body, and if the assembly after reconsideration again strikes out or reduces such expenses, the chief executive may budget the expenses (and the revenue necessary to cover them) on his/her own responsibility. In addition, if the assembly strikes out or reduces the expenses necessary for emergency recovery measures in case of a disaster or the prevention of epidemics, and if after reconsideration it again strikes out or reduces such expenses, the chief executive may regard such resolution as a nonconfidence resolution (sections 176 and 177 of the Local Autonomy Act).

201. The assembly may pass a resolution of nonconfidence against the chief executive at any time. The chief executive may declare the dissolution of the assembly only when it passes a nonconfidence resolution. The resolution of nonconfidence requires a concurring vote of more than three-quarters of the members present provided that more than two-thirds of the total members shall be present. The chief executive shall lose office either if it fails to dissolve the assembly within the specified period, or if a nonconfidence resolution is again approved at the first assembly session after the general election caused by the assembly dissolution. In the latter case, a concurring vote of more than one-half of the members present is required provided that more than two-thirds of the total members shall be present (section 178 of the Local Autonomy Act). If the chief executive loses office, a new chief executive is to be elected for the term of four years by popular vote.

The device of checks and balances through the nonconfidence resolution and the dissolution of local government has not often been used and has had less importance than in the case of the national government.

II. Administrative Branch

202. Chief executives of prefectures and municipalities are governors of prefectures, mayors of cities, and heads of towns and villages. They are elected by direct popular vote for a four-year term of office and may be reelected. The office of the chief executive is incompatible with membership in the Diet or membership in any local assembly.

The chief executive has the power to manage and execute the affairs of a local government and to represent it.

203. Before the major amendment of 1999 to the Local Autonomy Act, which took effect in April 2000, chief executives were also to act as agents of the national government concerning national functions deputed to them either by statutes or cabinet orders (*see* paragraph 201). As long as a governor of a prefecture acted as an agent of the national government, he was assumed to be under the direction and supervision of the competent Minister. Likewise, mayors and other heads of municipalities were considered to be under the direction and supervision of the competent governor who, in turn, acted in the capacity of a national administrative organ. If a governor, acting as such, violated statutes, cabinet orders, or ministerial orders, or if he was in default of performance, the competent Minister could file a suit with the High Court for a writ of mandamus to overcome serious hindrances to administration. Likewise, a governor could file a suit with the District Court for a writ of mandamus against deputed executive organs, such as a mayor.

As explained before (paragraph 202), the whole system of "deputed" functions of local administrative organs was abolished by the major amendment to the Local Autonomy Act, which took effect in April 2000.

204. With the consent of the assemblies concerned, a governor may appoint one or more vice-governors and a mayor may appoint one or more vice-mayors (sections 161–162 of the Local Autonomy Act). No assembly consent is required for the removal of such officers. The chief accountant of a prefecture and the treasurer of a municipality are in charge of monetary matters relating to the local government. The procedures for their appointment and removal are the same as those for the vice-governors and vice-mayors.

The chief executive may appoint and promote officials and other employees based on their merit. Most of the members of administrative boards and commissions are appointed by the chief executive, but the administrative boards and commissions are independent of the chief executive in discharging their responsibilities.

Part IV. Citizenship and the Administration of Justice

Chapter 1. Rules Concerning Nationality and Relevance of Nationality

by Prof. Hiroyuki Hata with updates by Prof. Takehisa Nakagawa

§1. Constitutional and Statutory Provisions Concerning Nationality

205. Article 10 of the Constitution of Japan states, "The conditions necessary for being a Japanese national shall be determined by law." This means that the conditions for establishing Japanese nationality must be determined by the Legislature and not by the Executive. The Constitution does not have any other provisions concerning nationality except for Article 22, paragraph 2, which stipulates, "Freedom of all persons to move to a foreign country and to divest themselves of their nationality shall be inviolate." Rules concerning the acquisition and loss of Japanese nationality are laid down by the Nationality Act (enacted in 1950; revised in 1952, 1984, etc.).

I. Acquisition of Japanese Nationality

206. There are two ways of acquiring Japanese nationality under the Nationality Act. One way of acquiring Japanese nationality is by birth, and the other is by means of naturalization.

A. Acquisition of Nationality by Birth

207. According to section 2 of the Nationality Act, Japanese nationality is accorded to:

(1) a child born to a father or mother who is a Japanese national at the time of its birth;
(2) a child whose father died before it was born, but was a Japanese national at the time of his death; or

(3) a child born in Japan, whose parents are unknown at the time of its birth, or have no nationality.

208. Section 3 of the Nationality Act provides for the acquisition of Japanese nationality by notification. In cases where a child whom the father or mother acknowledges is under 20 years of age (excluding a child who was once a Japanese citizen), the child may acquire Japanese nationality through notification to the Minister of Justice if the acknowledging father or mother was a Japanese citizen at the time of the child's birth, and the father or mother is currently a Japanese citizen or was so at the time of death.

B. Acquisition of Nationality by Naturalization

209. Any person who is not a Japanese national may acquire Japanese nationality through naturalization (section 4 of the Nationality Act). In order to apply to the Minister of Justice for naturalization, the applicant must meet the following requirements (section 5, paragraph 1):

(1) he or she has continuously resided in Japan for seven years or longer;
(2) he or she is over 19 years of age, and legally competent under the laws of his or her home country;
(3) he or she is a person of good conduct;
(4) he or she is able to make a living with his or her own assets or skill, or with those of his or her spouse or other relatives with whom he or she shares the household;
(5) he or she has no nationality, or will lose his or her prior nationality if he or she acquires Japanese nationality; and
(6) he or she has neither plotted nor advocated to destroy by force the Constitution of Japan or a government which has been organized under it nor, after the Constitution went into effect, organized or joined a political party or other organization which plots or advocates to do so.

In spite of Proviso (5) of the preceding paragraph, paragraph 2 authorizes the Minister of Justice to grant naturalization to an alien who cannot legally lose his or her existing nationality notwithstanding his or her wish when the Minister considers it appropriate to do so in the light of the alien's relationship with a Japanese national or because of special circumstances.

210. There are also some cases in which the Minister of Justice may especially grant naturalization to an alien, even if the alien has not satisfied the requirements set out in section 5. At first, any person (adopted children excluded) whose father or mother was a Japanese national and who has continuously resided or been domiciled in Japan for three years or longer, as well as persons who were born and have continuously resided in Japan for three years or longer, or whose parent (adoptive parent excluded) was born in Japan, and persons who have continuously resided in Japan for ten years or longer are eligible for naturalization into Japanese nationality (section 6).

211. Also eligible for naturalization are:

(1) alien spouses of Japanese nationals who have continuously resided in or been domiciled in Japan for three years or longer, and are currently domiciled in Japan;
(2) those who are married to Japanese nationals for three years or longer and have continuously resided in Japan for one year or longer (section 7);
(3) those who are the children (adopted children excluded) of Japanese nationals and are currently domiciled in Japan;
(4) those who are the adopted children of Japanese nationals and have continuously resided in Japan for one year or longer, and were minors under the laws of their home country when they were adopted;
(5) those who lost Japanese nationality (except for those who had acquired their Japanese nationality by naturalization) but are domiciled in Japan; or
(6) those born in Japan who have had no Japanese nationality since their birth, but have been continuously residing in Japan for three years or longer (section 8).

Furthermore, the Minister, with the consent of the Diet, may make an exceptional grant of naturalization to an alien who has made a special contribution to Japan even if such alien has not met the conditions prescribed in section 5, paragraph 1 (section 9).

II. Loss of Japanese Nationality

212. Section 11 of the Nationality Act stipulates, "A Japanese national who has acquired the nationality of a foreign country on his or her own will shall lose Japanese nationality" and "A Japanese national who has the nationality of a foreign country shall lose Japanese nationality when he or she has chosen the former in accordance with the laws and ordinances of the foreign country." Also, Japanese nationals who were born abroad and obtained the nationality of a foreign country by birth shall lose Japanese nationality retroactively from the date of their birth unless they express their will to keep Japanese nationality in accordance with the provisions of the Family Register Act (enacted in 1947 and as amended) (section 12 of the Nationality Act). Japanese nationals who have the nationality of a foreign country can divest themselves of their Japanese nationality by notifying the Minister of Justice (section 13, paragraph 1 of the Nationality Act). Upon such a notification they will lose their Japanese nationality (section 13, paragraph 2).

III. Choice of Nationality

213. Japanese nationals who are also nationals of a foreign country and who have obtained two nationalities before they reach 20 years of age must, before their 22nd birthday, opt for one of such nationalities. However, in the event dual nationality was acquired after reaching the age of 20, opting must take place within two years after acquiring such dual nationality (section 14, paragraph 1 of the Nationality Act). The selection of Japanese nationality is effected by making a declaration that they will choose Japanese nationality and renounce foreign nationality, in accordance with the provisions of the Family Register Act, as well as by divesting themselves of foreign nationality (section 14, paragraph 2).

§2. Relevance of Nationality

214. Scholarly opinion concerning whether the constitutional provisions which guarantee rights and liberties are applicable to foreigners who have no Japanese nationality is divided. Some constitutional law scholars and lawyers who are of the negative view refer to the nature of a constitution, which they consider to be the basis for the operation of national power for the people to whom the constitution belongs. As a further ground for their contention, they also point to the statement in the Constitution which states, "The fundamental human rights by this Constitution guaranteed to the people of Japan are fruits of the age-old struggle of man to be free" (Article 97).

215. However, the majority of constitutional law scholars and lawyers are of the opinion that all the fundamental rights and liberties provided for in the Constitution, except for those which, from the nature of things, must be limited to Japanese nationals, must be guaranteed to foreigners living in Japan who have no Japanese nationality. This opinion derives from the pre-State nature of human rights and the spirit of international cooperation and harmony upon which the Constitution of Japan is based.

216. Needless to say, foreigners have no freedom of entry into Japan. The decision concerning residence in Japan by foreigners is considered to be a continuation of power to regulate entry and thus is a matter under the discretion of the Japanese government. As to the alleged right of an alien to freedom of entry, the Supreme Court has stated, "It is an international customary law that whether or not to admit an alien into a country is under the discretionary power of the State concerned" (11 *Keishu* 1663, Sup. Ct., G.B., June 19, 1957). With respect to the question of aliens' freedom of residence, the Court later declared that aliens residing in our country have no constitutional right to reside or to seek to continue to reside, for the decision about an alien's residence is left to the discretion of the country. (32 *Minshu* 1223, Sup. Ct., G.B., October 4, 1978)

217. It has generally been agreed that although foreigners in Japan are entitled to most of the freedoms and rights contained in the Constitution, such as the right to a trial before the court, alien residents are denied certain rights which the State grants solely to its nationals, such as the right to participate in the political process.

In addition, various socioeconomic rights, such as the right to make a wholesome and cultured livelihood (Article 25 of the Constitution), the right to receive an education (Article 26), the right to work (Article 27), and the right of workers to organize, bargain collectively and strike (Article 28) have traditionally been considered to be limited to Japanese nationals. As a matter of fact, the Public Offices Election Act (sections 9 and 10) limits the rights to vote and run for public office to Japanese nationals (*see infra* paragraph 234).

218. However, a considerable number of influential scholars and lawyers have begun to question the government's position which denies alien residents the right to be appointed to nonmanagerial posts in the civil service. These scholars and lawyers also question the legitimacy of unconditionally denying socioeconomic rights to aliens.

219. In the sphere of economic freedoms and property rights, aliens are subject to special governmental regulations. Referring to the freedom to choose an occupation, for example, an alien cannot become a notary public (section 12 of the Notary Public Act). Also, with respect to the freedom of economic activities, aliens are neither permitted to obtain mining licenses (sections 17 and 87 of the Mining Act) nor to open radio stations (section 5 of the Electric Wave Act).

220. Aliens are also subject to governmental restriction in the enjoyment of legal rights related to land, as well as in the acquisition of land, buildings, factories, business establishments, mining rights and other property rights related to them. Such rights are usually granted on a reciprocal basis (section 1 of the Alien Land Act).

221. The Alien Land Act, enacted in 1925, provides in section 1 that imperial decrees, based on the principle of reciprocity, may restrict foreigners or foreign corporations' enjoyment of land rights. The Act also provides in section 4 that imperial decrees may limit the acquisition of land rights by foreigners or foreign corporations in areas necessary for national defense. These imperial decrees are now read as Cabinet orders under the Constitution of 1947. No such Cabinet orders have been issued.

In recent years, a sense of alarm has been growing over foreigners and foreign corporations' active acquisition of land. In response to calls for legislative measures, the Act on the Survey of Land Use and Regulation of Land Use around Important Facilities and Remote Islands was enacted in June 2021. This Act does not, however, regulate the acquisition of land by foreign nationals or foreign corporations as such. Also, it controls the transactions by Japanese citizens or Japanese corporations. Section 1 of the Act states that its purpose is "to prevent land in the area around important facilities and in the area of border islands from being used for acts that interfere with the functions of such important facilities or border islands." It remains unclear how the government will enforce this Act.

222. Except for the freedom to enter and reside in Japan, the right to participate in the political process, and socioeconomic and property rights, aliens are entitled to all other constitutional rights to the same extent as are Japanese nationals. In addition, the Constitution has been interpreted to mean that aliens are prohibited from engaging in such political activities as exerting an undue influence on the political choice of the Japanese people.

223. Influential Japanese constitutional law scholars agree that it is constitutionally permissible for alien residents to take action through appropriate means to express their opinions on matters directly related to their status. In this respect, in a case regarding the political activities of an alien who attended a rally held to defeat the Japan-United States Security Treaty and who worked to support the hunger strike staged to oppose the government-proposed immigration act, the Supreme Court stated that the protection of the freedom of political activities extended to aliens unless their activities were such as to unduly influence the decision and execution of the political will of the State (*McLean v. Minister of Justice*, 32 *Minshu* 1223, Sup. Ct., G.B., October 4, 1978).

Chapter 2. Fundamental Human Rights and Liberties

by Prof. Hiroyuki Hata with updates by Prof. Hiromi Nishimura and Prof. Takayoshi Okada

§1. General

I. Sources

A. *Constitution of Japan, Chapter III (Rights and Duties of the People)*

224. Article 11 provides, "The people shall not be prevented from enjoying any of the fundamental human rights" and "These fundamental human rights guaranteed to the people by this Constitution shall be conferred upon the people of this and future generations as eternal and inviolate rights." Also, Article 97 states:

> The fundamental human rights by this Constitution guaranteed to the people of Japan are fruits of the age-old struggle of man to be free; they have survived the many exacting tests for durability and are conferred upon this and future generations in trust, to be held for all time inviolate.

The Constitution further enumerates in Chapter III various individual rights and liberties (Articles 13 to 40) necessary to safeguard the human dignity of all individuals.

B. *International Covenant on Civil and Political Rights*

225. On August 4, 1979, Japan ratified two legally binding treaties, namely, the International Covenant on Economic, Social and Cultural Rights (ICESCR) and the International Covenant on Civil and Political Rights (ICCPR). Both treaties went into effect on September 21 of the same year. As a signatory to these treaties, Japan is obligated to take all appropriate means to progressively achieve the full realization of the rights recognized in the Covenant (ICESCR) (Article 2, paragraph 1 of the ICESCR). Japan must also submit reports on the measures adopted which give effect to the rights recognized in the Covenant (ICCPR) and on the progress made in the enjoyment of those rights (Article 40, paragraph 1 of the ICCPR). In light of its content (Articles 2–27) and pursuant to Article 98, paragraph 2 of the Constitution which stipulates, "The treaties concluded by Japan and established laws of nations shall be faithfully observed," the Covenant (ICCPR) is considered to be self-executing in Japan and therefore to constitute a source of human rights. In this regard, it differs from the ICESCR which is not considered self-executing.

C. Ordinary Legislation to Implement Constitutional Provisions and Provisions of Treaties

226. The Diet has to enact laws to implement constitutional provisions and provisions of treaties that guarantee rights but are not self-executing.

227. The Constitution has several provisions dealing with socioeconomic rights which cannot be realized without legislation. For example, Article 25 guarantees the right to maintain the minimum standards of wholesome and cultured living. Both leading scholarly opinion and judicial precedent take the stand that this provision is not self-executing (*Asahi*, 21 *Minshu* 1043, Sup. Ct., G.B., May 24, 1967). It is agreed that the right to a decent life which Article 25 guarantees is, as a matter of fact, guaranteed and carried out by a statute, namely, the Livelihood Protection Act. There are many such rights that can only be realized through ordinary legislation.

II. Historical Outline

A. Pre-Meiji Constitution Period

228. On March 14, 1867, the newly created Meiji government issued the Proclamation of Five Articles and thereby declared that Japan would proceed in the direction of a new modern State. By carrying out various drastic reforms in the fields of public administration, taxation, land ownership (e.g., the abolition of *Han* (feudal province) and establishment of *Ken* (prefecture) in 1871, land tax reform in 1872, etc.), as well as abolishing the feudalistic social status system (the Emancipation Proclamation of 1870, etc.), the new government dealt a fatal blow to the feudalistic old regime on the verge of collapse, contributing to the establishment of a strong centralized State.

As a result, various rights, such as the people's freedom to choose and change their residence, freedom of economic activities, and private ownership of land were recognized. This helped lay the foundation for the subsequent development of a capitalistic economy in Japan.

Though economic freedoms were thus expanded, the government, in the face of mounting anti-government activities by discontented samurais, adopted several executive ordinances, such as the Publication Ordinance (1873), the Newspaper Ordinance (1875), the Assembly Ordinance (1879), etc., which grossly curtailed freedom of expression and freedom of assembly. This period of time, however, also witnessed a very active human rights movement which produced various constitution drafts prepared by private citizens. The most notable of these was Emori Ueki's epoch-making draft containing a detailed bill of rights (1880). The year before Ueki's draft was announced, the Senate had proposed a contrasting draft that guaranteed civil rights and liberties, though only within the framework of legislative enactment. However, the Senate draft was rejected by the government as too progressive.

B. Enactment of the Meiji Constitution

229. On October 12, 1880, an imperial order promising to establish a popularly elected legislature by 1889 was issued as the people's demand for the guarantee of civil rights and liberties and the establishment of a legislature mounted. In order to fulfill the commitment it was necessary to prepare a constitution, and Count Hirobumi Ito was charged with the responsibility to study and make a draft constitution. In 1881, Ito went to Europe for research. He then made a draft modeled after the Prussian Constitution of 1850. This draft subsequently became the Meiji Constitution (enacted in 1889).

230. Needless to say, the Meiji Constitution, Japan's first modern constitution, guaranteed various rights and liberties: namely, freedom to choose and change residence (Article 22); freedom of one's own body (Article 23); right to a trial before a judge (Article 24); privacy of housing (Article 25); secrecy of correspondence (Article 26); inviolability of property rights (Article 27); freedom of religion (Article 28); freedom of speech, press, assembly and association (Article 29); and right to petition (Article 30). However, it must be noted that these rights were only guaranteed within the limits of statutes. For example, Article 29 of the Meiji Constitution which guaranteed the freedom of expression, assembly and association provided, "Japanese subjects shall, within the limits of law, enjoy the freedom of speech, writing, publication, assembly and association." Article 26 also stated, "Except in cases stipulated by law, the secrecy of the letters of every Japanese subject shall remain inviolate." Therefore, it is not too much to say that the Diet could curtail any rights and liberties that it wished.

231. It must also be noted that the judiciary under the Meiji Constitution, like that of its model the Prussian Constitution of 1850, did not have the power to review the constitutionality of legislation. The courts were required to consider as constitutional any laws which the Diet passed and to which the Emperor gave his assent. In addition to such structural deficiencies, there were some other problems with the guarantee of rights and liberties under the Meiji Constitution. One problem was that the Constitution lacked a provision incorporating the principle of equality under the law. Another one was that any constitutional rights and liberties could be curtailed by the executive authority in times of national crises based on provisions for a state of siege (Article 14) and executive emergency legislation (Article 8) (*infra* paragraph 449). This was corroborated by Article 31 which stated, "The provisions contained in the present Chapter shall not affect the exercise of the powers appertaining to the Emperor, in times of war or cases of a national emergency."

C. Enactment of the Constitution of Japan

232. Unlike the Meiji Constitution, the Constitution of Japan (1947) has a complete set of human rights provisions, including equal rights, which are deemed indispensable guarantees of human dignity. Moreover, the Constitution declares all those rights "eternal and inviolate" (Articles 11 and 97). Furthermore, to safeguard constitutional rights, the Constitution gives the courts of law the power to review legislation for constitutionality (Article 81).

III. General Rules

A. *Who Is Entitled to the Protection of Rights and Liberties?*

233. From the provisions of the Constitution (Articles 11 and 97), there are no questions whatsoever about the fact that all Japanese nationals are fully entitled to the protection of rights and liberties guaranteed by the Constitution irrespective of their race, creed, sex, social status, family origin or other traits. The problem being discussed in Japan is whether alien residents or corporations are entitled to the same protection of constitutional rights and liberties as are Japanese nationals. As to the rights and liberties guaranteed to aliens, *see* §2 of Chapter 1 (*supra* paragraphs 189–196).

1. Alien Residents

234. Scholarly opinion as to whether alien residents are entitled to constitutionally protected rights and liberties is divided. One theory insists that since a constitution is a document of the agreement by the people who constitute a State, only such people are entitled to the protection of rights and liberties guaranteed in the Constitution unless otherwise specifically provided. Those scholars and lawyers who take this stand do not, however, object to the view, based on the spirit of the Constitution of Japan, which in turn is based on principles of international cooperation and harmony, that the protection of the rights and liberties which are guaranteed therein should be as far as possible extended to resident aliens. However, they assert that extension should be provided by individual legislation.

Unlike the abovementioned theory, the leading opinion on this problem is that constitutional rights and liberties are in principle guaranteed to resident aliens as well as to Japanese nationals. This view is taken in the light of the pre-State nature of human rights as well as paragraph 2 of the Preamble to the Constitution which stipulates, "We recognize that all peoples of the world have the right to live in peace, free from fear and want." The leading opinion further states that whether or not specific rights are guaranteed to aliens should be determined according to the nature of the right at issue.

235. Judicial precedent is based on this latter opinion. For example, the Supreme Court in 1950 declared, "It should be recognized that any person who stays in Japan is entitled to human rights which he or she should naturally have as a human being even if his or her entry into the country was illegal" (4 *Minshu* 683, Sup. Ct., G.B., December 28, 1950). In 1978, the Court again held, "It should be understood that all rights and liberties guaranteed by the provisions of Chapter III of the Constitution, except for those deemed to be guaranteed only to Japanese nationals from the nature of the right, are equally applied to aliens staying in our country" (*McLean v. Minister of Justice*, 32 *Minshu* 1223, Sup. Ct., G.B., October 4, 1978, 32 *Minshu* 1223, Sup. Ct., G.B., October 4, 1978).

236. The rights and liberties which are considered not available to aliens include rights to participate in the political process and thereby form and execute the will of the people. Included therein are the right to vote and run for public office, the right to referendum, the right to recall public officials, the right to be employed by the government in certain categories of civil service where the duties are regulatory or greatly affect the decision of the State will, etc. It is also generally agreed that there is a limitation imposed on the political activities of aliens in so far as such activities have an important effect on the political process of the State. For example, aliens are prevented from forming or joining a political association with the intent to intervene in Japan's politics; initiating or engaging in political activities to support or oppose a particular government in Japan; etc. (*see supra* paragraph 215).

However, it should not be inferred from the above that alien residents are prohibited from expressing, or meeting and uniting to express, their opinions on matters directly related to their status or living in Japan. In sum, all civil rights and liberties should be extended to aliens so far as the exercise thereof does not unduly influence the political process of the State. As mentioned above, judicial precedent supports this stand (*McLean v. Minister of Justice*, 32 *Minshu* 1223, Sup. Ct., G.B., October 4, 1978, 32 *Minshu* 1223, Sup. Ct., G.B., October 4, 1978) (*see supra* paragraph 233).

There has been a growing demand among aliens with permanent resident status in Japan for the right to vote in local elections. In 1990, a group of Korean residents in Osaka filed suit with the Osaka District Court seeking registration on the voter's list, though sections 11 and 18 of the Local Autonomy Act and section 9, paragraph 2 of the Public Offices Election Act require Japanese nationality to vote in local elections. Plaintiffs contended that such requirement violated Article 93, paragraph 2, which provides, *inter alia,* "The chief executive officers of all local public entities, the members, their assemblies, and such other local officials as may be determined by law shall be elected by direct popular vote within several communities." Though the District Court and the Supreme Court (3rd Petty Bench) denied the claim, the latter in obiter dictum expressed the significant view that the Diet had authority, in its discretion, to confer the right to vote in local elections on alien permanent residents (*Kim v. Osaka City North Ward Elections Commission*, 49 *Minshu* 639, Sup. Ct., G.B., February 28, 1995).

237. There are also issues relating to the extension to aliens of the constitutional guarantees of economic and property rights, such as the freedom to enter and leave the country, the freedom to choose an occupation, the right to property, and so on. The most controversial problem is whether resident aliens have the freedom of reentry into Japan. There are two different points of view on the meaning of reentry. One view is that each reentry is a new entry, while the other regards temporary travel from Japan as a base of life and return not as involving a new entry. As far as the re-entry of resident aliens is concerned, influential constitutional law scholars are in favor of the latter viewpoint. Now that they are permitted to reside in Japan, whether permanently or for a certain period of time, resident aliens may well have the freedom of reentry while they maintain their abode in Japan. This freedom may be limited in exceptional cases where there is a special reason to disapprove entry.

238. The freedom to choose and pursue an occupation and the right to property must also be guaranteed to aliens because these rights are vital to their subsistence. However, as aliens are neither a constituent of the State nor directly responsible for its existence, their rights are unavoidably subject to extensive curtailment as seen in such laws as the Alien Land Act, the Shipping Act, the Aircraft Act, and so on.

As previously mentioned, such socioeconomic rights as the right to live a decent life, the right to education, the right to work, etc., have also been traditionally considered not guaranteed to aliens. However, the number of constitutional law scholars and lawyers who oppose the traditional view is increasing on the basis of paragraph 2 of the Preamble which states, "We recognize that all peoples of the world have the right to live in peace, free from fear and want."

2. Corporations

239. Scholarly opinions on whether corporations are entitled to the enjoyment of fundamental human rights guaranteed by the Constitution are also divided. Those who take the negative view insist that human rights are guaranteed to preserve the human dignity of men and women. Needless to say, what they mean by men and women, in this case, are natural persons, not corporations. According to this view, a corporation is a legal fiction created by law as a means for people to exercise their rights (e.g., the freedom of assembly and association, the freedom of economic activities, the right of property, etc.), and benefits accruing from the corporation's acts revert to the natural persons who constitute it. It is further insisted that private corporations, to say nothing of public corporations (e.g., the State, local public entities, public-owned enterprises, etc.), have become so big, powerful and influential that the corporations themselves are a threat to the preservation of the human dignity of the natural persons.

240. What the negative view asserts is partly true, and worth considering, but it is neither realistic nor reasonable to deny corporations constitutional rights in a highly developed and complex contemporary industrial society. In this respect, Article 19, paragraph 3 of the Basic Law of the German Federal Republic (1949) is noteworthy. It stipulates, "the basic rights shall also apply to domestic corporations to the extent that the nature of such rights permits." In Japan also, the leading scholarly opinion is to the effect that corporations are entitled, to the extent possible, to all constitutional rights and liberties, except for those which, from their nature, are considered limited to natural persons. The Supreme Court of Japan in announcing its famous decision for the so-called.

The *Yawata Steel Company Political Contribution* case of 1970 stated that the provisions of rights and duties contained in Chapter III of the Constitution should be understood to extend to domestic corporations as far as is possible from their nature/ and upheld the constitutionality of the corporation's political contribution

(24 *Minshu* 625, Sup. Ct., G.B., June 24, 1970). In the final analysis, the question of which rights are applied to corporations is to be determined on a case-by-case analysis according to the nature of the right at issue.

B. In What Cases May Limitations Be Imposed on Rights and Liberties?

241. The Constitution of Japan declares a set of rights and liberties as "eternal and inviolate" (Articles 11 and 97). However, this does not mean that the rights and liberties guaranteed by the Constitution are without limits. In this respect, the Declaration of the Rights of Man and of the Citizen issued in evolutionary France on August 26, 1789, stated that:

> Liberty consists in being able to do anything which does not injure another: therefore, the exercise of the natural rights of each man has no limits other than those which assure to other members of society the enjoyment of these same rights. These limits may be determined only by the law (loi): (IV.)

This is nothing but a manifestation of the fact that rights and liberties are not absolutely limitless.

242. The Japanese Constitution, in Article 12, likewise stipulates that:

> The freedoms and rights guaranteed to the people by this Constitution shall be maintained by the constant endeavor of the people, who shall refrain from any abuse of these freedoms and rights and shall always be responsible for utilizing them for the public welfare.

The Constitution further states in Article 13 that:

> All of the people shall be respected as individuals. Their right to life, liberty, and the pursuit of happiness shall, to the extent that it does not interfere with the public welfare, be the supreme consideration in legislation and in other governmental affairs.

243. In addition to Article 12 and Article 13, there are two additional articles that contain the term "public welfare" in their respective provisions. They are Article 22 and Article 29. Article 22, paragraph 1 provides, "Every person shall have the freedom to choose and change his residence and to choose his occupation to the extent that it does not interfere with the public welfare." Article 29 states, "The right to own and hold property is inviolable" in paragraph 1 and "Property rights shall be defined by law, in conformity with the public welfare" in paragraph 2. The leading scholarly theory and judicial precedents take the position that Articles 12 and 13 are provisions containing a general rule governing all constitutional rights and freedoms. These two articles are designed to show that all rights and freedoms are guaranteed insofar as they do not invade others' rights. In other words, they show that even though "eternal and inviolate," individual constitutional rights are subject to minimum restriction from the standpoint of harmonious guarantee of everyone's rights.

244. If Article 12 and Article 13 are provisions containing a general rule concerning all constitutional rights and liberties, the question arises why the term "public welfare" is repeatedly used in Article 22 and Article 29. An answer is that the rights and freedoms guaranteed in these provisions are such economic and property rights as the freedom to choose and change a residence, the freedom to choose and pursue an occupation and the right of property and that unlimited pursuit of such rights will inevitably undermine the foundation of the twentieth-century welfare state which has the role of realizing substantial equality for all its people. It is a fact that economic and property rights are given a weaker status than civil and political rights under twentieth-century constitutions. The same is true of the Japanese Constitution, which is based on the idea of a modern welfare state. A restrictive phrase, such as "to the extent that it does not interfere with the public welfare" or "in the conformity with the public welfare" is placed in the provisions of the Constitution guaranteeing economic and property rights in order to make it easier to regulate such rights for the welfare of all the people. The Supreme Court of Japan, relying on the idea of a "double standard" which was adopted by its United States counterpart as early as 1937, held that the Diet could, in the interests of the public welfare, actively regulate an individual's freedom of economic activities if the regulation was based on reasonable grounds (26 *Keishu* 586, Sup. Ct., G.B., November 22, 1972).

245. In conclusion, it can be said that there are two kinds of "public welfare" used in the Japanese Constitution. One is the public welfare used in Article 12 and Article 13, which has the role of negatively adjusting conflicting rights and freedoms from a standpoint of the idea of a free State, and the other is that used in Article 22 and Article 29, which is based on the idea of distributive justice and is aimed at actively correcting social inequalities and injustices caused by the concentration of wealth.

C. Are Constitutional Rights and Liberties Applicable among Private Parties?

246. Traditionally, constitutional rights and liberties were considered guarantees against abuses by public authorities. Therefore, constitutional provisions were thought to be inapplicable to a case of invasion of rights by private persons unless otherwise stipulated in the Constitution. Until fairly recently the same view was applied in Western Europe and the United States.

After the end of World War II, Japanese scholars and lawyers began to discuss the problem of the applicability of constitutional rights to actions among private persons under the influence of the American theory of "private government" and the

German counterpart of "Drittwirkung." Unlike the traditional view that constitutional rights are only guarantees against abuses by the public authorities, and therefore not applied to controversies between private parties, there are two theories which insist that constitutional provisions have an effect on private persons, either directly or indirectly.

247. One is called the direct effect theory, and the other is the indirect effect theory. The former is based on the view that in today's society where various organized interest groups, such as big businesses, political parties, labor unions, etc., exist as a possible threat to human rights, the Constitution is not only a legal norm to govern the structure of and operation of State power but also represents an objective value system to govern social, political, economic and all other aspects of the life of the people. While this is a persuasive theory, it has a serious defect. If constitutional rights were to apply to actions among private parties, those rights might create benefits for one party but would create obligations for the opposite party. Constitutional provisions are usually written in such abstract and ambiguous terms that either party to a private constitutional controversy will inevitably shoulder an unpredictable burden.

248. Unlike the above theory (the direct effect theory), the indirect effect theory takes the stand that the rights and liberties guaranteed by the Constitution are not directly applied but are indirectly applied to disputes and activities among private persons. This indirect application comes through such general provisions of private law as section 90 of the Civil Code which provides, "Any legal act injurious to the public order or the good morals shall be null and void." For example, the Tokyo District Court held that a company regulation that forced women employees to retire at younger ages than men or to quit upon marriage was invalid because it injured the "public order or the good morals" (17 *Rominshu* 1407, Tokyo Dist. Ct., December 20, 1966). In this case, the court adjudged the company regulation to be injurious to public order or good morals and therefore null and void because it violated Article 14 of the Constitution which prohibited sex discrimination. Thus, the import of Article 14 was indirectly applied to the controversy between the private parties through section 90 of the Civil Code. The Supreme Court also relied on the indirect effect theory in the famous Grand Bench Decision in the *Mitsubishi Resin Company* case in which the validity of the company's dismissal of an employee who had hidden his connection with political activities during his university days was challenged (27 *Minshu* 1536, Sup. Ct., December 12, 1973).

249. Seven years later, the Supreme Court again affirmed the indirect effect theory, holding as invalid a Nissan Motor Company regulation which required female employees to retire five years earlier than male workers, finding such regulation injurious to public order or good morals (35 *Minshu* 300, Sup. Ct., March 24, 1981). If, as the traditional view holds, constitutional rights and freedoms are not to be applied among private persons, then there exists the great possibility that those rights might be invaded by big enterprises, political parties, labor unions, etc., and the substantial meaning of the constitutional guarantee of rights and freedoms would be lost. However, if constitutional rights were to be directly applied to actions among private parties, either side of the dispute would, as mentioned above, shoulder an unpredictable burden. Both the traditional view and the direct effect theory have a defect. In this sense, the indirect effect theory, a theory contrived to reconcile the above two theories, is the most proper view.

Of course, such constitutional provisions as Article 15, paragraph 4; Article 18; Article 27, paragraph 3; Article 28, etc., which apparently stipulate that they are directly applicable between private parties are exceptions.

§2. Civil Rights and Liberties

I. Equal Rights

A. *Equality under the Law*

250. Under the Meiji Constitution (enacted in 1889), there was no provision encompassing the principle of equality under the law. One provision, however, guaranteed Japanese subjects the right to be appointed to civil service offices, though with limitations. Article 19 of the Meiji Constitution stipulated, "Japanese subjects may, according to qualifications determined by law or ordinance, be appointed to civil and military or any other public offices equally." Because of the limiting qualifications, women were substantially kept from engaging in civil service.

251. Article 14, paragraph 1 of the Constitution of Japan stipulates, "All of the people are equal under the law and there shall be no discrimination in political, economic or social relations because of race, creed, sex, social status or family origin." In addition to the principle of equality under the law, the Constitution provides for:

(a) the abolition of peers and peerage (Article 14, paragraph 2);
(b) the prohibition of awarding honor, decoration or distinction with privilege (Article 14, paragraph 3);
(c) the essential equality of the sexes in family life (Article 24, paragraph 2);
(d) the equal opportunity to education (Article 26, paragraph 1); and
(e) the guarantee of universal suffrage in public office elections (Article 15, paragraph 3) and equality in the qualifications for membership in the Diet and for voting (Article 44, Proviso).In order to achieve substantial equality, the Constitution also guarantees such social rights as the right to maintain the minimum standards of wholesome and cultured living (Article 25, paragraph 1), the right to receive an equal education (Article 26, paragraph 1), the right to work (Article 27, paragraph 1), and the right of workers to organize and to bargain and act collectively (Article 28). At the same time, the Constitution makes it possible to restrict economic and property rights from the standpoint of distributive justice (Article 22, paragraph 1 and Article 29, paragraph 2).

252. When the Constitution of Japan was promulgated, scholarly opinion was sharply divided as to whether Article 14, paragraph 1 (which provided for the principle of equality under the law) bound only the law enforcement organ or whether it also bound the lawmaking organ. Constitutional law scholars who were generally strict constructionists insisted that the term "equality under the law" did not bind the lawmaking organ. In their opinion, this provision only requires that all laws that have been made be equally applied. In other words, the term "equality" used in Article 14 means equality in the application of laws, not in the contents of laws. Of course, as the latter part of Article 14, paragraph 1 has a provision stipulating that there shall be no discrimination "because of race, creed, sex, social status or family origin," it is obvious that the lawmaking body is prohibited from making a law which constitutes discrimination based on any of the abovementioned features. According to this view, however, even if a law made by the lawmaking organ is discriminatory in contents, it will not be violative of Article 14, paragraph 1 unless the discrimination is based on "race, creed, sex, social status or family origin."

253. However, the leading scholarly theory and judicial precedents are opposed to such a construction. They take the position that Article 14, paragraph 1 binds both the law enforcement and lawmaking bodies. Under this theory, the lawmaking body is prohibited from making a law that is discriminatory in content, whatever the reason may be. This view regards the features enumerated in the latter part of Article 14, paragraph 1 (e.g., "race, creed, sex,") as examples. Therefore, it will be unconstitutional to make a discriminatory law, whatever the ground of discrimination may be.

254. There is also a scholarly controversy as to whether the equality which the Constitution guarantees is absolute equality or relative equality. The absolute equality theory requires that all persons be treated equally regardless of their age, gender, talent and other traits. However, the relative equality theory insists that persons with the same ability must be treated equally. According to the latter theory, it is impossible and unrealistic to treat people with different personality traits equally in all aspects of life. The problem with the absolute equality theory is that, if that theory were adopted, section 733 of the Civil Code which prohibits women from remarrying for one hundred days after the date of divorce, sections 65 to 67 of the Labor Standards Act which gives women workers a physiological leave, section 61 of the Labor Standards Act which prohibits boys under 18 years of age and women from engaging in late-night work, etc., would all be unconstitutional.

255. The leading scholarly opinions and judicial precedents support the relative equality theory: a theory that recognizes different treatment of persons with different talents and other personal traits. In sum, Article 14, paragraph 1 is designed to prohibit unreasonable discrimination, not to deny a distinction based on a "reasonable" ground. Of course, what is "reasonable" cannot be so easily decided, for the term "reasonable" is a relative concept, and changes from time to time and from place to place. Nevertheless, there is no other way to determine whether a specific act violates equality under the law than to decide according to the indefinite concept of "reasonableness." The problem is that there exists the possibility that the determination of reasonableness may be done on the basis of out-of-date concepts and stereotypes.

256. In its decision in a *patricide* case, the Fukuoka District Court held that section 205 of the Penal Code which stipulated a more severe punishment for bodily injury resulting in the death of a lineal ascendant than a similar offense against a non-ascendant, was unreasonable and, therefore, unconstitutional, because the provision originated in feudalistic, undemocratic and anti-human-right philosophies (4 *Keishu* 2070, Sup. Ct., January 9, 1950). However, this decision was reversed by the Supreme Court, which stated that it would not be unreasonable discrimination to take into consideration the relationship between parents and children in meting out punishment. This decision was based on the theory that the morality which ruled the relationship between husbands and wives, parents and children, and brothers and sisters was a universally recognized moral principle (4 *Keishu* 2037, Sup. Ct., G.B., October 11, 1950). The decision was by a vote of 13 to 2.

257. Twenty-three years later, however, the Supreme Court changed its attitude by holding that section 200 of the Penal Code, which made it an aggravated crime punishable by death or life imprisonment to intentionally kill a lineal ascendant, was violative of equality under the law and, therefore, null and void (27 *Keishu* 265, Sup. Ct., G.B., April 4, 1973) (*supra* paragraph 157). The penalty for committing an ordinary premeditated murder (section 199 of the Penal Code) was death, life imprisonment, or imprisonment of not less than three years. The decision was by a vote of 14 to 1. It must be noted, however, that eight of the fourteen Justices who supported the opinion of the Court did not disavow all differences in punishment between patricide and ordinary murder. They only invalidated section 200 of the Penal Code because it imposed too severe a penalty on one who committed a patricide as compared with one who committed an ordinary murder.

B. Discriminations in Japan

1. Women

258. There is no denying that Japanese women were discriminated against in all aspects of life, including family life, under the Meiji Constitution. For example, women were not given the right to vote or run for public office until December 17, 1945, when the old Election Act for Members of the House of Representatives was revised. They were also denied equal opportunities in employment in the private sector as well as in the national and local civil services. Furthermore, they were legally subjected to gross discrimination in marriage and other family relations. Discriminatory provisions in the Civil Code and the Penal Code entitled only the oldest son to inherit all family property as head of a family (section 970 [eliminated] of the Civil Code), denied a wife's legal competence (section 14 [eliminated] of the Civil Code), empowered a husband to manage and make a profit on a wife's property (section 799 and section 801 [eliminated] of the Civil Code) and to designate a wife's domicile (section 789 [eliminated] of the Civil Code) as well as to exercise sole parental prerogative over a child (section 877 [eliminated] of the Civil Code), obligated solely the wife to preserve virtue (section 813 [eliminated] of the Civil Code), stipulated a discriminatory punishment for a wife's adultery (section 183 [eliminated] of the Penal Code), and so on. Needless to say, all of these provisions were eliminated from the Civil Code and the Penal Code when the Constitution of Japan was adopted.

259. In order to get rid of the extreme inequalities based on gender which existed under the Meiji Constitution, the Constitution of Japan has a specific provision, in addition to the general principle of equality under the law (section 14, paragraph 1), stipulating, "Marriage shall be based only on the mutual consent of both sexes and it shall be maintained through mutual co-operation with the equal rights of the sexes" (section 24, paragraph 1) and "With regard to choice of spouse, property rights, inheritance, choice of domicile, divorce and other matters pertaining to marriage and the family, laws shall be enacted from the standpoint of individual dignity and the essential equality of the sexes" (section 24, paragraph 2). Considering the fact that men and women differ physiologically and physically, it must be noted that the framers of the Constitution put the terms "individual dignity and the essential equality of the sexes" in Article 24, paragraph 2.

260. The present Civil Code has some provisions under which men and women are treated differently. For example, section 733 prohibits women (but not men) from being remarried for six months after their marriages have been canceled or terminated. This latter provision is based on the fear that the paternity of a newborn baby may be unknown if women are allowed to be remarried soon after divorce. The Supreme Court has so far sustained the constitutionality of the limitation of women's remarriage as a reasonable distinction based on the physiological difference of the sexes (1563 *Hanji* 81, Sup. Ct., December 5, 1995).

However, in 2015, the Supreme Court ruled that section 733, paragraph 1 of the Civil Code is unconstitutional, holding as follows. The legislative purpose of this provision is understood to be to avoid the duplication of the presumption of paternity and thereby prevent the occurrence of paternity disputes. In light of the provisions of section 772, paragraph 2 of the Civil Code, the duplication of the presumption of paternity is avoided by providing a calculated hundred-day ban on remarriage for children born after a woman's second marriage. However, the portion of the provision in question that exceeds a hundred days cannot be regarded as the period necessary to avoid the duplication of the presumption of paternity as stipulated in section 772 of the Civil Code. This part of the provision imposes excessive restrictions that lack rationality and violates Article 14, paragraph 1 and Article 24, paragraph 2 of the Constitution (69 *Minshu* 2427, Sup. Ct., G.B., December 16, 2015). As a result, the Diet acted swiftly. It amended the Code by shortening the ban on remarriage to one hundred days and establishing a new provision that the prohibition does not apply to women who are not pregnant at the time of divorce.

261. Other problems with Japan's Civil Code include section 750 which requires that a family name shall be determined at the time of marriage by the consultation of a married couple, section 762 which stipulates that a husband and a wife shall, respectively, own properties which they had before marriage and which they each acquire after marriage. Some people insist that these systems have, as a matter of fact, been functioning in favor of a husband and accordingly should be revised. The constitutionality of the latter provision has, however, been affirmed by the Supreme Court (15 *Minshu* 2047, Sup. Ct., G.B., September 6, 1961).

The Supreme Court held that 96% of couples choose the husband's surname under a system of the same surname for married couples based on the provision of section 750 of the Civil Code, "Married couples shall assume the surnames of their husbands or wives as determined at the time of marriage." In this case, the Supreme Court ruled that the fact that the overwhelming majority of couples in Japan choose their husbands' surnames is not the result of this provision itself. Therefore, this provision does not violate Article 14, paragraph 1 of the Constitution.

Furthermore, the Supreme Court has held that the system of the same surname for married couples does not violate Article 24, paragraph 2 of the Constitution (69 *Minshu* 2586, Sup. Ct., G.B., December 16, 2015). It found that there are cases where a person who changes his or her surname due to marriage suffers disadvantages such as loss of identity and difficulty in maintaining the social trust, reputation, and honor that he or she has developed while using the surname before marriage. However, the system of the same surname for married couples permits the use of the surname before marriage as a common name. Since this common name is widespread in society, the above disadvantages can be mitigated to a certain extent. Considering these points, the system of the same surname for married couples is not a system that lacks rationality in light of the demands for individual dignity and the essential equality of the sexes. It thus does not violate Article 24 of the Constitution.

262. On July 1, 1985, Japan ratified the Convention on the Elimination of All Forms of Discrimination Against Women which was adopted by the General Assembly of the United Nations in 1979. In order to fulfill better its obligation as a Member State signatory to the Convention, Japan began to revise some statutes which had been criticized as constitutionally questionable before ratification. In 1984, Japan revised section 2 of the Nationality Act so that Japanese nationality might be given to any child born to a father or mother who was a Japanese national at the time of its birth. Before the 1984 amendment, Japanese nationality was accorded only to a child born to a father who was a Japanese national (*supra* paragraph 205). In addition, the Equal Employment Opportunity Act was enacted in 1985, which for the first time comprehensively prohibited sex discrimination in employment. The Act has been amended several times and now prohibits discrimination based on sex in recruitment and employment (section 5), and discrimination based on sex in assignment, promotion, demotion, education and training (section 6). Furthermore, the Act prohibits so-called indirect discrimination (section 7). Indirect discrimination refers to measures that require a reason other than the worker's sex but are substantially equivalent to discrimination based on sex. These provisions prohibiting sex discrimination do not prevent the implementation of special treatment of female workers, i.e., positive action, to improve the circumstances that hinder the securing of equal opportunity and treatment between men and women (section 8). The Act further stipulates the prohibition of disadvantageous treatment based on marriage, pregnancy, childbirth, and the like (section 9) and the implementation of measures against sexual harassment in the workplace (section 11).

2. *Buraku*

263. One of the most serious discriminations that exist in contemporary Japanese society is what is called the *Buraku* discrimination, systematic discrimination by socially and politically created class distinction which was built up in the course of about 260 years of rule by the Tokugawa Shogunate (1603–1867). During this period, a group of Japanese people was unjustly forced to live in villages (*Burakus*) isolated from other groups of people and were subjected to ruthless and inhumane restrictions.

264. In 1871, the Meiji government issued the Emancipation Proclamation which announced the formal liberation of *Burakumins* (persons who lived in *Burakus*) from the feudal status which had long bound them. The government, however, did not take any measures to help these people adjust to the new environs, though it gave substantial aid to former samurais who lost their fiefs or stipends as a result of the abolition of the old regime. Therefore, though legally liberated, they were obliged to live in poverty and misery and undergo continued discrimination in all aspects of their life, especially in marriage, employment, etc.

The problem of *Buraku* discrimination which is peculiar to Japanese society is the fact that a group of people called *Burakumins* are still alienated from the protection of civil rights and liberties which the people of modern society are naturally entitled to. In August of 1965, the Deliberative Council for the Measures for *Dowa* Problems, a Prime Minister's advisory panel, submitted a report declaring the elimination of *Buraku* discrimination to be a task for the entire nation to tackle and proposing that a comprehensive affirmative action program should be carried out by the government. Prompted by the report, the national government finally decided to squarely cope with the task of eliminating both economic and psychological discrimination. (The term "*Dowa*" which is made up of characters which mean "sameness" and "harmony" was created by the government to express the elimination of *Buraku* discrimination.).

265. In 1969, the Diet enacted a ten-year temporary law entitled "Act on the Special Measures for *Dowa* Projects" (ASMDP) to carry out a series of affirmative action programs. The law was extended for three additional years. Then, in 1982, a new five-year temporary law entitled "Act on the Special Measures for the Improvement of Areas" (ASMIA) was enacted following the expiration of the ASMDP. Furthermore, in order to make it possible to carry on *Dowa* projects which would possibly be left incomplete when the existing law expired, the Deliberative Council for the Special Measures for the Improvement of Areas, a new Prime Minister's advisory body, proposed an additional law. Thus, in 1987, the Act on the State's Special Financial measures concerning Specific Projects for the Improvement of Areas, a five-year temporary law, came into being. Though this law formally expired on March 31, 1992, modifications enacted in 1992 and 1997 extended the validity of some specified provisions for an additional ten years, namely, until March 31, 2002 (section 1 of the Supplementary Provision of the Act on the State's Special Financial measures concerning Specific Projects for the Improvement of Areas). Now, the series of special measure laws have all expired.

It must be noted that these laws were all project laws made with a view to eliminating "economic discrimination" and that at the moment, there were no effective means under the existing laws to eliminate "psychological discrimination." It is true that *Burakus*' economic situation has considerably improved, but it is still an undeniable fact that there persistently exists psychological discrimination against people from *Burakus* in various aspects of life, especially in marriage, employment, etc. Therefore, there is a strong demand for new legislation which would stipulate, among others, a regulatory means to effectively cope with the elimination of "psychological discrimination." In response to these demands, the Act for the Elimination of Buraku Discrimination was enacted in 2016. It consists of six sections and is the first statute to use the expression "Buraku discrimination." It can be said that the Act newly recognizes that discrimination against Buraku people still exists today. This Act clearly states that discrimination against the Buraku people is "unacceptable" and "an important issue to be resolved" in light of the Constitution (section 1). In addition, it clearly states the necessity of education and enlightenment regarding the elimination of discrimination against the Buraku people (section 5).

3. *Ainu*

266. The *Ainu* are indigenous inhabitants of Japan, living mainly on Hokkaido, the northernmost island of Japan. According to a survey made by the prefectural government of Hokkaido in 2013, the population of *Ainu* in Hokkaido, including their non-*Ainu* spouses, adopted children, etc., who constitute a household, numbers 16,786. Under the Meiji government's coercive policy of developing Hokkaido, the *Ainu* had their ethnic rights denied and were forced to assimilate into ethnic Japanese. In 1877, the land called "*aynu mosir*" (land of human beings), on which they had been living in their traditional way for centuries, was incorporated into the government's territory as "un-owned" land. In this way, the *Ainus*' ancestral land in Hokkaido was taken from them. The following year, 1878, they were also forced to renounce their traditional names in the family registry. In 1899, the government enacted a law entitled the Hokkaido Former Aboriginal Persons Protection Act. The purpose of this law was said to be to save the *Ainu*, who were economically pinched because they had lost their traditional land and means to make a livelihood. However, as a matter of fact, this law forced them to engage in farming on a limited tract of land (about 5 acres per family) leased to them by the government. Although the farmland was eventually given to the *Ainu* people who kept cultivating it for fifteen years, most of the land was subsequently lost for one reason or another.

Years of government assimilation policy has not only deprived the *Ainu* of their native language (*Ainu* language) as a mother tongue for daily use but also made it difficult for the *Ainu* to leave their traditional culture to posterity. Prompted by such a critical situation and encouraged by a rising international movement for the promotion of indigenous people's human rights, *the Ainu* people have been demanding that the government officially recognize them as the original inhabitants of Japan. In March 1997, the Sapporo District Court, in the *Nibutani Dam Construction* case in which the legality of the Hokkaido Expropriation Commission's permission to construct a flood prevention dam in a valley deemed by the Ainu to be "sacred land" was contested, recognized for the first time in Japan's judicial history that the Ainu are the indigenous people of Hokkaido, in the northernmost part of Japan.

A month and a half later, the Diet finally enacted a law entitled "Act concerning the Promotion of the Ainu Culture and the Spread and Enlightenment of Knowledge of the Tradition of the Ainu" (hereinafter referred to as "the Ainu Culture Promotion Act"). Under the law, the government is obligated to take measures to protect and promote the Ainu culture and tradition in order to create a society in which the Ainu people's pride as a race is respected and for the additional purpose of contributing to the development of diverse cultures in Japan. Though this law does not provide for the return of the land rights which the Ainu people claim, it is significant because the government has openly recognized that Japan is inhabited not only by ethnic Japanese but also by people of a different race.

On September 13, 2007, the United Nations Declaration on the Rights of Indigenous Peoples was adopted by the United Nations General Assembly. Subsequently, on June 6, 2008, the Japanese Diet unanimously adopted a resolution calling for the Ainu people to be recognized as indigenous people by both houses of the Diet. Then, on April 19, 2019, a new Ainu law was enacted, which for the first time clearly states that the Ainu people are "indigenous people." The exact name of this law is the "Act on the Promotion of Measures to Realize a Society in which the Pride of the Ainu People is Respected." This new law replaces the Ainu Culture Promotion Act, stipulates the prohibition of discrimination, and includes a new subsidy system to support the promotion of tourism and industry.

4. Sexual Minorities (LGBT)

267. Until now, the issue of social discrimination against so-called "sexual minorities," or LGBT (lesbian, gay, bisexual, transgender), has not been fully recognized in Japan. In recent years, however, public understanding of LGBT has rapidly increased and legal reforms have been implemented. First, the Gender Identity Disorder Special Law enacted in 2004 established requirements and procedures for gender reassignment in the family register. One of the requirements for a person with gender identity disorder to request a trial for gender reassignment is that he/she must undergo sterilization surgery (Article 3, paragraph 1, Item 4 of the same law). In a 2019 case in which the constitutionality of this requirement was disputed, the Supreme Court held that "it is undeniable that there is an aspect that restricts the freedom of a person not to have his/her body invaded against his/her will," but that it is based on considerations such as avoiding sudden changes that may cause confusion in society. The necessity of these considerations and the appropriateness of the method can change according to changes in social conditions regarding the treatment of gender according to gender identity and the understanding of the family system, and the constitutionality of such a provision should require constant consideration. When the purpose of this provision, the manner of the above restrictions, and the current social situation are comprehensively weighed, it cannot be said that this provision violates Articles 13 and 14(1) of the Constitution at this point in time. (261 *Shumin* 1, Sup. Ct., January 23, 2019).

Then, in June 2013, the Law for the Promotion of Understanding of LGBT was enacted to promote public understanding of diversity of sexual orientation. Based on the principle that all citizens, regardless of their sexual orientation, are respected as irreplaceable individuals who equally enjoy fundamental human rights, the law imposes on the national government, local governments, and employers the obligation to make efforts to implement measures to promote public understanding of the diversity of sexual orientation. In a case in which a national public servant with gender identity disorder requested the National Personnel Authority to take administrative measures, including allowing him to freely use the women's restroom at his workplace, and which were not granted, the Supreme Court ruled that the National Personnel Authority's measures were illegal. The Supreme Court concluded, "The National Personnel Authority's decision, without taking into account the specific circumstances of the case, placed undue emphasis on consideration for other employees and unreasonably disregarded the disadvantage of the appellant, and as the decision was not made from the standpoint of fairness to all concerned and the exercise and promotion of efficiency of the employees including the appellant, it was extremely lacking in validity." (Sup. Ct., July 11, 2023)

There have been five district court decisions in suits alleging that Japan's Civil Code and Family Registration Law do not recognize same-sex marriage and that this violates the Constitution, and four of them have ruled that the law is unconstitutional. The plaintiffs, all of whom are homosexuals, lived together and received a written oath of partnership under the "Partnership Oath System" of Kumamoto City. They submitted a marriage certificate to the city office of their place of residence, but the marriage certificate was rejected because of their homosexuality.

In this case, the Fukuoka District Court held as follows (Fukuoka Dist. Ct., June 8, 2023). Same-sex couples cannot enjoy any of the benefits provided by the institution of marriage and suffer a serious disadvantage in not being legally recognized as a family. It must be said that this provision, which does not give them the means to legally become a family with the partner of their choice, is in violation of Article 24, paragraph 2 of the Constitution, which states that the dignity of the individual should be the foundation of the family. However, with regard to the system to eliminate the serious disadvantages of homosexuals, various considerations and adjustments are inevitable, taking into account the traditions of Japan and social conditions, including national sentiment, as well as the welfare of the child, and it must be left to the legislature to consider and deal with the issue. As concrete facts showing the change in the social situation surrounding same-sex marriage, the Court cites the fact that the population coverage rate of local governments that have introduced the partnership system has reached 62.1%, and the percentage of those in favor of same-sex marriage in various opinion surveys has increased to over 60% since 2018, and that even in Japan, there are doubts about the socially accepted notion that marriage is a heterosexual union. The Supreme Court's decision on same-sex marriage is awaited.

In October 2023, the Supreme Court unanimously ruled unconstitutional the aforementioned requirement of sterilization to change the sex in the family register (Article 3, paragraph 1, Item 4 of the Gender Identity Disorder Special Law of 2004). The Court held as follows. The freedom not to have one's body invaded against one's will is guaranteed in Article 13 of the Constitution as an important right related to personal survival. It is understood that this provision is based on the following considerations: if a person who has undergone a gender reassignment trial gives birth with the reproductive function of the sex before the reassignment to a child, problems related to parent-child relationships may arise and cause confusion in society. It is necessary to avoid drastic changes in the long-standing distinction between men and women based on their biological sex. This provision required a harsh choice between two options: with the development of medical knowledge, a person with gender identity disorder who does not require gonadectomy as medical treatment is required either to give up his/her freedom not to undergo physical invasion to undergo gonadectomy, which is a severe physical invasion, or to give up the important legal interest of being treated in accordance with his/her gender identity and thus renounce gender reassignment. The restriction on freedom from bodily harm by this provision is excessive, and the degree of restriction is so severe that it cannot be considered necessary and reasonable. It violates Article 13 of the Constitution and is invalid. (77 *Minshu* 1792, Sup. Ct., G.B., October 25, 2023).

However, the Supreme Court did not render its decision on another requirement for gender reassignment, namely, that the genitals have an appearance similar to that of the gender to be changed (Article 3, paragraph 1, Item 5 of the same law), since it had not been considered at the High Court level; it sent the case back to the High Court for further proceedings. Nevertheless, in their dissenting opinion, the three judges did find that the appearance requirement was also unconstitutional and that the petitioner's gender change should be approved.

II. Intellectual Freedoms

A. *Right to Life, Liberty, and the Pursuit of Happiness*

268. Article 13 of the Constitution of Japan provides, "All of the people shall be respected as individuals" and "Their right to life, liberty, and the pursuit of happiness shall, to the extent that it does not interfere with the public welfare, be the supreme consideration in legislation and in other governmental affairs." The leading scholarly opinions and judicial precedents had long been of the view that the latter part of this article was a general rule that all rights and liberties guaranteed by the Constitution were subject to restriction for the public welfare and that the "right to life, liberty, and the pursuit of happiness" was not a concrete constitutional right, but merely a general term for all individual constitutional rights beginning from Article 14 (4 *Keishu* 2380, Sup. Ct., G.B., November 22, 1950). However, this interpretation began to change after Justice Kotaro Tanaka stated in a concurring opinion to the *Passport Issuance Denial* case that, though the freedom to travel abroad temporarily was not included among the rights guaranteed by Article 22, paragraph 2, it was guaranteed as part of the right to life, liberty, and the pursuit of happiness stipulated by Article 13 (12 *Minshu* 1969, Sup. Ct., G.B., September 10, 1958).

269. In 1969, the Supreme Court finally recognized the Article 13 right to life, liberty, and the pursuit of happiness to be more than a general term for all individual rights and liberties expressly or implicitly guaranteed by the Constitution, holding that:

> It can be said that Article 13 ... stipulates the people's freedoms in private life to be protected against the exercise of State powers, such as the police power, etc. And it should be said that anyone has freedom not to have his or her looks or figure indiscriminately photographed, as one of the individual's freedoms in private life ... . At least, it must be said that it is violative of Article 13 of the Constitution and therefore impermissible for a police officer to photograph an individual's looks, etc., without sufficient reason. (23 *Keishu* 1625, Sup. Ct., G.B., December 24, 1969.)

Nowadays, many influential constitutional law scholars in Japan are of the opinion that Article 13 guarantees rights that are not prescribed in the following individual constitutional provisions but are considered to be indispensable for living with human dignity, which include, among others, the right of privacy, the right to environmental protection, etc. These rights can be explained as follows.

1. The Right of Privacy

270. The term "privacy" was unknown to the Japanese people for a long time. The invasion of others' privacy, namely, the indiscriminate disclosure of others' private matters, finally came to be considered a tort that was remediable under section 709 of the Civil Code. In the famous *"After the Banquet"* case, the Tokyo District Court for the first time in Japan's legal history drew the right of privacy from the spirit of Article 13 which stipulated respect for the people as individuals (15 *Kaminshu* 2317, Tokyo Dist. Ct., September 28, 1964). The Court held that an invasion of privacy could be recognized as a tort, and so legal protection is given:

(1) when the disclosed private affairs of an individual are or may be taken as, a fact in his or her private life;
(2) when such matters are recognized as those which the private person involved does not want to have disclosed in the light of a normal person's sensitivity; and
(3) when such matters are not yet known to the general public.

271. Later, in 1969, the Supreme Court, too, endorsed an individual's right not to have his or her looks photographed without sufficient reason as a constitutional right, relying on the spirit of Article 13 as mentioned above (23 *Keishu* 1625, Sup. Ct., G.B., December 24, 1969). The following year, the Court again recognized the freedom of smoking as a sort of constitutional right of privacy (24 *Minshu* 1410, Sup. Ct., G.B., September 16, 1970).

272. However, a new theory which construes the right of privacy to be a right to "selectively disclose information about himself or herself" or to "control information about himself or herself" has been proposed under the influence of the theoretical developments in the United States since the 1960s. This new theory (right to control one's own information) has been gaining more and more support among academics, lawyers and human rights activists. These days, many governmental agencies have been accumulating information about individuals for various administrative purposes. Such accumulation of information may well give anxiety to people or may seriously influence their way of life, for no one can say that there is no possibility that important information about an individual's private matters may be gathered without such individual's knowledge, or that inaccurate information about individuals may be accumulated. In addition, there is no guarantee that even if accurate and legitimately acquired, the information may not be misused. In light of these points, it is indispensable for the protection of privacy in contemporary society (reasonably called the "information society" or "high-technology society"), that the right of individuals to obtain the disclosure of information about themselves be guaranteed, so that its accuracy may be confirmed, and if inaccurate, be corrected.

273. At the moment, Japan has not yet passed national legislation such as the Privacy Act of the United States (1974) to protect the right of privacy in this sense. The number of prefectural and local governments which have the right to privacy ordinances is gradually increasing. By 2006, a total of 1,890 prefectural and local governments (at that time) had enacted ordinances, and the enactment rate had reached 100%. However, partly because the concept of "privacy" is not necessarily clear, and partly because it is feared that the expansion of the right of privacy may inevitably narrow the scope of the freedom of expression, special care must be taken in legislating for the protection of privacy.

Local ordinances preceded national legislation on the protection of privacy in Japan. In 2003, the Diet passed the first comprehensive statute to protect "personal information" (information that can identify a specific individual), which does not use the word "privacy." Hence, the name is "Act on the Protection of Personal Information." The concept of "personal information" is limited to identifying an individual and includes any information that can lead to identifying a specific individual. The concept of personal information is so comprehensive that it can be called an open concept. Moreover, the Act did not provide criteria to determine what kind of personal information would be subject to legal protection. Therefore, when the Act was first enacted, it caused confusion and overreaction that all personal information should not be disclosed.

Subsequently, in light of rapid changes, such as the development of information and communication technologies and the globalization of business activities, the Act was revised in 2015 to ensure the proper use and distribution of personal information and the concept of "anonymously processed information" was introduced. Anonymously processed information is, in essence, information in which personal information has been processed so those specific individuals cannot be identified. For example, it is created by processing personal information from a personal information database by deleting their names or abstracting their addresses or birth dates so that specific individuals cannot be identified. Anonymously processed information was introduced to promote data utilization among businesses. As an exception to the prohibition on the provision of personal information to a third party, anonymously processed information can be provided to a third party without the individual's consent. Still, certain obligations are imposed on the business operator to handle it (sections 36–39 of the Act).

The Act was revised in 2020. A concept called "pseudonym-processed information" has been newly established to promote innovation and the effective use of data. This type of information has been processed by deleting or replacing information in the data which can identify a particular individual, such as a name, with other information, which is called "pseudonymization," to make it impossible to identify a specific individual from the processed data alone. In other words, pseudonym-processed information has been processed so that a specific individual cannot be identified unless it is cross-checked with other information. However, the existing anonymously processed information is information in which personal information is processed so that a specific individual cannot be identified, and the personal information cannot be recovered. The new "pseudonym-processed information" is information whose usefulness as data is maintained at the same level as "personal information," but the scope of processing is reduced, and the restrictions on use are expanded (restrictions on the purpose of use, deletion upon achievement of the purpose of use, etc., section 35-2, paragraphs 3 and 5 of the Act) compared to "anonymously processed information." Pseudonym-processed information was established to promote the utilization of big data within companies as information that enables detailed data analysis with a relatively simple processing method. In principle, the provision of pseudonym-processed information to third parties is prohibited (section 35-2, paragraph 6 of the Act on the Protection of Personal Information).

2. The Right to Environmental Protection

274. Natural environments, such as water, air, sunshine, tranquility, landscape, etc., are indispensable for human subsistence. With these factors conserved in good shape, people can live a life that, as human beings, they deserve. In the mid-1960s, as Japan's economy achieved high growth, so-called environmental problems, such as water pollution, atmospheric pollution, obstruction of sunlight, noise pollution, destruction of landscape, etc., began to arise and threaten the disruption of human life. The occurrence of such a situation had not been expected when the Constitution of Japan was adopted the year following the end of World War II. To cope with such environmental problems the idea of a right to environmental protection came to be proposed as part of the right to life, liberty and the pursuit of happiness guaranteed by Article 13 of the Constitution. If the right to life, liberty, and the pursuit of happiness is a constitutional right to enjoy "various interests indispensable for living with human dignity," the view which construes Article 13 to include a right to enjoy good natural environments, namely, the right to environmental protection, is fully understandable.

275. There are two kinds of legal remedies that may be given against the invasion of a legal right or interest caused by pollution: an after-the-fact remedy and a preventive remedy. The former requires a tortfeasor to pay damages after an illegal act has been done. The latter is by way of restraining an illegal act by injunction before it is done.

Needless to say, when a harmful act that is likely to imperil people's lives and health is going to be committed, what is necessary is a preventive remedial measure, namely, restraint of the act before its danger becomes clear. The significance of proposing the concept of environmental protection as a constitutional right is based on this point.

276. The right to environmental protection, which is asserted as the legal basis on which to restrain the pollution or destruction of the environment, is guaranteed both by Article 13 (referred to above) and Article 25, which provides for the right to maintain a wholesome and cultured life. However, while both Article 13 and Article 25 can be used to protect the natural environs, the latter should be invoked, for a right guaranteed by the former (Article 13) is an inclusive one which is not necessarily clear in contents and therefore may be limited in its use.

277. Though the right to environmental protection has not yet been recognized as a full-fledged right, there are some lower court decisions that seem to have recognized the substance of this right (631 *Hanji* 24, Hiroshima Dist. Ct., May 20, 1971; 729 *Hanji* 24, Osaka Dist. Ct., February 27, 1974; the below mentioned Osaka High Ct. decision). For example, the Osaka High Court held in the *Osaka International Airport Pollution* case, relying on Article 13 and Article 25, that even if a real physical injury had not yet occurred anyone could ask the court to enjoin an act that would bring about an extreme mental hardship or an extreme inconvenience in daily life, as well as bodily injury which might cause illnesses, when such a danger was imminent (797 *Hanji* 37, Osaka High Ct., November 27, 1975). Though it did not specifically say so, this decision appears to have recognized the substance of the right to environmental protection, for the decision sustained the District Court order enjoining nighttime flights from 9.00 p.m. to 7.00 a.m. on the ground that the use of an airport in the nighttime, especially, for an hour after 9.00 p.m., would disturb the lives of nearby inhabitants. The Supreme Court, however, rejected the portion of the decision related to the prohibition of nighttime flights after 9.00 p.m. without referring to the right to environmental protection (35 *Minshu* 1369, Sup. Ct., December 16, 1981.) The plaintiffs were, however, given a damage award for injury sustained in the past.

B. Freedom of Thought and Conscience

278. Article 19 of the Constitution states, "Freedom of Thought and Conscience shall not be violated." Under the Meiji Constitution, there was no express provision that guaranteed the freedom of thought and conscience. Modern constitutions guarantee such intellectual freedoms as freedom of thought, freedom of religion, freedom of expression, freedom of assembly and association, academic freedom, secrecy of communication, etc. The most basic of these freedoms is the freedom of thought; other intellectual freedoms mentioned above are stipulated to strengthen this freedom from all sides.

It is evident that the content of Article 19 was framed under the influence of the Potsdam Declaration which demanded, "Freedom of speech, of religion, and of thought, as well as respect for the fundamental human rights, shall be established" (section 10), and on General MacArthur's Memorandum to the Japanese government on Removal of Restrictions on Political, Civil, and Religious Liberties (issued on October 4, 1945) which directed the Japanese government to eliminate "restrictions on freedom of thought, of religion, of assembly and of speech" (l-a-(l)).

279. Though freedom of thought and conscience is from time to time used as a generic term for all intellectual freedoms such as freedom of expression, freedom of religion, etc., its own significance is to guarantee the right of persons to free mental activities. Therefore, the term "thought" therein used is not the knowledge of a mere fact, but includes systematic thinking or belief based on a sense of value, such as political or religious belief or opinion, a view of life, a view of the world, etc.

280. What is the meaning of "conscience"? In other countries, it is used as a synonym for religion. For instance, Article 4, paragraph 1 of the German Constitution (the Bonner Grundgesetz) states, "Freedom of religion and conscience shall not be invaded." In the Constitution of Japan, however, judging from the fact that freedom of religion is provided for in a separate article (Article 20), while freedom of conscience is stipulated side by side with that of thought in the same article (Article 19), the word "conscience" is reasonably considered to be a term broader than "religion" and of the same nature as "thought." To sum up, the meaning of "thought" stipulated in Article 19 is a logical aspect of thought, while that of "conscience" is an ethical aspect of thought.

281. One's thought is not generally recognized while it remains in his or her mind. However, once expressed, it is constitutionally protected as a part of speech, press or other forms of expression (Article 21). Also, when it involves religion or academic research, such thought is protected either by Article 20 which guarantees freedom of religion or by Article 23 which guarantees academic freedom. Since there are provisions to protect expressed thought, Article 19 may well have its own meaning different from the above provisions. One such meaning is a guarantee that no one is compelled to express his or her inner thought; namely, the right to remain silent. Article 19 in this sense is interpreted not only to prohibit the governmental authorities from directly coercing people to express their thoughts but also to prohibit governmental authorities from compelling people to perform acts that would betray or disclose their inner thought, such as compelling suspected Christians to trample upon a tablet of the crucifix as occurred in Japan during the Edo era, or compelling civil servants to take an anti-Communist oath as occurred in the United States during the cold war.

282. Of course, knowledge of a mere fact or technical knowledge does not fall under the term "thought" as guaranteed by Article 19. Therefore, refusal to answer about specific facts or knowledge is not per se protected by the right to remain silent. However, if it is related to one's political belief or view of the world, the knowledge of a mere fact will come under the protection of Article 19. Another intent of Article 19 is to guarantee that no one is compelled to act against his or her own thought and conscience. The conscientious objector system as seen in, e.g., the United States and Germany, might be cited as a good example.

283. The famous Grand Bench Decision of the Supreme Court called the *Apology Advertisement* case is a judicial precedent concerning freedom of thought and conscience. The appellant was ordered by lower courts to have carried in newspapers an apology advertisement reading "my broadcast and newspaper article were contrary to the fact, and damaged your honor and caused you much trouble. Here I make an apology for it." The appellant immediately appealed to the Supreme Court insisting that to compel him to make such an apology against his will violated Article 19 which guaranteed freedom of conscience. The Supreme Court, however, rejected the petition as groundless (10 *Minshu* 785, Sup. Ct., G.B., July 4, 1956).

In Japan, the Act Concerning the National Flag and National Anthem was enacted in 1999 (*see* paragraph 28). This law itself only stipulates that the national flag shall be the rising sun flag (*Hinomaru*) and the national anthem shall be the *Kimigayo*. It does not obligate citizens or even public officials to salute the flag or sing the *Kimigayo*. However, raising the national flag and singing the national anthem are required at school events. Forcing citizens to salute the national flag and sing the national anthem would mean they would be required to express a particular ideology of loyalty to the nation through external actions. This poses a problem about freedom of thought and conscience under Article 19 of the Constitution. If this were to be enforced on children, students, or their parents, it would be considered an infringement of freedom of thought and conscience. What of the coercion of school staff? In Japan, the constitutionality of standing and singing orders as job orders has been challenged in many courts. It is noteworthy that the Tokyo District Court ruled in 2006 that it is a historical fact that *Hinomaru* and *Kimigayo* have been used as the spiritual pillars of imperialist and militarist ideologies and that imposing the obligation to stand and sing through disciplinary measures is an infringement of the freedom of thought and conscience.

However, the Supreme Court has ruled that the order for school staff to stand and sing is constitutional (65 *Minshu* 2148, Sup. Ct., June 14, 2011): (1) Some believe that they cannot express their respect for the *Hinomaru* and *Kimigayo* in light of their own historical and world views. For those individuals, the standing and singing order (job order) would require an external action (an action that includes an element of expression of respect) that is different from the action (refusal to express respect) which originates from that individual's view of history or worldview. Therefore, this job order is an indirect restriction on the person's freedom of thought and conscience. (2) Judgment as to whether or not indirect restrictions are permissible is made by comprehensively weighing the purpose and content of the job order and the manner of restrictions, and then from the perspective of whether or not the job order is deemed to be necessary and reasonable to an acceptable degree. (3) The job order is in line with the purpose of the various provisions of the relevant laws and regulations that stipulate the goals of school education and the significance and nature of ceremonial events such as graduation ceremonies. The order also considers the nature of the position of local government officials and the public nature of their duties. It intends to ensure consideration for students, etc., and ensure orderliness appropriate for educational events and smooth progress of such ceremonies. Therefore, the job order does not violate Article 19 of the Constitution.

C. *Freedom of Religion and the Separation of Church and State*

1. Freedom of Religion

284. Article 28 of the Meiji Constitution provided that Japanese subjects shall, within limits not prejudicial to peace and order, and not antagonistic to their duties as subjects, enjoy freedom of religion. Partly because it was interpreted that compliance with ordinances or orders was also included among their "duties as subjects," and partly because Shintoism was considered not to be a religion, people were forced by government orders to attend Shinto rites or ceremonies against their will.

Also, it must be noted that big Shinto shrines were publicly supported and that Shinto priests serving therein were paid out of public funds as civil servants. It was considered that Shinto shrines were not religious facilities but public establishments for paying respects to those who were enshrined therein as a result of their remarkable contribution to the founding and development of the country.

285. Unlike its predecessor, the Constitution of Japan stipulates, "Freedom of religion is guaranteed to all" (the former part of paragraph 1 of Article 20) and "No person shall be compelled to take part in any religious act, celebration, rite or practice" (Article 20, paragraph 2). It also provides, "The State and its organs shall refrain from religious education or any other religious activity" (Article 20, paragraph 3). Belief in religion is to believe and be devoted to a supernatural or superhuman entity (e.g., a god or gods, Buddha, Supreme Being, Absolute Being, etc.). This is the essence of religion, and the freedom of religion is the right to practice a religion in which one believes, in such a manner as he or she likes. It naturally includes: (1) the freedom to hold or attend a religious rite or ceremony; (2) to propagate a religion or to engage in religious education or other religious activities; and (3) to assemble or to combine for religious purposes.

There are some court decisions which consider limitations on the freedom of religion:

a. *Incense Offering Incantation Treatment* Case

286. A preacher performed an incantation by burning incense sticks for a mentally disabled person to cure her disability. However, as a result of this activity, the person died of a heart attack four hours later. When indicted on the charge of infliction of injury resulting in death (section 205 of the Penal Code), the preacher asserted both that the incantation in question was conducted as a religious act and that it was a generally recognized medical cure for mental retardation. However, the assertion was rejected by lower courts. Eventually, the case was appealed to the Supreme Court which turned down the appeal holding that the freedom of religion was in no way constitutionally limitless and that the incantation performed was an extreme anti-social practice deviating from the guarantee of the freedom of religion (17 *Keishu* 302, Sup. Ct., G.B., May 15, 1963).

b. *Cultural Sightseeing Tax* Case

287. The Prefecture of Nara enacted an ordinance imposing JPY 5–10 as a cultural sightseeing tax on each person who paid an admission fee and entered the Golden Pavilion of Todaiji Temple and the West Pavilion of Horyuji Temple. The tax money thus collected was to be appropriated for the conservation and repair of facilities for sightseeing within the prefecture. Both temples filed suit challenging the constitutionality of the prefectural ordinance on the ground that the imposition of such a tax deterred people from visiting the temples for worship and therefore violated Article 20 which guaranteed freedom of religion. The Nara District Court turned down the suit and sustained the constitutionality of the ordinance, holding that, in light of various factors, it could not be concluded that the ordinance was designed to make a religious act an object of taxation. Factors considered by the Court included the meaning and purpose of taxation, the nature and object of taxation, the degree of involvement with religion, the amount of tax, and the range of people to be taxed. (19 *Gyoshu* 1221, Nara Dist. Ct., July 17, 1968).

2. The Separation of Church and State

288. History shows that when a country establishes a State church or connects itself with a particular religion by giving it a special privilege there inevitably arises State persecution against dissenters and atheists. Therefore, most modern constitutions provide for the separation of Church and State as an institutional guarantee of freedom of religion. Thus, the policy of a State to leave religious matters entirely to religious organizations and neither to interfere with nor support them is called the principle of separation of Church and State.

289. Under the Meiji Constitution, there was no express provision that adopted the principle of separation of Church and State. However, since freedom of religion was guaranteed, excessive entanglement of the State with religion should have been prohibited. In other words, some scheme to separate Church and State should have been established. On the contrary, however, Shintoism was regarded as essentially different from ordinary religious teachings, and placed outside the scope of Article 28, and Shinto shrines were virtually treated as quasi-State churches and public establishments.

290. It was shortly after General MacArthur's Memorandum on Removal of Restrictions on Political, Civil, and Religious Liberties was issued on October 4, 1945 (*supra* paragraph 276), thereby carrying out section 10 of the Potsdam Declaration, that such a state of affairs in Japan was drastically altered. Needless to say, the Constitution of Japan which was adopted following the issuance of this Memorandum expressly provided for the separation of Church and State. Concretely speaking, the Constitution stipulates, "No religious organization shall receive any privileges from the State, nor exercise any political authority" (the latter part of paragraph 1 of Article 20), and "The State and its organs shall refrain from religious education or any other activity" (Article 20, paragraph 3). It also provides, "No public money or other property shall be expended or appropriated for the use, benefit or maintenance of any religious institution or association ..." (Article 89). All of these provisions are designed to prohibit the State from having a connection with a specific religion and thus to secure the freedom of religion. The following court decisions concern the separation of Church and State.

a. *Tsu Shinto Groundbreaking Ceremony* Case

291. The mayor of Tsu City, a mid-size city located near Nagoya, held a Shinto-style groundbreaking ceremony when his city built a municipal gymnasium. The mayor expended approximately JPY 7,000 as the cost for the ceremony, including the fee of Shinto priests. A citizen filed suit (based on section 242-2 of the Local Autonomy Act) contending that the holding of the religious ceremony and the payment of money to the priests by the mayor violated both Article 20, paragraph 3, which prohibits the State and its organs from performing religious acts, and Article 86, which prohibits the expenditure of public money for religious organizations.

The Tsu District Court rejected the plaintiff's contention holding that the groundbreaking ceremony in question was a mere customary act and was not a religious act prohibited by Article 20 of the Constitution (18 *Gyoshu* 246, Tsu Dist. Ct., March 16, 1967).

292. On appeal, the Nagoya High Court reversed the district court decision and held that the Shinto-style groundbreaking ceremony was violative of the constitutional principle of separation of Church and State and that the expenditure of money for it was unlawful. The reasons for the decision were three-fold: (1) the ceremony was administered by a professional Shinto priest; (2) it was conducted in accordance with the order of ceremony prescribed by a religious denomination; and (3) the history of a Shinto groundbreaking ceremony was not sufficiently old to make the ceremony generally accepted as a customary act (the general custom of holding a Shinto groundbreaking rite started in 1907 when the Shrine Act was enacted) (22 *Gyoshu* 680, Nagoya High Ct., May 14, 1971). Thereupon, the appellee (mayor) appealed to the Supreme Court.

293. In reviewing the petition, the Supreme Court apparently relied on the so-called *Lemon* test which had been enunciated by the United States Supreme Court in the case of *Lemon v. Kurtzman*, 403 U.S. 602 (1971). The *Lemon* test is a judicial test which requires a court to examine the following three elements in deciding on the constitutionality of legislation challenged under the Church and State doctrine: (1) whether the legislation in question has been made for a religious purpose; (2) whether it has had the effect of assisting, promoting and encouraging a particular religious organization or oppressing and interfering with others; and (3) whether it entangles the government excessively with religion.

294. Unlike its American counterpart, the Supreme Court of Japan only considered the first and second elements and concluded that the mayor's holding of the groundbreaking ceremony and defrayal of public funds therefore did not exceed its limits in light of those elements and therefore did not violate the separation of Church and State doctrine guaranteed by Article 20, paragraph 3 and Article 89 (31 *Minshu* 533, Sup. Ct., G.B., July 13, 1977).

This modified test, announced by the Japanese Supreme Court in the *Tsu Shinto Ground-breaking Ceremony* case, is called the purpose-effect (*MokutekiKoka*) test. In 1992 the Court, using this test, declared the Ehime Prefecture governor's expenditure of public funds for the official rites of the Gokoku shrine held in the spring and fall (on nine occasions over five years) unconstitutional (51 *Minshu* 1673, Sup. Ct., G.B., April 2, 1997).

The Court emphasized that though the expenditure of money was made in the name of an offering or in the name of the charge for a sacred tree branch or a candle to be offered at the altar, the Governor's use of public money for important functions of the Gokoku shrine unavoidably gave the impression that the State supported a particular religion. Accordingly, such action was adjudged to violate the doctrine of separation of Church and State, even though the amount of money expended was minimal.

The Supreme Court has applied the purpose-effect standard in cases involving violations of the principle of the separation of Church and State. This was considered to be the established precedent. Recently, however, the Supreme Court issued a decision based on a different standard, which attracted much attention. In this case, the constitutionality of a local government's act of allowing a group of shrine parishioners, who were included in a neighborhood association, to use public land as a site for a religious organization without compensation was challenged. The Supreme Court stated that, in determining whether or not the act violated the principle of the separation of Church and State, it is reasonable to consider various circumstances, such as the nature of the religious facility, the circumstances that led to the land being used as the site of the facility without compensation, how the land was provided without compensation, and the public's evaluation of these circumstances, and to make a comprehensive judgment in light of socially accepted ideas. In light of this careful consideration, the Supreme Court held that the provision of public land free of charge for religious facilities violates the principle of the separation of Church and State and is a violation of the Constitution (64 *Minshu* 1, Sup. Ct., G.B., January 20, 2010).

Scholars have pointed out various readings of this Supreme Court decision. The supplementary opinion states that applying the purpose-effect standard is limited to instances where religiousness and secularity are mixed. The standard does not apply to acts such as offering public land free of charge for purely religious facilities or events, as in this case. There is also a view that the purpose-effect standard should only apply to one-time acts in the previous cases, but not to a continuous, long-time inaction, as found in this case.

b. *Gokoku Shrine Co-enshrinement* Case

295. A Self-Defense Force officer who had died in a traffic accident while performing his duties, over his wife's protest, was enshrined in Gokoku Shrine, originally a Shinto shrine to enshrine war dead, by a local chapter of the organization of veterans of the Self-Defense Forces. The wife filed suit against the chapter president and the State, seeking both damages for the mental pain she had undergone and the cancellation of the procedures the chapter president had taken to enshrine her deceased husband. The plaintiff insisted that the procedure to enshrine her husband had been taken with the active participation of the Self-Defense Forces and that this State involvement with a religious act violated the separation of Church and State and infringed on her "religious personal right to mourn over her husband's death, pray for his bliss and to quietly think of the meaning of his death" which she asserted was included in the freedom of religion.

296. Both the Yamaguchi District Court and the Hiroshima High Court found that even though the procedure to enshrine was taken in the name of the Yamaguchi chapter of the Veterans' Association, the State had been directly entangled with taking the procedure to enshrine the deceased former Self-Defense officer. The defendants were ordered to pay damages for invading the plaintiff's "religious personal right" (921 *Hanji* 44, Yamaguchi Dist. Ct., March 22, 1979; 1046 *Hanji* 3, Hiroshima High Ct., June 1, 1982). Both lower courts, however, denied the plaintiff's claim seeking the cancellation of the enshrinement because such action was up to the shrine.

297. On appeal, the Supreme Court reversed the High Court decision holding that the procedure to enshrine the deceased officer had been taken by the Veterans' Association, a private organization, and there had been no direct State entanglement with religion which could constitute a violation of the principle of separation of Church and State. The Court also held that the appellee (plaintiff) had no standing to sue because there was no legally protected interest or right such as the "religious personal right" on which she relied (42 *Minshu* 277, Sup. Ct., G.B., June 1, 1988).

D. Academic Freedom

298. The Meiji Constitution did not have any provisions which guaranteed academic freedom. However, university professors maintained (on the basis of reason and practice) that universities that were established to do research for the pursuit of truth should be given academic freedom and autonomy so that they could perform their missions. The government was fairly tolerant toward academics and institutions of higher learning for a certain period of time. This was especially so during the era of *Taisho* Democracy (1912–1930), and it seemed that academic freedom and autonomy had been established to some extent. However, as ultranationalist forces in Japan gained power in the early 1930s, academic freedom and autonomy began to be circumscribed and were eventually lost.

Article 23 of the Constitution of Japan provides, "Academic freedom is guaranteed." What this provision encompasses can be summarized as follows.

1. Freedom of Research

299. This is a freedom not to be compelled by the governmental authorities to accept a theory against one's will, as well as not to be restricted in selecting a subject for research and method of research.

2. Freedom to Publish the Results of Research

300. In order to reach the truth, the results of the research must be under constant examination and criticism from other researchers. In this sense, this freedom is indispensable for the development of scholarship.

3. Freedom to Teach

301. This is a freedom to teach one's own theories, which are the results of his or her research, either on a platform or in classrooms. This can be said to be a kind of freedom to publish the results of research. However, scholars are divided as to whether this freedom is applicable to teachers of lower schools, namely, elementary and secondary schools. The leading scholarly theory in this respect is that while the freedom of research and the freedom to publish the results of one's research are applied to the general public, the freedom to teach is guaranteed only to those teaching or doing research at universities. Also, there is a theory close to the leading theory which insists that since the freedoms of research and publication can also be guaranteed by the freedom of thought and conscience (Article 19) as well as the freedom of expression (Article 21), the significance of Article 23 lies in guaranteeing the freedom to teach at universities. The Grand Bench Decision of the Supreme Court in the so-called *Poporo Theatrical Troupe* case (17 *Keishu* 370, Sup. Ct., G.B., May 22, 1963) apparently supports the leading theory.

4. Academic Autonomy

302. Most constitutional law scholars in Japan agree that Article 23's academic freedom includes the guarantee of academic autonomy. The Meiji Constitution did not have any express provisions for academic freedom. Nevertheless, professors of such State universities as Tokyo and Kyoto Imperial Universities asserted on the basis of the imperial order which had established those institutions that faculties of universities should, as a matter of logic, be given autonomy in the appointment and dismissal of professors. Autonomy was considered necessary to fulfill the mission to do research for the pursuit of the truth, even if there was no express constitutional provision for autonomy. During the era of *Taisho* Democracy, Tokyo, Kyoto, and some other Imperial Universities enjoyed a considerable range of autonomy as far as the appointment and dismissal of professors were concerned. However, as Japan turned ultranationalist in the 1930s, such freedom began to be suppressed, and professors who protested the government's interference were ruthlessly oppressed.

The Special Act for Education Civil Servants enacted on the basis of Article 23 of the Constitution of Japan guarantees a wide range of academic autonomy in the appointment, promotion, dismissal, demotion, etc., of presidents, deans and professors of State and other public universities (sections 3 to 10).

E. Freedom of Expression

303. The Constitution of Japan states, "Freedom of assembly and association as well as speech, press and all other forms of expression are guaranteed" (Article 21, paragraph 1) and "No censorship shall be maintained, nor shall the secrecy of any means of communication be violated" (Article 21, paragraph 2). Unlike the Meiji Constitution, the present Constitution extends its protection to "other forms of expression" as well as to speech and the press. The other forms of expression include painting, sculpture, music, movies, plays, and such symbolic forms of speech as picketing, demonstrations, etc. Though the Constitution declares "freedoms and rights" to be "permanent and inviolate" (Articles 12 and 97), it also stipulates that these rights are subject to restriction for the public welfare (Articles 12 and 13). Also, it is the courts of law that ultimately decide the limits of constitutional rights (Article 81). Therefore, it is important to see how the courts have interpreted the constitutional provisions which guarantee rights and freedoms.

304. Freedom of expression (e.g., speech, press and other forms of expression) is the freedom to express one's view in words, printing, or other means, without any interference from the government. In order to effectively guarantee freedom of the press, the Constitution expressly prohibits the governmental authorities from censoring publications before they are published (Article 21, paragraph 2). The guarantee of freedom of expression is indispensable not only for an individual's self-realization but also for the maintenance of democratic government. A popularly elected legislature in our contemporary mass society tends to be merely a place in which various interest groups compete to achieve their own ends and make self-serving compromises and inevitably disregards the will of the people it represents. Under such circumstances, freedom of expression is playing a more and more important role as the means to make up for shortcomings in representative democracy. Japan is not an exception.

305. It is an undeniable fact that American theories concerning freedom of expression have had much influence on theoretical developments in Japan since the end of World War II. One of the theories introduced to Japan soon after the war was the "clear and present danger" test, a doctrine enunciated by Justice Oliver Wendell Holmes of the United States Supreme Court in the famous case *Schenck v. United States*, 249 U.S. 47 (1919). On the basis of this test, some Japanese lower courts acquitted defendants who had been indicted on the charge of distributing handouts in which they advocated the overthrow of the government by force in violation of the Subversive Activities Prevention Act. Though the spirit of this test was resorted to by the Japanese Supreme Court in the *Niigata Prefecture Public Safety Ordinance* case (8 *Keishu* 1866, Sup. Ct., G.B., November 24, 1954), the test was ignored six years later in the *Tokyo Metropolitan Public Safety Ordinance* case (14 *Keishu* 1243, Sup. Ct., G.B., July 20, 1960) which adopted the "balancing test," a rather conservative doctrine used by conservative courts in the United States. In addition, the "less restrictive alternative" doctrine, a judicial test used by the United States Supreme Court (*Shelton v. Tucker*, 364 U.S. 479 (1960)) to determine the constitutionality of a particular act, was adopted in some cases (*Sarufutsu*, 10 *Kakeishu* 293, Asahikawa Dist. Ct., March 25, 1968; the *Drugstore*, 29 *Minshu* 572, Sup. Ct., G.B., April 30, 1975). This test holds that the restriction on freedom of expression is permissible only when there is no "less restrictive alternative" by which to achieve a permissible objective.

306. Freedom of expression is the freedom to express one's thoughts freely. However, in order to express his or her opinion on a particular problem, a person must have ample information related to it. For it is not until he/she has enough information that he/she can form an informed opinion. From such a point of view, scholars in the mid-1960s began to insist that Article 21, paragraph 1 guarantees the right to know as the premise for freedom of expression. Accordingly, it was urged that in response to the people's right to know the media's right to collect and edit data for a news report and to report them as the news was also guaranteed. In 1969, the Supreme Court finally declared the media's right to gather and report news materials was "worth receiving constitutional protection" (23 *Keishu* 1490, Sup. Ct., G.B., November 26, 1969).

The following are some of the decisions concerning the freedom of expression.

1. *Hakata Station* Case (on the Court Order to Produce TV News Films)

307. In the trial of police officers who were indicted on the charge of abusing their powers and of committing an assault and battery on a group of student activists in Fukuoka, the Fukuoka District Court requested NHK and three other TV companies to produce news films that had already been televised. The companies declined the request on the ground that it infringed their right to collect data for news reporting and thus constituted a violation of Article 21, paragraph 1. The District Court ordered the TV companies to produce the films in evidence in accordance with section 99 of the Code of Criminal Procedure. The companies refused to comply with the order and appealed the case to the Fukuoka High Court, which sustained the District Court's order, holding that:

(1) the use of the TV films as evidence was indispensable to a fair trial;
(2) the freedom to report news was subject to the public welfare; and
(3) the court's order to produce the films was appropriate when the importance of the films as evidence was weighed against the disadvantages which the TV companies would suffer as a result of submitting the films. Thereupon, the

appellants (TV companies) filed a petition with the Supreme Court to reverse the high court decision and vacate the order to produce the films.

308. The Supreme Court rejected the petition, holding that:

(1) the freedom to report facts as news is guaranteed by Article 21;
(2) the freedom to collect data for news reports is also worth receiving constitutional protection in light of the spirit of Article 21 of the Constitution;
(3) the constitutionality of the order to produce the films in accordance with section 99, paragraph 2 of the Code of Criminal Procedure was to be determined by weighing two constitutional values, namely, the freedom to gather news materials and report them as news and the right to a fair trial.

In light of these holdings, the Court found that the order to produce the films, the disputed point in the case, was not violative of Article 21 of the Constitution (23 *Keishu* 1490, Sup. Ct., G.B., November 26, 1969). The decision was unanimous.

2. *Matsue Campaign Law Violation* Case (on the Prohibition of House-to-House Campaign Visits)

309. Section 138, paragraph 1 of the Public Offices Election Act makes house-to-house visits for the purpose of persuading electors to vote or not to vote for a particular candidate a crime punishable by imprisonment without forced labor for no less than one year or fines of no less than JPY 100,000 (section 239, paragraph 1, No. 3). The leading case on this provision is the 1950 Supreme Court decision, which sustained its constitutionality by simply stating that the prohibition of house-to-house campaign visits secured the execution of a fair election which, in turn, came within the public welfare exception (4 *Keishu* 1799, Sup. Ct., G.B., September 27, 1950). As freedom of expression was constitutionally subject to the public welfare exception, the house-to-house visit restriction did not violate Article 21 of the Constitution even though it might limit, to some extent, freedom of expression.

In 1979, however, the Izumo Branch of the Matsue District Court, ignoring the abovementioned precedent, acquitted two defendants indicted on the charge of illegally making a house-to-house visit during the campaign period on the ground that section 138, paragraph 1 violated freedom of speech (923 *Hanji* 141, Matsue Dist. Ct., Izumo Br., January 24, 1979). Rejecting as groundless the idea that a house-to-house visit might give rise to corrupt practices like the buying of votes or the promising of favors, the Court held that it was apparent that to prohibit a house-to-house visit far exceeded the minimum reasonable limit allowable to restrict freedom of speech which was among the "preferred rights" guaranteed by the Constitution. Accordingly, since there was no reasonable basis on which to punish a house-to-house visit, section 138, paragraph 1 and section 239, paragraph 1, No. 3 were null and void as being in violation of Article 21 of the Constitution. This decision was affirmed by the Matsue Branch of the Hiroshima High Court (964 *Hanji* 134, Hiroshima High Ct., Matsue Br, April 28, 1980).

On further appeal, the Supreme Court, on the basis of its decision of 1950, reaffirmed the constitutionality of section 138, paragraph 1, and reversed and remanded the case to the lower court (35 *Keishu* 205, Sup. Ct., June 15, 1981).

3. *Sarufutsu* Case (on the Prohibition of Political Activities of Civil Servants)

310. A civil servant working for a post office in Sarufutsu, Hokkaido, was indicted on the charge of violating section 102, paragraph 1 of the National Civil Service Act and Rule 14-7, paragraph 6, No. 13 of the National Personnel Authority, which prohibits civil servants of the national government from distributing or posting papers written for political purposes. These activities by civil servants are punishable under section 110, paragraph 1, No. 19 of the National Civil Service Act. Although the defendant had posted or distributed for posting election posters for a particular candidate on the designated public bulletin-boards in accordance with the decision made by the regional council of labor unions as alleged, he did so after working hours and without utilizing either his official position or governmental facilities. In addition, the charged employee was a nonmanagerial civil servant assigned simple and mechanical work with no discretion, and all posters he had posted or distributed had the official stamp of approval of the board of elections. The Asahikawa District Court resorted to the "less restrictive alternative" test and acquitted the defendant, holding that to impose a criminal sanction as stipulated by section 110, paragraph 1, No. 19 on acts done after working hours by such low-level civil servants as part of labor union activities, without utilizing governmental facilities or taking advantage of his official duties, with no intent to impair the fair performance of official duties exceeded the minimum allowable rational and necessary limit imposed by the test (10 *Kakeishu* 293, Asahikawa Dist. Ct., March 25, 1968). Accordingly, the District Court found that the provision, as applied to the defendant's acts at issue in this case, was violative of Articles 31 and 21 of the Constitution. The Sapporo High Court struck down the prosecution's appeal and sustained the District Court decision (560 *Hanji* 32, Sapporo High Ct., June 24, 1969).

311. On further appeal, however, the Supreme Court reversed the High Court decision, rejecting the test of "less restrictive alternative" and adopting a balancing test. It held that the constitutionality of regulation of civil servants' political activities was to be decided in light of the purpose of the regulation, the connection between this purpose and political activities to be regulated, and the balance between the benefit to be gained from regulating political activities and that to be lost by the regulation. It also held that what was decided by legislative discretion with regard to the necessity of imposing criminal sanctions must be respected in so far as there were no special circumstances to make it unconstitutional (28 *Keishu* 393, Sup. Ct., G.B., November 6, 1974).

312. The issue of the constitutionality of the National Public Service Act, which prohibits the distribution of political leaflets by national public officials, was again challenged in the *Horikoshi* case (Tokyo High Court decision, March 29, 2010) and the *Ujibashi* case (Tokyo High Court decision, May 13, 2010).

In both cases, the issue was whether the defendant, a national public servant, violated the National Public Service Act and the Rules of the National Personnel Authority by distributing Communist Party bulletins and leaflets to the residences of others on his day off, without the appearance of a public servant, and in a manner unrelated to his duties. Relying on the framework of the Supreme Court's decision in *Sarufutsu*, the Tokyo High Court found the defendant not guilty in *Horikoshi* and guilty in *Ujibashi*. Still, the difference between the two cases stems from the nature of the defendant's duties. The defendant in *Horikoshi* was a pension examiner at the Social Insurance Office, a job that left no room for discretion. In contrast, the defendant in *Ujibashi* was an assistant director of the Ministry of Health, Labor, and Welfare, a managerial position. The High Court acquitted the defendant in *Horikoshi* because it was difficult to imagine that his actions would raise questions about the neutrality of the entire public administration and found him guilty of violating Articles 21 and 31 of the Constitution (unconstitutional application) insofar as the statutes and regulations in question were applied to the case but found him guilty in *Ujibashi* because the statutes and regulations in question were constitutional.

The Supreme Court ruled in favor of the respective appellate court decisions in both cases. The Supreme Court ruled that the Constitution guarantees freedom of political activity to the people and that public officials' prohibition of political acts to ensure administrative neutrality should be limited to unavoidable limits. In this regard, the Supreme Court held that the prohibited political acts are limited to those that can be practically recognized as having the potential to impair the political neutrality of the performance of duties. In this case, the Supreme Court raised the following eight requirements as factors for judgment: (1) whether or not there is a managerial position; (2) whether or not there is job content or discretion; (3) whether or not it is during working hours; (4) whether or not there is use of facilities of the government or workplace; (5) whether or not there is use of the position of a public servant; (6) whether or not it is collective action by public servants; (7) whether or not the act is directly recognizable as an act by a public servant; and (8) whether or not the act has a purpose or content that conflicts with administrative neutrality. As a result, the accused in *Horikoshi*, who was not in a managerial position and had no discretion in the content or authority of his duties, was found not guilty (66 *Keishu*, 1337, Sup. Ct., December 7, 2012), and the accused in *Ujibashi*, who was in a position to direct his subordinates and could influence them following his political leanings, was found guilty with a fine of JPY 100,000 (66 *Keishu*, 1722, Sup. Ct., December 7, 2012).

Two District Court rulings that acquitted a man of trespassing under the Penal Code for distributing leaflets as a means of expression have attracted attention. In the first case, a member of a citizens' group that has been engaged in the anti-war and peace movement was charged with trespassing on a dwelling (section 130 of the Penal Code) for entering the former Defense Agency dormitory and posting leaflets opposing the deployment of the Self-Defense Forces in Iraq in the newspaper receptacles on the doors of each room. The Hachioji Branch of the Tokyo District Court acquitted him, applying the so-called theory of punishable illegality. The judgment states, "The motive for the defendants to enter the dormitory was legitimate, and the manner of entry did not deviate from reasonableness. The resulting infringement of the legal interests of the residents and the manager was only very minor. Furthermore, the posting of leaflets by the defendants is a form of political expression guaranteed by Article 21, paragraph 1 of the Constitution of Japan, and as a fundamental part of a democratic society, it has a so-called superior status compared to the posting of commercial advertising leaflets, which is a type of business activity understood to be guaranteed by Article 22, paragraph 1 of the same constitution. In light of the above circumstances, the act of the defendants entering the dormitory is not considered illegal from the standpoint of law and order as a whole to the extent that it deserves criminal punishment" (1892 *Hanji* 150, Tokyo Dist. Ct., Hachioji Branch, December 16, 2004).

In the second case, when political party leaflets were put into the doors and mailboxes of each unit of a private condominium that anyone could enter and leave, the residents arrested them and charged them with breaking and entering. The Tokyo District Court ruled that the act was not an act of entry without "just cause" as defined in section 130 of the Penal Code and that the act did not meet the requirements for the crime of trespassing and that he was not guilty. The Tokyo District Court said, "Even taking into account the recent increase in awareness of privacy protection and crime prevention, it is difficult to say that a social consensus has yet been established that briefly entering a corridor or stairway of an ordinary residential apartment building during the daytime to distribute doorposts of each unit is an unacceptable and illegal act of trespass" (Tokyo Dist. Ct., August 28, 2006).

However, the Supreme Court convicted the accused in both cases, stating, "The place where the accused entered is not a place where people generally have free access. Even if it is to exercise freedom of expression, entering such a place against the will of the administrator is not only an infringement of the administrator's right to control the place but also an infringement of the peace of private life of those who live there" (63 *Keishu* 1765, Sup. Ct., November 30, 2009).

F. Freedom of Assembly and Association

313. The term "assembly" means getting together with a common purpose, while the term "association" means continuously combining or being united for a common cause. The freedom of assembly means freedom to assemble peacefully, and the freedom of association permits one to form, join and withdraw from an organization, whether for political, economic, social, religious, scholarly, artistic or other purposes. Thus, freedom of assembly and association is an individual's freedom to collectively act with other people. In contemporary society, the mass media has a strong influence on all aspects of people's lives. However, unlike big businesses, political parties, labor unions, religious organizations, etc., the masses have no direct access to the media. For them, therefore, this freedom plays a very important role as a means to unify the opinions of many people through discussions and debates and collectively assert the resulting opinion to realize a common aim. Two cases concerning freedom of assembly and association should be discussed:

1. *Niigata Prefecture Public Safety Ordinance* Case (1954)

314. Most prefectures in Japan have a public safety ordinance which requires prior permission from a relevant prefectural Public Safety Commission for assembly or demonstration. A handful of prefectures have an ordinance that requires a mere notification. In Niigata Prefecture, two persons who had led a rally and procession in protest of the arrest of illicit brewers without first obtaining a permit from the public safety commission were indicted for violating a provision of the Public Safety Ordinance of Niigata Prefecture. The defendants pleaded innocent, contending that the permit system infringed on their freedom of expression. After they were convicted in the lower courts, they appealed to the Supreme Court, which held that:

(1) it is constitutionally impermissible to use a permit system to restrain in advance a mass action;
(2) it is not against the intent of the Constitution to adopt a permit system affecting a particular place and manner of demonstration, utilizing a reasonable and clear standard; and
(3) it does not constitute a violation of the Constitution to disallow or prohibit a mass action when it is predicted that such action may give rise to a clear and imminent danger to public safety (8 *Keishu* 1866, Sup. Ct., G.B., November 24, 1954).

In light of the above test, the Court upheld the conviction of the defendants, concluding that the Niigata ordinance was constitutional.

2. *Tokyo Metropolitan Public Safety Ordinance* Case (1960)

315. Relying on the test set forth by the Grand Bench Decision of 1954 concerning the Niigata Prefecture's Public Safety Ordinance student activists, who had been arrested on the charge of sponsoring or leading a demonstration in protest to the signing of the Japan-Korea normalization of relations treaty, insisted that the provision of the Tokyo Metropolitan Public Safety Ordinance which required a prior permit for assembly and demonstration violated Article 21 of the Constitution. The Tokyo District Court found the defendants innocent on the basis of the abovementioned test, and the case was appealed by the prosecution to the High Court, which transferred it to the Supreme Court in accordance with section 247 of the Rule of Criminal Procedure.

The Supreme Court struck down the decision of the original court, holding that the provision of the Tokyo Metropolitan Public Safety Ordinance at issue was not violative of the Constitution. It held that when suddenly stimulated or incited from within or outside:

> it is evident both from the rule of mass psychology and the actual experiences that even a peaceful and quiet group is at times drawn into a whirlpool of excitement and rage, instantly turns into a mob in an extreme case, tramples upon the law and order with force depending on the circumstances, giving rise

to such a dangerous situation as even a police force, to say nothing of leaders of the group, cannot control (14 *Keishu* 1243, Sup. Ct, G.B, July 20, 1960).

Without much reference to its own decision in the *Niigata* case, the Court upheld the Ordinance (which provides for a permit system) as constitutional based on a point of view that regards mass action as potentially dangerous, holding that the minimum necessary prior measure was needed to provide for the maintenance of law and order.

316. The Court also held that though the Tokyo Ordinance adopted a permit system for assembly and demonstration, the system was not different in essence from a notification system and that the constitutionality of the ordinance should not be determined by technical differences between a permit system or a notification system.

3. *Izumisano Civic Hall* Case (1995)

317. Many local governments have adopted a permit system for the use of public facilities. If a permit is denied, the use of the public facility is not allowed, and the "freedom of assembly" guaranteed in Article 21 of the Constitution is restricted. In the *Izumisano Civic Hall* case, the organizers of a rally against the construction of Kansai International Airport sought permission to hold a rally at the civic hall but were denied permission because the event fell under the category of "a case where there is a risk of disturbing public order" as stipulated in the ordinance. The organizers then challenged the unconstitutionality of the denial. The Supreme Court held that the non-permission did not violate the Constitution, reasoning as follows:

(1) Those who have the authority to manage public facilities should be able to deny the use of such facilities only when there is a danger that other fundamental human rights will be violated and the public welfare will be impaired by allowing the facilities to be used for such gatherings, except in cases where there are competing applicants for use. In such a case, to avoid or prevent such danger, the holding of the assembly at the facility may be restricted to the extent necessary and reasonable.

(2) Whether or not there is a "risk of disturbing public order" should be interpreted in a limited way to mean a case in which the need to avoid or prevent the risk of infringement of life, body, or property of a person or damage to public safety by the holding of an assembly prevails over the importance of guaranteeing the freedom of assembly. In light of the purpose of the *Niigata Public Safety Ordinance* case, it is not enough to say that there is a mere possibility of a dangerous situation occurring, but it is necessary to specifically foresee the occurrence of a clear and imminent danger as the degree of danger.

(3) In this case, it is foreseeable that the life, body, or property of the hall staff, passersby, or nearby residents will be violated, and therefore, the non-permission is constitutional (49 *Minshu* 687, Sup. Ct., March 7, 1995).

This decision is considered a revival of the so-called clear and present danger test, which has been developed in American law, adopted in *Niigata Prefecture Public Safety Ordinance* and yet rejected in *Tokyo Metropolitan Public Safety Ordinance*. In other words, it can be said that the idea that the mere occurrence of an abstract danger is not sufficient as a justification for restricting the freedom of assembly, but that the event of a concrete danger called "clear and present danger" is required was revived. Similarly, there is another Supreme Court decision that ruled that the disapproval of the use of public facilities for gatherings was illegal because it was not foreseeable in light of the objective facts that there would be obstacles to the management of the facilities (50 *Minshu* 549, Sup. Ct., March 15, 1996).

G. Secrecy of Communication

318. Article 21, paragraph 2 guarantees the "secrecy of any means of communication." This clause protects the secret communication of expression from one specific person to another while freedom of expression is designed to guarantee open expressions. The means of communication being protected include mail, telegram, telephone, fax, electric mail, conversations between individual persons and all other means of communication. The secrecy of communication is designed to protect privacy in communication, and together with Article 35, which protects the security of homes, guarantees the freedom of private life.

In order to guarantee the secrecy of communication, the Penal Code prohibits disclosure of mail addressed to other people (section 133) and the Mail Act obligates those engaged in the postal service not to divulge secrets either while in office or after retirement (section 9). In addition, the Mail Act prohibits censorship of the mail (section 8). The Electric Communication Business Act has provisions to the same effect (sections 3 and 4).

319. It has also been held to be unconstitutional to wiretap a telephone communication or to overhear others' private conversation through a hidden microphone. TA High Court decision held that the overhearing of Communist Party members' conversations through a microphone planted by policemen in an adjoining room did not constitute an abuse of official authority prohibited by section 193 of the Penal Code even if such activity constituted a minor harmful effect on the fundamental rights of the involved persons. The basis of this decision was that eavesdropping was exercised within the scope and to an extent necessary to achieve a legitimate investigative purpose (9 *Hanji* 3, Tokyo High Ct., July 7, 1953). This is the only decision dealing with wiretapping and human rights.

Debate continued on the constitutionality of interception of communications for criminal investigation, and in 1999 the Communications Interception Act was enacted. This law allowed for criminal investigation of the interception of communications on the condition that; (1) there is no alternative means for the investigation of the legally designated target crime; (2) it can be reasonably assumed that the crime will be committed through the communications in question; and (3) the interception is based on an interception warrant issued by the court with a limited period of interception. When the law was first enacted, the target crimes were limited to four categories; drugs, firearms, mass smuggling, and organized murder, but after the law was revised, most crimes are now covered. Problems remain, however, including unclear requirements for issuing interception warrants and inadequate after-the-fact remedies for intercepted persons.

§3. Economic Freedom and Property Rights

320. Article 22, paragraph 1 of the Constitution of Japan states, "Every person shall have the freedom to choose and change his residence and to choose his occupation to the extent that it does not interfere with the public welfare." Article 29 of the Constitution further stipulates, "The right to own or hold property is inviolable" (paragraph 1); "Property rights shall be defined by law, in conformity with the public welfare" (paragraph 2); and "Private property may be taken for public use upon just compensation therefor" (paragraph 3). These constitutional provisions, which guarantee economic freedom and property rights, apparently make it easier for the Diet, in the context of public welfare, to regulate economic rights than to regulate civil rights and civil liberties (26 *Keishu* 586, Sup. Ct., G.B., November 22, 1972). Scholars agree that such difference exists because the Constitution of 1947 was drafted under the strong influence of the philosophy of the New Dealers of the United States. In other words, regulation of economic freedom and property rights for the public welfare is given a legal presumption of constitutionality.

I. Freedom to Choose and Change One's Residence

321. The freedom to choose and change one's residence is a freedom to decide where to live. In the feudal age, people were forced to live in a specific area throughout their lives under the constraint of a rigid social status system. However, the decay of the feudalistic social status system made the movement possible. This, in turn, prompted the collapse of the feudal system and the realization of modern society.

The freedom to choose and change one's residence was originally designed to guarantee the freedom to choose a place wherein to pursue an occupation or to do business. In that sense, it belongs, broadly speaking, to the category of economic freedoms. That is why this freedom is provided for in Article 22, paragraph 1 side by side with the freedom to choose an occupation. However, nowadays when people's social life has become highly complex, it is not appropriate to regard the freedom to choose and change a residence as part of economic freedom. Rather, it must be noted that the freedom to choose and change a residence, namely, that of movement, not only accrues from the guarantee of bodily freedom but also has an additional aspect as a means to participate in mass action included in the freedom of expression.

322. Statutory restrictions imposed on the freedom to choose and change a residence based upon the public welfare include:

(1) the forced hospitalization of people suspected of having an infectious disease (section 19 of the Act on the Prevention of Infectious Diseases and Medical Care for Patients with Infectious Diseases);
(2) the forced hospitalization of mentally disabled persons (section 29 of the Mental Health Preservation Act);
(3) the prohibition against insolvent people leaving their place of residence without court permission (section 37 of the Bankruptcy Act);
(4) the limitation on criminal defendants' place of residence (section 95 of the Code of Criminal Procedure).

II. Freedom to Move to a Foreign Country and Renounce One's Nationality

323. Article 22, paragraph 2 of the Constitution stipulates, "Freedom of all persons to move to a foreign country and to divest themselves of their nationality shall be inviolate." The freedom to move to a foreign country is, as a matter of fact, merely a freedom to leave one's own country, for whether or not to admit such person is up to the country which he or she wishes to enter. The majority of scholars (and judicial precedents) take the position that the freedom to move to a foreign country includes the right to visit a foreign country temporarily (e.g., on a sightseeing trip) (12 *Minshu* 1969, Sup. Ct., G.B., September 10, 1958). However, there are two views that oppose this majority theory. One view insists that the freedom to go to a foreign country for a short period is included in the freedom of movement guaranteed by Article 22, paragraph 1, and the other asserts that such right is guaranteed as part of the Article 13 right to the pursuit of happiness (Tanaka and Shimoiizaka, JJ, concurring opinion to the above decision, 12 *Minshu* 1969).

324. Article 22, paragraph 2 of the Constitution guarantees the freedom of people to divest themselves of their nationality. However, under the Nationality Act, only those who have a foreign nationality are allowed to renounce their Japanese nationality. No one can renounce his or her nationality in order to become a stateless person. This requirement is to comply with the international endeavor to reduce the number of denationalized people.

III. Property Rights

325. Paragraph 1 of Article 29 of the Constitution stipulates that the right to own or to hold property is inviolable. This provision not only guarantees an individual's personal right to property but also secures the system of private ownership. In light of the fact that the absolute guarantee of property rights and of freedom of economic activities under eighteenth and nineteenth-century constitutions threatened the lives of the socially and economically weak, virtually all constitutions enacted in the Western world after 1919 make it possible for the government to regulate these rights for the public welfare. The Constitution of Japan is not an exception in this regard. For example, while declaring that the right to own or hold property is inviolable (paragraph 1), Article 29 of the Constitution provides that property rights shall be defined by law, in conformity with the public welfare (paragraph 2) and that private property may be taken for public use upon just compensation therefor (paragraph 3). These provisions explicitly show that contrary to the practice in the eighteenth and nineteenth centuries, the guarantee of property rights under the present Constitution is not absolute.

Although Article 29, paragraph 3 stipulates that due compensation shall be made for any losses caused by the expropriation of private property, no compensation is deemed to be necessary for losses that every person may undergo (and should as a matter of course endure) for the common good (*supra* paragraph 318).

326. Statutory restrictions on property rights are numerous. Examples include restrictions on the construction of houses and other buildings (sections 43–68 of the Building Standards Act; section 37 of the Urban Planning Act), regulation of land use for prevention of pollution (section 11 of the Basic Act for Anti-pollution Measures), imposition of obligations to preserve important cultural assets (section 31, paragraph 1 of the Cultural Asset Protection Act), prohibition on the export of important cultural assets (section 44 of the Cultural Asset Protection Act), expropriation of private property for emergency use (section 78, paragraph 1 of the Basic Act for Countermeasures Against Disasters), and regulation of ownership and use of land (sections 2, 3, 5, 6 and 7 of the Land Expropriation Act).

Supreme Court decisions on economic and property rights include, among others, the *Drug Store* case (*supra* paragraph 158), the *Nara Reservoir* case, and the *Small Marketplace Permit System* case.

A. Nara Reservoir *Case (1963)*

327. In 1954, the Prefecture of Nara, in order to prevent a disaster that might be caused by the collapse of the banks of reservoirs, enacted an ordinance to prohibit the planting of trees, bamboo, agricultural products, etc., on such banks. The defendants, who had long cultivated the bank of a reservoir they co-owned, were indicted in the summary court when they failed to stop cultivating the land, even though the ordinance had taken effect. The court found them guilty and sentenced them to fines. The Osaka High Court reversed the decision and acquitted the defendants on the following grounds: (1) the regulation of private property by a local ordinance, not by a statute, violated Article 29, paragraph 2; and (2) the restriction of the ordinance on the use of private property without compensation violated Article 29, paragraph 3 of the Constitution.

On appeal, the Supreme Court held: (1) that it was appropriate to restrict the use of the bank of a reservoir by a prefectural ordinance in order to preserve the public welfare, namely, the safety of a reservoir; (2) that prohibition on the use of the bank of a reservoir in order to prevent disaster is an unavoidable restriction one must endure as part of social life; and (3) therefore, the use of the bank of a reservoir is not a legally protected right and no compensation is necessary for any losses resulting from its regulation (17 *Keishu* 521, Sup. Ct., G.B., June 26, 1963).

B. Small Marketplace Permit System *Case (1972)*

328. The Act for the Special Measures for Adjustment of Retail Businesses prohibits the sale or lease of a building to be used as a small marketplace located within the area of a city designated by a cabinet order unless a prefectural governor's permit has been obtained. According to the Act, a small market is a commercial establishment containing ten or more retail stores, all or some of which deal in the sale of perishable foods. The purpose of the Act is to protect economically weak retail businesses and ensure the harmonious social and economic development of the area by preventing excessive competition. Defendants, who had built a building and leased it to forty-eight retailers without obtaining a permit, were indicted and found guilty in both the summary and high courts. Thereupon, they filed a petition to vacate the original decision with the Supreme Court arguing mainly that: (1) to regulate a private person's economic activities through a permit system in order to carry out a socioeconomic policy and the imposition of a distance requirement in order to prevent excessive competition not only contravene Japan's basic economic system which is based on the principle of free competition but also serves monopolistic interests of existing business establishments at the expense of consumers; and (2) a distance requirement which allows a monopoly of retail business within an area and prevents consumers from buying foodstuffs at less cost violates Article 25 of the Constitution which guarantees the right to maintain minimum standards of wholesome and cultured living.

The Supreme Court, however, held the Act constitutional and rejected the petition (26 *Keishu* 586, Sup. Ct., G.B., November 22, 1972). The Court found, as far as the regulation of economic and property rights to carry out a socioeconomic policy was concerned, that the Diet had discretion in deciding the necessity, object, means and manner of regulation and that a law to regulate such rights should be presumed constitutional as long as its purpose was legitimate, and the means and manner of regulation were not "extremely unreasonable."

§4. Freedom of an Individual's Body and Person

329. The Constitution of Japan has nine articles to guarantee the freedom of an individual's body and person, in contrast with the Meiji Constitution which had only two. An individual's bodily and personal freedoms were remarkably jeopardized under the Meiji Constitution.

I. Freedom from Bondage and Involuntary Servitude

330. Article 18 of the Constitution stipulates, "No person shall be held in bondage of any kind. Involuntary servitude, except as a punishment for crime, is prohibited." It is said that this provision is modeled after Amendment XIII to the United States Constitution which prohibits slavery and involuntary servitude. The term "bondage" refers to restraints on bodily freedom to the extent that a person's personality is ignored. Prostitutes and laborers who are forced to work under the constraint of debts or under the threat of force can be said to be "held in bondage." Also, the term "servitude" means to labor with pain. By Article 18, every individual is guaranteed freedom from bondage and involuntary servitude. Labor with pain (i.e., hard labor) imposed as a sanction for a crime is a constitutional exception to this provision.

II. Right to Due Process

331. Article 31 of the Constitution states, "No person shall be deprived of life or liberty, nor shall any other criminal penalty be imposed, except according to procedure established by law." This provision is interpreted to guarantee both:

(1) the principle of *poena sine lege* which is one of the most important principles of modern criminal law in Continental Europe; and
(2) the due process doctrine which constitutes a basic doctrine of Anglo-American constitutional law and which is said to date back to Article 36 of the Magna Carta of 1215.

The principle of *poena sine lege* is a requirement that no one shall be punished for an act which is not expressly stipulated by a statute to be a crime in advance of the activities involved and also that no one shall be punished to a greater extent than the punishment prescribed by a statute. The doctrine of due process, however, is a principle that requires that both the substance of legislation and the procedure for enforcing it meet certain fundamental principles of fairness and thus be considered "due process."

332. As to the principle of *poena sine lege*, some scholars insist that Article 31 does not provide for it but simply requires that the procedure for enforcing legislation be prescribed by a statute. They do not deny, however, that the principle of *poena sine lege* is guaranteed by the Constitution; rather they claim the principle is not expressly prescribed. These scholars base the principle on such other provisions as Articles 39 and 73 (Proviso of No. 6), which implicitly guarantee it. Article 39 stipulates, "No person shall be held criminally liable for an act which was lawful at the time it was committed." Also, Proviso No. 6 of Article 73 provides, "it cannot include penal provisions in such cabinet orders unless authorized by such law." However, the majority of scholars and the Court take the view that Article 31 is a provision that guarantees the principle of *poena sine lege*. For example, in the Grand Bench Decision of Tokushima City Public Safety Ordinance, the Supreme Court stated that the ordinance at issue was so vague in content that a person with ordinary comprehension could not well understand what was made criminal conduct and therefore violated Article 31 (29 *Keishu* 489, Sup. Ct., G.B., September 10, 1975).

333. As regards the due process aspect of Article 31, the leading scholarly theory is that though Article 31, unlike the due process clauses of the United States Constitution, has not employed the term "due process," it nonetheless requires not only that the substance of law but also that the procedure for enforcing it be "due." This means that Article 31 requires governmental organs to provide due process, namely, notice and opportunity to be heard in defense, before depriving citizens of their legally protected interests or rights. The following Supreme Court decision is one of those which supports this interpretation.

334. In the *Third-Party's Property Confiscation* case, defendants were arrested and indicted on the charge of attempting to smuggle goods to Korea by a motor-powered sailing vessel which they had chartered from a third-party owner. Section 118, paragraph 1 of the Customs Act provides for the confiscation of ships used for smuggling as well as the confiscation of cargoes involved in smuggling. Defendants were found guilty in the first- and second-instance courts. As a result, the ship, as well as the cargo, was confiscated. Thereupon, a petition was filed with the Supreme Court to vacate the original decision, asserting that the confiscation of the vessel without giving the owner of the vessel the opportunity to defend was violative of Article 29, paragraph 1 of the Constitution which guarantees the inviolability of the right to property and which only permits confiscation of a third-party's property after making sure the owner had knowingly leased it for a criminal purpose. The Court declared that it was constitutionally necessary to provide notice and an opportunity for explanation and defense to a third-party owner whose property was taken and that to confiscate the owner's property without providing this opportunity constituted an imposition of a criminal sanction infringing on the owner's property right in violation of the due process requirement of Article 31 (16 *Keishu* 1593, Sup. Ct., G.B., November 28, 1962).

III. Freedom from Unlawful Arrest

335. Article 33 of the Constitution stipulates that:

> No person shall be apprehended except upon warrant issued by a competent judicial officer which specifies the offense with which the person is charged, unless he is apprehended, the offense being committed.

This provision requires the law enforcement officers to obtain a warrant issued by a judge before arresting a suspect in order to prevent an arbitrary arrest. An exception is made when one is arrested while in the act of committing the offense. Though Article 33 specifies only two requirements concerning the warrant itself, namely, that it be issued by a competent judicial officer (judge) and that it specifies the offense charged, the Code of Criminal Procedure provides that a warrant must contain the name and address of the suspect, the name of an offense with which the suspect is charged, the gist of the offense charged, the name and location of the office to which the suspect is to be taken, the period of validity of the warrant, a provision which requires that the warrant be returned after the expiration of the period, the date of its issuance and other items prescribed by court regulation (section 200, paragraph 1).

336. If the statement of Article 33 is literally read, there should be no more than two categories of arrest, namely, arrest based on a warrant and arrest during the performance of the act, which later does not require a warrant. As a matter of fact, however, the Code of Criminal Procedure provides for emergency arrest as a third category (section 210). According to section 210, public prosecutors, police officers, and so on, are empowered to summarily arrest a suspect if they have found that there is adequate cause to suspect that he or she has committed a crime punishable by death, life imprisonment or imprisonment for no less than three years and because of the urgency of the necessity of arrest, the arresting official cannot afford the time required to obtain a warrant. Of course, law enforcement officers must apply to the court for a warrant immediately after the emergency arrest of a suspect is completed, and if a warrant is not granted, the suspect must be released immediately. Some scholars insist that the emergency arrest is unconstitutional. However, the majority of scholars and judicial precedent support its constitutionality on the ground that it is a limited procedure allowed only when: (1) a suspect is charged with a serious crime, namely, a "crime punishable by death, life imprisonment or imprisonment for no less than three years"; (2) there is "adequate cause" (unlike "probable cause" which is needed to obtain a warrant); and (3) the necessity of arrest is "urgent" (9 *Keishu* 2760, Sup. Ct., G.B., December 14, 1955).

IV. Right to Be Informed of the Cause for Arrest and Detention

337. Article 34 of the Constitution provides that:

> No person shall be arrested or detained without being at once informed of the charges against him or without the immediate privilege of counsel; nor shall he be detained without adequate cause; and upon demand of any person such cause must be immediately shown in open court in his presence and the presence of his counsel.

Whether temporarily or continuously, the confinement of the body causes a person mental pain. Therefore, law enforcement officers are not only prohibited from arresting or detaining suspects without adequate cause but also are obligated to inform detainees of the cause for arrest or detention and of the right to counsel. Also, in order to prevent unlawful detention, the cause for detention must be shown in open court when detainees or related persons have so demanded. The details of the procedure for a show cause demand are prescribed in the Code of Criminal Procedure (sections 82–87).

V. Freedom from Torture or Cruel Punishment

338. It is an undeniable fact that even though it had been prohibited under the old Penal Code which took effect in 1892, law enforcement officers in prewar Japan often illegally inflicted torture on suspects. In order to eliminate such an evil practice, Article 36 of the Constitution provides that the infliction of torture by any public officer and cruel punishments are absolutely forbidden. Torture was usually inflicted to coerce a confession. Therefore, the Constitution, while providing for an absolute prohibition of torture, also stipulates that confessions obtained by torture are not admitted in evidence (Article 38, paragraph 2) and that no one can be convicted or punished in cases where the only proof against him is his own statement (Article 38, paragraph 3).

339. Also, the present Penal Code makes it a special crime punishable by imprisonment of no more than seven years for special public officers (judges, public prosecutors, police officers, etc.) to commit an assault and battery on accused and criminal suspects (sections 195 and 196). And, if a public prosecutor in charge has decided not to indict a special public officer charged with one or more of the crimes prescribed in sections 193–196 of the Penal Code (abuse of authority by special public officers) or in section 45 of the Subversive Activities Prevention Act (abuse of authority by public safety investigators), a person who has brought the charge can ask a court exercising jurisdiction over the district of a prosecution office to which the prosecutor belongs to refer the case to judgment by a court (section 262, paragraph 1 of the Code of Criminal Procedure). If the court has found the claim reasonable, it should refer the trial and judgment of the case to a court that has jurisdiction (section 266 of the Code of Criminal Procedure). In that case, the court must appoint an attorney to act as prosecutor and to perform the prosecution (section 268 of the Code of Criminal Procedure).

340. The term "cruel punishment" means criminal sanctions which cause a person unnecessary mental and physical pain and which are considered cruel and unusual from the standpoint of humanity. Examples include crucifixion, burning, exposing a cut-off head to the public, boiling in a caldron, etc. Section 11, paragraph 1 of the Penal Code provides that the death penalty shall be executed in prison by hanging. When the constitutionality of this provision was challenged, the Supreme Court sustained capital punishment as constitutional on the basis of Article 13 and Article 31 of the Constitution (2 *Keishu* 191, Sup. Ct., G.B., March 12, 1948). It must be noted, however, that a concurring opinion by Justices Shima, Iwamatsu and Kawamura pointed out the possibility that, though the death penalty did not constitute "cruel punishments" at the time of the decision, it might become unconstitutional in the future in accordance with the vicissitudes of public sentiment. The Court also held that execution by hanging was not unconstitutional (9 *Keishu* 663, Sup. Ct., G.B., April 6, 1955).

VI. Rights of Criminal Defendants

A. *Right to a Speedy and Public Trial by an Impartial Tribunal*

341. Article 37, paragraph 1 of the Constitution states that in all criminal cases, the accused shall enjoy the right to a speedy and public trial by an impartial tribunal. This provision encompasses three requirements. First, a criminal trial must be conducted by an "impartial tribunal." This means that the court must be manned by an impartial judge or judges. In order to secure the impartiality of the court, the Code of Criminal Procedure provides that judges shall be disqualified from trying cases in which: (1) they are victims, or the relatives, legal representatives or guardians of victims or defendants; (2) they have served as witnesses or expert witnesses, or attorneys, counsels or advisors; (3) they have performed duties as public prosecutors or police officers (section 20). The Code also stipulates that both prosecutors and the accused can challenge judges whom they reasonably believe might not perform their duties impartially (section 21).

342. The second requirement is that a trial must be "speedy." This not only requires that the Diet and the organ of judicial administration take necessary measures to generally guarantee a speedy trial but also empowers a court to take the drastic remedial step of terminating proceedings against a defendant whose right to a speedy trial has been impaired due to an extreme delay of the trial. This judicial remedy exists even though there is no concrete statutory ground for it. In the famous *Takata* case, the Supreme Court sustained the District Court decision which had invalidated the indictment of a defendant because of a violation of the constitutional provision for a speedy trial. In that case, the trial had been discontinued for fifteen years—a period of time which was long enough to complete the running of the period of prescription for the alleged crime (26 *Keishu* 631, Sup. Ct., G.B., December 20, 1972). The Nagoya High Court had reversed the District Court decision on the ground that even though the trial had been interrupted for such a long period, there was no statutory basis to close the case.

In 2003, the Act for Expediting Trials was enacted, which requires that court proceedings in first instance be completed within the shortest possible time, no longer than two years (section 2). Especially in trials with the participation of lay judges, it is required to make the trial proceedings quick and easy to understand. For this purpose, provisions were introduced to make it possible to open the trial on consecutive days as much as possible (section 281-6 of the Code of Criminal Procedure), and a system of pre-trial arrangement procedures to make the trial proceedings continuous, systematic, and expeditious (section 316-2 and 316-3 of the Code).

343. The third requirement is that a trial must be "public." In addition to this requirement, Article 82 of the Constitution more concretely guarantees a public trial. It states that trials "shall be conducted and judgment declared publicly" (paragraph 1) and "[w]here a court unanimously determines publicity to be dangerous to public order or morals, a trial may be conducted privately, but trials of political offenses, offenses involving the press or cases wherein the rights of people as guaranteed in Chapter III of this Constitution are in question shall always be conducted publicly" (paragraph 2).

B. Right to Obtain Witnesses and Examine All Witnesses

344. Article 37, paragraph 2 stipulates that the accused "shall be permitted full opportunity to examine all witnesses, and he shall have the right of compulsory process for obtaining witnesses on his behalf at public expense." Needless to say, the accused has a right to cross-examine prosecution witnesses who testify against him.

C. Right to Counsel

345. Article 37, paragraph 3 provides that at all times the accused shall have "the assistance of competent counsel who shall, if the accused is unable to secure the same by his own efforts, be assigned to his use by the State." Most criminal suspects and defendants do not have a good knowledge of the law. In addition, suspects are usually psychologically, socially and economically very unstable. Therefore, it is indispensable for them to have the assistance of competent lawyers to protect their legitimate interests as suspects or accused persons. This is especially true as the investigation or prosecution is in the hands of police officers or public prosecutors who are specialists in the law. Indigent suspects or accused persons are entitled to be provided with defense counsel at State expense. Under the Code of Criminal Procedure, no one may be either arrested or detained without being provided the right to counsel (section 77, paragraph 1; section 203, paragraph 1 and section 204, paragraph 1). Also, the trial of cases involving crimes punishable by death, life imprisonment or imprisonment for no less than three years cannot be initiated without defense counsel (section 289).

Furthermore, the Code of Criminal Procedure guarantees suspects and accused persons the right to an interview with defense attorneys, and the right to give to or receive from counsel papers or goods (section 39, paragraph 1). However, these rights are very limited because, when deemed necessary for the investigation, the relevant officials (prosecutors, police investigators, etc.) can designate the date, time and place regarding the interview, or the giving or receiving of the above items and may limit such time to the period preceding indictment (section 39, paragraph 3).

D. Right to Remain Silent

346. Article 38, paragraph 1 of the Constitution stipulates that no person shall be compelled to testify against himself. This provision originates from a famous English legal maxim: "No one is compelled to incriminate himself." This right was established as a common-law right in England during the latter part of the sixteenth century and later came to be adopted as the privilege against self-incrimination in

Amendment V to the United States Constitution (adopted in 1791). It is apparent that Article 38, paragraph 1 is modeled after this self-incrimination clause of the U.S. Constitution.

The right to refuse to testify against oneself, guaranteed by Article 38, paragraph 1, is not only guaranteed to criminal suspects or those accused of criminal conduct as the right to keep silent (section 198, paragraph 2; section 291, paragraph 4 and section 311, paragraph 1 of the Code of Criminal Procedure), but the right also extends to witnesses, who can refuse to testify against their relatives as well as against themselves (sections 146 and 147 of the Code of Criminal Procedure).

347. To date, Article 38, paragraph 1 has become an issue mainly in connection with regulatory legislation for administrative purposes. For example, such statutes as the Income Tax Act, the Road Traffic Act, and the Narcotics Control Act obligate certain people to make a report about the income they have received, the traffic accidents they have been involved in, the narcotics they have handled, etc. These reports are required to be made to related administrative agencies in order to achieve particular public purposes (section 120 of the Income Tax Act, section 72 of the Road Traffic Act, and sections 37–49 of the Narcotics Control Act). As one who has not complied with the reporting regulation is subjected to a criminal sanction, a constitutional question arises as to whether the imposition of such an obligation constitutes compelling one to testify against oneself. For example, the Income Tax Act requires everyone to file a return with a taxation office reporting income which he or she has gained, whether legally or illegally. Therefore, one who has illegally gained income has either to opt for the failure to report such income (and as a result being punished for violation of the obligation to report) or report such income (thereby risking punishment since the violation may be discovered as a result of filing the return). Though scholars' opinions on the constitutionality of such an obligation vary, leading scholarly opinion and judicial precedent take the stand that the imposition of such an obligation is constitutionally permissible as long as it is done to achieve an administrative purpose, not to investigate a crime (16 *Keishu* 495, Sup. Ct., G.B., May 2, 1962; 29 *Keishu* 1, Sup. Ct., January 21, 1975; etc.).

E. Freedom from Double Jeopardy

348. Article 39 of the Constitution states that no person "shall be held criminally liable for an act […] of which he has been acquitted, nor shall he be placed in double jeopardy." The Code of Criminal Procedure allows the prosecution to appeal to a higher court to seek either a guilty verdict or a heavier penalty in a case where a defendant has either been found innocent or has been given a light punishment by a lower court. Scholars' views are divided on the constitutionality of the prosecution's authority to appeal. In a 1950 case, a defendant who was sentenced to a heavier penalty as a result of the appeal taken by the prosecution filed a petition with the Supreme Court to vacate the conviction on the ground that the filing of an appeal by the prosecution constitutes double jeopardy prohibited by Article 39. The

Court struck down the petition holding that Article 39 is not a provision to guarantee the Anglo-American type of double jeopardy. Rather, it held that the provision was designed to guarantee a principle generally established in Continental European countries that no one can be repeatedly prosecuted for an act the judicial determination of which has become final (4 *Keishu* 1805, Sup. Ct., G.B., September 27, 1950).

F. Freedom from Unlawful Search and Seizure

349. Article 35 of the Constitution provides:

> The right of all persons to be secure in their homes, papers and effects against entries, searches and seizures shall not be impaired except upon warrant issued for adequate cause and particularly describing the place to be searched and things to be seized, or except as provided by Article 33 (paragraph 1).

Moreover, each search or seizure "shall be made upon separate warrant issued by a competent judicial officer" (paragraph 2). This article is aimed at guaranteeing the security of the private life of people by keeping their homes, papers and possessions inviolable. The term "home" is not limited to a person's domicile or residence within the meaning of the Civil Code. "Home" includes all parts of buildings that are personally occupied in order to lead one's private life. Therefore, personally occupied hotel rooms, dormitory rooms, business offices, and so on fall under the term "home."

350. Though paragraph 2 of Article 35 stipulates that each search or seizure must be made upon a separate warrant, this does not mean that the permission to search and the authority to seize must be described in separate warrants.

There is no constitutional problem if the search of a particular home and the seizure of a particular thing are separately described in a single warrant (6 *Keishu* 502, Sup. Ct., G.B., March 19, 1952). Furthermore, paragraph 2 of Article 35 authorizes prosecutors, police officers, etc., to enter a suspect's home to make a lawful arrest and undertake a search of the scene of the arrest and make a seizure pursuant to such search. The details of the search and seizure incident to a lawful arrest are contained in sections 218 to 220 of the Code of Criminal Procedure.

351. It must be noted that although Article 35 requires that a thing to be seized be particularly described in the warrant, judicial precedents are not as strict in this regard as the language of the article appears to be. For example, in 1958, the police performed a search and seizure in the headquarters of the Tokyo Metropolitan teachers' union in connection with an allegedly illegal strike. The strike had been staged to protest the method of evaluation of teachers' performance directed by the Board of Education. The warrant under which the police acted described the alleged crime as a "Case of Alleged Violation of the Local Civil Service Act." The union asserted that this description was so vague that the search and seizure violated Article 35. The Supreme Court rejected the union's objection, holding that Article 35 only requires that the warrant specify the place to be searched and the thing to be seized. The Court found that Article 35 does not go so far as to require that the warrant specify that it was issued for adequate cause (12 *Keishu* 2776, Sup. Ct., G.B., July 29, 1958). The grounds for the union's assertion was that although the warrant at issue enumerated as objects to be seized "the minutes of meetings, the diary of the strike, directives from the headquarters, memos and all other papers and things considered to be related to this case" since the name of the crime was not clearly described in the warrant, the items to be seized could not be determined.

352. Article 35 of the Constitution was originally designed to prevent law enforcement officers from making an unlawful search and seizure while performing their duties as part of a criminal procedure. However, this provision, together with Article 38, paragraph 1 (guaranteeing the right to keep silent), has come to be broadly interpreted as applicable to any criminal investigative procedure as well as noncriminal investigations that are directly connected with activities that substantially involve or could lead to criminal responsibility (26 *Keishu* 554, Sup. Ct., G.B., November 22, 1972).

§5. Right to Demand Governmental Actions

353. The Constitution of Japan guarantees the people four rights which are considered rights to demand governmental actions. They are as follows:

I. Right to File a Petition for the Redress of Grievances

354. Article 16 of the Constitution stipulates:

> Every person shall have the right of peaceful petition for the redress of damage, for the removal of public officials, for the enactment, repeal or amendment of laws, ordinances or regulations and for other matters, nor shall any person be in any way discriminated against for sponsoring such a petition.

The details concerning the procedure for filing a petition are described in the Petition Act. According to section 5 of the Petition Act, governmental agencies must accept and deal bona fide with any petitions which have been lawfully filed.

Though the Meiji Constitution guaranteed the right to petition for the redress of grievances, the scope of such right was limited (Article 30). For example, people were prohibited from filing petitions dealing with amendments to the Constitution or the Imperial House Act. Moreover, seeking action which might interfere with court decisions was prohibited (section 11 of the Petition Ordinance). Under the present Constitution, there is no limitation placed on the right to petition and people can petition the government concerning all matters. Although the relative value of the right to petition has undeniably diminished as a consequence of the protection afforded by freedom of speech, its importance is still significant.

II. Right to Sue the State for Redress

355. Article 17 of the Constitution stipulates, "Every person may sue for redress as provided by law from the State or public entity, in case he has suffered damage through illegal act of any public official." Under the Meiji Constitution, neither the State nor other public entities assumed legal responsibility for damages accruing from illegal acts of government officials who had the authority to restrict people's rights. Article 17 of the present Constitution, however, makes it clear that people can sue for redress from the State or other public entities for damage caused by unlawful acts of civil servants or employees or resulting from defects in the construction or administration of rivers, roads or other public facilities which they administer. This means that the Constitution has abandoned the sovereign immunity adopted by the Meiji Constitution. The detailed requirements and procedures for a damage claim are contained in the State Tort Liabilities Act.

356. Section 1 of the State Tort Liabilities Act provides that when public officials of the State or public entity who exercise governmental authority have willfully or negligently done damage to others in performing their duties the State or public entity shall assume the responsibility for such damage (paragraph 1) and "[i]n the case of the preceding paragraph when civil servants are either willfully or grossly negligent, the State or public entity can claim damages against such officials" (paragraph 2). This provision clarifies the following two points:

(1) that the responsibility which the State assumes is its own, not one which it assumes in place of negligent officials; and
(2) that even if there is negligence on the part of a public official, such an official cannot be personally liable for damage resulting from such negligence unless he/she is guilty of gross negligence.

357. Section 2 of the State Tort Liabilities Act states, "When damage has accrued to others because of deficits in the construction or administration of rivers, roads and other public facilities, the State or public entity shall assume the responsibility for such damage" (paragraph 1) and "In the case of the preceding paragraph when there is another person to assume the liability, the State or public entity shall claim damages against that person" (paragraph 2). It must be noted that the responsibility which the State or public entity assumes under this provision is a "no-fault" liability or a strict liability.

III. Right of Access to the Courts

358. Article 32 provides that no person shall be denied the right of access to the courts. The "courts" herein described are judicial courts, namely, the Supreme Court and such inferior courts as are established by law, i.e., High Courts, District Courts, Family Courts and Summary Courts, which are established by law (Article 76, paragraph 1 and section 2, paragraph 1 of the Judiciary Act). By this provision, anyone whose legal rights or interests have been impaired is given the right to file a suit with and seek a remedy from judicial courts. This provision also means that judicial courts cannot refuse to adjudicate cases which have been lawfully filed.

Under the Meiji Constitution, the judicial courts reviewed only civil and criminal cases and did not have jurisdiction over administrative cases. Therefore, those who had their rights invaded by unlawful governmental acts could not seek a remedy from judicial courts. They were only allowed to sue for redress in the Administrative Court, a one-instance special tribunal, which was not connected with the ordinary courts of law (*supra* paragraph 138). Under the present Constitution, however, the judicial power extends to administrative cases as well as to civil and criminal cases. This means that the ordinary courts are empowered to review the legality of administrative acts.

359. Article 76, paragraph 2 of the Constitution prohibits the exercise of final judicial power by agencies or bodies of the Executive. It also prohibits the establishment of "extraordinary tribunals" such as courts-martial, the Imperial House Court and the Administrative Court which had existed in prewar days. Nonetheless, it is established that agencies and bodies of the Executive are not prevented from exercising judicial functions so long as such exercise is not final (section 3, paragraph 2 of the Judiciary Act) (*supra* paragraph 139). For example, under the Patent Act complaints concerning the validity of a patent right must first be lodged with the Patent Bureau for adjudication. If either party to the dispute is not satisfied with the result of the adjudication, an appeal can be taken to the Tokyo High Court (section 178, paragraph 1 of the Patent Act). Similarly, complaints challenging the validity of the dismissal, demotion or other disciplinary actions taken against national civil servants must first be filed with the National Personnel Agency, an independent administrative commission, and then can be taken to the courts (section 92-2 of the National Civil Service Act). The Supreme Court takes the position that compelling one to first file a complaint with an administrative organ to seek a remedy before going to the judicial court does not infringe on the right of access to the courts as long as it does not constitute an unreasonable restriction tantamount to a virtual denial of justice (5 *Minshu* 759, Sup. Ct., G.B., November 30, 1951). The Court has also upheld statutes of limitation which, in the interests of public welfare, shorten the period of time for filing an administrative suit with a court of law, as long as such limited period is not such an unreasonably short one as to substantially deny people access to the courts (3 *Minshu* 199, Sup. Ct., G.B., May 18, 1949).

360. It is judicially settled that Article 32 not only guarantees the right of access to the courts but also guarantees litigants the right to a public and adversarial trial (14 *Minshu* 1657, Sup. Ct., G.B., July 6, 1960).

361. In order that indigent people can enjoy the benefit of Article 32, a legal aid system has been established by the national government. Under this system, those who cannot afford to hire a lawyer can ask for a loan from a governmental fund earmarked to assist people seeking a judicial remedy. If it is adjudged that the party seeking such a loan has a reasonable prospect of winning the proposed litigation, the funds will be provided.

IV. Right to Compensation Arising from Improper Criminal Charges

362. For the purpose of protecting the human rights of criminal suspects, the Constitution of Japan has a set of elaborate and detailed provisions concerning both the procedure governing the trial of criminal defendants as well as procedures for the arrest, detention and indictment of suspects. It is nevertheless impossible to completely prevent an invasion of defendants' and suspects' bodily and personal freedoms. Therefore, from the point of view of equity, it is essential to establish a system to provide equitable compensation to those who have suffered mental, physical and economic losses caused by an error in the criminal process (herein referred to as "criminal compensation").

In prewar days criminal compensation was, to some extent, available under the old Criminal Compensation Act (enacted in 1931). However, as there was no constitutional basis for compensation, it is not too much to say that the Act was considered more favor from the State than a right. In this sense, the decision as to whether to grant compensation was left entirely to the discretion of the State.

Unlike the Meiji Constitution, the Constitution of Japan expressly stipulates, "[a]ny person, in case he is acquitted after he has been arrested or detained, may sue the State for redress as provided by law" (Article 40). Compensation is available for arrest or detention, even where the original arrest was not unlawful. It must be noted that the relief provided in Article 40 is different in nature from damages to be given to victims whose legal interests have been impaired by tortious acts of public officials as prescribed by Article 17. It has also to be noted that the compensation provided by Article 40 is given to victims after the verdict of not guilty has become final. The details of the procedure for criminal compensation are provided in the Criminal Compensation Act. According to the Act, a claim for criminal compensation must be lodged with the court which has handed down the verdict of not guilty (section 6) within three years from the day when the verdict has become final (section 7). Compensation for the arrest or detention ranges from JPY 1,000 to JPY 12,500 per day (section 4).

To do justice to those who have either been arrested or detained but have not been found not guilty because no indictment was ever obtained, the Rule of Compensation for Criminal Suspects (a directive issued by the Minister of Justice in April of 1948) provides for compensation in such cases. The amount of compensation, as well as the decision to give compensation, is determined by a prosecutor of the prosecution bureau which has decided not to indict.

§6. Social Rights

363. What the eighteenth and nineteenth-century constitutions guaranteed to the people were equal rights and freedoms, the core of which were property rights and economic freedoms. The guarantee of these rights made a tremendous contribution to the development of capitalist economies, which in turn inevitably brought about an extreme gap between the rich and the poor. In order to correct social inequalities and eliminate social injustices caused by the maldistribution of wealth, active State intervention was required. Apparently, under the strong influence of the German

Constitution of 1919, most of the constitutions adopted after the end of World War II provided for social rights such as the right to live a decent life, the right to have an education, the right to work, the right of workers to unite, bargain collectively and strike, etc. The Constitution of Japan which went into effect in 1947 was no exception. In addition to the traditional rights and liberties, it incorporates the following four social rights designed to create substantive equality for all people and to protect human dignity. At the same time, it also restricts property and economic rights to achieve the same purpose.

I. Right to Maintain the Minimum Standards of Wholesome and Cultured Living

364. Article 25 of the Constitution stipulates, "All people shall have the right to maintain the minimum standards of wholesome and cultured living" (paragraph 1) and "In all spheres of life, the State shall use its endeavors for the promotion and extension of social welfare and security, and of public health" (paragraph 2). There are three theories on the nature of a right which Article 25, paragraph 1 guarantees, namely, the "Programmatic Declaration Theory," the "Abstract Right Theory" and the "Concrete Right Theory." This split of scholarly opinion arose partly because the provisions of Article 25 were vague and abstract and partly because there was a large gap between the guarantees of the Constitution and the economic realities in the years following the war when most people were barely living above the subsistence level and the government was unable to provide a living consistent with the language of Article 25.

365. According to the Programmatic Declaration Theory, the guarantee of Article 25, paragraph 1 establishes a goal that the State must seek to attain. Accordingly, no one can seek a judicial remedy for the failure of the government to provide him or her with substantial aid to reach the standard of living that Article 25 refers to. This stand was supported by the Supreme Court in the *Staple Food Control Act* case decided in 1948, in which a petitioner relying on Article 25 challenged the constitutionality of the Act which prohibited the sale and purchase of staple food (2 *Keishu* 1235, Sup. Ct., G.B., September 29, 1948).

366. Unlike this approach, the Concrete Right Theory (which is the most positive of the three theories) takes the position that one can get a judicial remedy when he or she is not able to make a livelihood at the level called for by Article 25. In other words, the courts are legally empowered not only to declare the Diet's failure to make a law to guarantee a decent life unconstitutional but also to force the Diet to legislate to realize the guarantee of Article 25. Most constitutional law scholars, however, regard this theory as too extreme in light of the doctrine of separation of powers, which they think makes it constitutionally impossible for the courts to force the Diet to legislate.

367. Most scholars favor the Abstract Right Theory. Those who favor this theory recognize that there can be no judicial remedy under Article 25 unless there is legislation to carry out the guarantee of Article 25. Nonetheless, this constitutional right to a minimum standard of living is not a mere programmatic declaration. It is a legal right in the sense that courts interpreting existing welfare legislation must do so in a way which conforms to and carries out Article 25. In the famous *Asahi* case, the Supreme Court stated in obiter dictum that though the decision as to the amount of a livelihood protection allowance to be provided to the needy by the Livelihood Protection Act was constitutionally left to the discretion of the Minister of Health and Welfare, that discretion was properly a matter for judicial review when the Minister was deemed to have greatly exceeded or abused his discretionary power under the Act (21 *Minshu* 1043, Sup. Ct., G.B., May 24, 1967).

368. The government is generally granted relatively broad discretion in how to realize the rights of Article 25 of the Constitution, due to state fiscal constraints. Thus, there is not much room for the unconstitutionality of the government's policy. It is problematic, however, to allow the government too broad a discretion in the realization of this right. The key issue is how to control this discretion. Even now, there are disputes in court as to whether or not public assistance based on the Livelihood Protection Act can really enable people to lead "the minimum standards of wholesome and cultured living."

369. The government has lowered the standard amount of livelihood assistance, which covers clothing, food, and utilities, in three steps since 2013. The average reduction was 6.5% and the maximum was 10%. In total, approximately JPY 67 billion is said to have been cut. Thus, lawsuits were filed in prefectures throughout Japan, claiming that the government's lowering of the standard amount of livelihood assistance violated the Constitution, which guarantees "the minimum standards of wholesome and cultured living." Of these, in February 2021, the Osaka District Court reversed the government's decision to lower the standard amount of livelihood assistance, stating that the original indexes used by the government in its calculations did not reflect the actual living conditions of recipients and that there were errors and omissions in the decision-making process (1490 *Hanta* 121, Osaka Dist. Ct., February 22, 2021).

370. This ruling did not decide whether it was unconstitutional, but it attracted attention. However, this ruling was overturned by the Osaka High Court of Appeals on April 14, 2023. The Osaka High Court found that the revision of the standard amount of livelihood assistance was reasonable, noting that since the standard amount was not reduced after the Lehman Shock in 2008, the disposable income of households receiving public assistance was relatively higher than that of ordinary households. A series of lawsuits have been filed in twenty-nine District Courts, and the Courts are divided on whether the lowering of the standard amount is illegal or legal.

II. Right to Receive Education

371. Article 26, paragraph 1 stipulates, "[a]ll people shall have the right to receive an equal education correspondent to their ability, as provided by law." In order to realize the guarantee of this right, the Basic Act on Education provides, "The people must be given equal opportunities to receive an education suited to their abilities, and must not be subjected to discrimination in education on account of race, creed, sex, social status, economic position, or family origin." (section 4, paragraph 1), and "The national and local governments shall provide the necessary educational support to ensure that persons with disabilities receive an adequate education in accordance with their level of disability" (section 4, paragraph 2). Also, "The national and local governments shall take measures to provide financial assistance to those who, despite their abilities, encounter difficulties in receiving education for economic reasons" (section 4, paragraph 3). However, since the matters referred to in paragraph 1 are basically matters within Article 14 (which guarantees equality under the law), the real significance of Article 26, as a provision stipulating social rights, lies in the guarantee given in paragraphs 2 and 3.

To receive education means not only a means to "maintain the minimum standards of wholesome and cultured living" (Article 25, paragraph 1) but also a cultural aspect of the right to live such life itself.

372. The right to have an education guaranteed by Article 26 is clearly not self-executing. However, the guarantee of such a right is nevertheless significant in the sense that the government is obligated to make laws to achieve substantive equality in education. It is also noteworthy that Article 26 requires that the right to have education be substantiated by law because the Meiji Constitution did not have any provision dealing with education. All matters concerning education were provided for by administrative ordinances, such as imperial orders, ministerial orders, etc., and as a consequence were outside the principle of government by law.

373. Article 26, paragraph 2 stipulates, "all people shall be obligated to have all boys and girls under their protection receive ordinary education as provided for by law. Such compulsory education shall be free." Instead of making "ordinary education" (nine years of schooling—section 16 of the School Education Act) compulsory, the Constitution obligates the government to provide "free education" during that period. Scholarly opinions as to the scope of free education are divided into three theories: (1) it is left to the discretion of the Diet; (2) it is limited to the exemption of tuition; and (3) it covers not only tuition but also textbooks, instructional materials and other articles indispensable for attending school. Most scholars and the Supreme Court support the second theory (18 *Minshu* 343, Sup. Ct., G.B., February 26, 1964). However, since 1963, textbooks for elementary and junior high schools have by law been distributed free of charge. Furthermore, since 2014, students from households with less than a certain amount of income who attend high schools, regardless of whether they are public or private, have been provided with a subsidy to support their tuition.

374. Though basically a social right, Article 26 right to receive education also contains aspects of freedom from governmental interference. Accordingly, people are at the same time guaranteed the right to be free from the State's unreasonable intervention in educating their children. In order to respond to the right of people to receive an education, the State has to establish a reasonable educational system and provide proper facilities. A problem arises as to the extent to which the State can intervene in decisions of the contents of and methods of education. There are two scholarly theories on this point, namely, the State's Right Theory and the People's Right Theory. The former is a theory that asserts that under parliamentary democracy the contents and method of education are to be decided by the State as representative of the people. The latter insists that it is the people and, as a matter of fact, teachers whom the people have trusted who decide the contents and method of education. In the famous *Asahikawa Scholastic Ability Test* case, the Supreme Court rejected both theories as too extreme and one-sided (30 *Keishu* 615, Sup. Ct., G.B., May 21, 1976). While admitting that parents, private schools and teachers had limited freedom of education in their respective spheres, the Court held that in spheres other than those to which their freedoms extend, the State had the authority to decide the contents of education within a necessary and proper limit in the interests of children themselves and the general public. Further, the Court held that such State intervention as to impede children growing as free and independent persons, for instance, to compel enforcement of such education to install a false knowledge or partial view into children's minds, was constitutionally impermissible in light of Article 26 (the right to receive education) and Article 13 (the right to life, liberty and the pursuit of happiness).

III. Right to Work

375. Article 27, paragraph 1 states that all people shall have the right and the obligation to work. Though it is not self-executing, the government is obligated to provide the opportunity to work to those people who have the ability and willingness but are not able to find jobs to make a living. In order to fulfill the obligation, the Diet has enacted such laws as the Employment Security Act, Employment Insurance Act, Human Resources Development Promotion Act, Handicapped Persons' Employment Promotion Act, and so on.

376. In order to protect the interests of working people, the Constitution restricts the employers' freedom of contract as to wages, working hours, and so on. Article 27, paragraph 2 stipulates, "Standards for wages, hours, rest and other working conditions shall be fixed by law." The Constitution also prohibits the exploitation of children (Article 27, paragraph 3).

IV. Right of Workers to Organize and to Bargain and Act Collectively

377. Article 28 provides that the right of workers to organize and to bargain and act collectively is guaranteed. The right to organize means a right to form a labor union to negotiate on the same footing with an employer. To dismiss or take an unfavorable action against an employee on the ground that he/she has organized, joined or worked for a union constitutes an "unfair labor practice" (section 7 of the Labor Union Act), and such employee can seek a remedy from the prefectural labor union (section 27). Next, the right to bargain is a right accorded to a representative of a labor union or a person entrusted by a union to negotiate and conclude an agreement on wages, hours and other working conditions with an employer for the interest of the union or its members (section 6). And the right to act collectively is a means to win a favorable result in negotiations, the core of which is the right to strike. In order to guarantee these rights, laws such as the Labor Union Act, Labor Relations Adjustment Act, National Enterprises Labor Relations Act, and others, have been enacted.

378. As to the right to organize, it is also guaranteed by Article 21, paragraph 1 which provides for freedom of association. However, these rights are different in nature, i.e., while freedom of association guarantees freedom to combine without governmental interference, the right to organize is a positive right to seek the government's guarantee that no employee shall be dismissed or transferred against his/her will on the ground that he/she has organized, joined or worked for a labor union.

379. In accordance with the National Civil Service Act and Local Civil Service Act, both national and local civil servants have all or part of their right to organize and to bargain and act collectively denied depending on the nature of their respective service. For example, members of the Self-Defense Forces, police officers, firefighters, corrections officers, maritime safety officers, and so on, do not even have the right to organize, while white-collar civil servants (including public school teachers) have the right to organize, but can neither conclude an agreement as a result of negotiation, nor go on strike, and blue-collar civil servants are only deprived of the right to strike (section 64 of the Self-Defense Forces Act; sections 98, 108-2 and 108-5 of the National Civil Service Act; sections 37 and 55 of the Local Civil Service Act; and section 17, paragraph 1 of the National Enterprises Labor Relations Act).

380. With respect to the constitutionality of those laws which deprive civil servants of the right to strike and punish one who incites or instigates these people to strike, the Supreme Court at first sustained such laws based on Article 13 which declares human rights as inviolable insofar as they do not interfere with the public welfare and on Article 15, paragraph 2 which stipulates that all public officials are servants of the whole community and not of any group thereof (*Cabinet Order, No. 201* case, 7 *Keishu* 775, Sup. Ct., G.B., April 8, 1953). However, as Japan recovered from the devastation of the war and her socioeconomic conditions changed, the Court began to change its attitude.

381. In 1966, in the famous case *Zentei Tokyo Central Post Office* (20 *Keishu* 901, Sup. Ct., G.B., October 26, 1966), the Supreme Court modified its precedence governing the right of civil servants to strike by holding that the restriction of the right could only be allowed to protect the interest of the whole people's life and that sanctions to be imposed on government employees who illegally resorted to a strike should be minimum. It further declared that criminal sanctions should not in principle be imposed on the organizers of a strike, to say nothing of its participants, unless (1) it was staged for a political purpose, (2) it was accompanied by violence, or (3) it brought about a grave hindrance to the people's life. Though this decision did not completely liberate civil servants from the threat of criminal sanctions, the decision is nevertheless significant in the sense that it exonerated from criminal liability union leaders who had allegedly incited postal workers to walk out of their posts. The stand of this case was further strengthened by two Supreme Court decisions handed down three years later, *Tokyo Metropolitan Teachers Union* (23 *Keishu* 305, Sup. Ct., G.B., April 2, 1969) and *Zen-shiho Sendai* (23 *Keishu* 685, Sup. Ct., G.B., April 2, 1969).

382. In 1973, however, the Supreme Court again changed its attitude toward the right of civil servants to strike, holding that to prohibit government employees from resorting to a strike and impose criminal sanctions on one who had instigated or incited them to join a strike was not unconstitutional because:

(1) the civil servants' resort to a strike was not only incompatible with the specialty of their status and the public nature of their service but also would bring about a more or less hindrance to the prosecution of public service which might seriously harm the common interest of the whole people; and
(2) because civil servants were accorded the guarantee of their status in return for the deprivation of the right to strike (*Zen-norin Police Officers' Duties Performance Act* case, 27 *Keishu* 547, Sup. Ct., G.B., April 25, 1973).

The trend in the case law has shifted from a respect for the right of public officials to strike to judgments that actively uphold as constitutional the severe and all-encompassing restrictions imposed by the current law.

§7. Rights to Participate in the Decision and Formation of the National Will

383. The Constitution of Japan stipulates, "We, the Japanese people, acting through our duly elected representatives in the National Diet, determined that ..." and "Government is a sacred trust of the people, the authority for which is derived from the people, the powers of which are exercised by the representatives of the people, and the benefits of which are enjoyed by the people" (paragraph 1 of the Preamble). These provisions show that Japan has adopted representative democracy as a principle. Under representative democracy, people do not directly participate in the decision of the national will but choose their representatives to decide it. It is not only impossible but also inappropriate, for all members of a State to get together at one place and decide the will of the State where various and complex competing interests exist.

I. Inalienable Right of People to Choose and Dismiss Public Officials

384. The Constitution provides that "The people have the inalienable right to choose their public officials and to dismiss them" (Article 15, paragraph 1), thus guaranteeing the right of people to indirectly participate in the decision and formation of the national will. The term "public officials" herein used includes members of the Diet, Ministers of State, members of local legislatures, governors, mayors, judges and all other national and local civil servants. This provision does not provide people with the right to directly appoint all public officials. Rather, it declares the basic principle of democracy that the right to choose and dismiss all public officials derives from the people with whom sovereign power resides. As a matter of fact, cases in which public officials are directly chosen or dismissed by people are limited. There are only three such cases: (1) the election of members of both Houses of the Diet (Article 43); (2) the election of heads of all local public entities, members of their assemblies, etc. (Article 93, paragraph 2); and (3) the recall of Supreme Court Justices (Article 79). Other public officials, including judges, civil servants serving in the executive branch, etc., are appointed and dismissed by the respective competent authorities in accordance with the procedures prescribed by laws enacted by the Diet representing the whole people. Therefore, even though the appointment and dismissal of these officials are exercised by organs other than the people, they are not violative of Article 15, paragraph 1.

II. Right to Directly Participate in the Determination of the National Will

385. Though Japan has adopted representative democracy as mentioned above, the Constitution provides that the people have the right to directly participate in the determination of the national will in the following two exceptional cases.

A. Right to Referendum Vote on Amendment to the Constitution

386. Article 96, paragraph 1 stipulates that:

> Amendments to this Constitution shall be initiated by the Diet, through a concurring vote of two thirds or more of all the members of each House and shall thereupon be submitted to the people for ratification, which shall require the affirmative vote of a majority of all votes cast thereon, at a special referendum or at such election as the Diet shall specify.

Though all matters including the passage of a bill are decided by a majority of those present at each House (one-third or more makes a quorum), the initiation of a constitutional amendment requires both: (1) a concurring vote of two-thirds or more of all the members of each House, and (2) approval by the people through the affirmative vote of a majority of all votes cast at a special referendum or at the time of the election specified by the Diet. Procedural laws for a constitutional amendment, however, had not been enacted for a long period of time.

In 2007, the Diet, for the first time, passed a procedural statute for amending the Constitution. It provides for the way the people directly vote on the amendments to the Constitution of Japan (viz., referendum). It was partially revised in 2014. Another revision was made in 2021 to allow the establishment of polling stations in commercial facilities. Currently, there is still debate on whether or not to regulate commercials about constitutional amendments.

B. Right to Referendum on the Enactment of a Special Law Applied Only to One Particular Local Public Entity

387. Article 95 provides, "A special law applicable only to one local public entity cannot be enacted by the Diet without the consent of the majority of the voters of the local public entity concerned, obtained in accordance with law." This means that though the Diet is the highest organ of State power and the sole law-making organ of the State it cannot enact a law applicable only to one particular local public entity without the consent of the inhabitants of that entity. The purpose of this provision is to prevent the Diet from pressing an unfavorable law on a particular prefecture, city, town or village. Examples of such laws include the Hiroshima Peace Memorial City Construction Act, the Nagasaki International Cultural City Construction Act, and the Former Naval Port Cities Conversion Act. The former two laws are designed to help reconstruct Hiroshima and Nagasaki which were completely devastated during the last war, and the latter is to help former naval port cities, such as Yokosuka, Kure, Sasebo and Maizuru, develop peacetime industries.

C. Basic Principles on the Election of Public Officials

388. Under representative democracy, the election of public officials is very important. Generally speaking, all modern democracies guarantee such election principles as universal suffrage, secret ballot, equal vote and direct ballot. The Constitution of Japan guarantees these principles as follows.

1. Universal Suffrage

389. Under this principle, all people who have reached a certain age are given an equal right to vote irrespective of their race, creed, sex, social status, family origin, education, property or income. On July 1, 1890, the first election of members of the House of Representatives was held. However, the qualification to vote and run for a seat in that House was limited to those who paid JPY 15 a year as direct national tax (land tax and income tax). In the face of mounting popular demand for universal suffrage, such a requirement was gradually loosened, and, as far as the qualification of male voters was concerned, finally abolished in 1925, when the Universal Suffrage Act was enacted.

However, it was not until December 15, 1945, the year when World War II ended, that a genuine universal suffrage law (which expanded the franchise to women) came into being. Based on this accomplishment, the Constitution of Japan which was adopted the following year stipulates, "Universal adult suffrage is guaranteed with regard to the election of public officials" (Article 15, paragraph 3), and "there shall be no discrimination because of race, creed, sex, social status, family origin, education, property or income" with respect to the qualification of voters (Article 44, Proviso).

2. Secret Ballot

390. The secret ballot is a way of voting in which the only person to know who has voted for whom is the voter himself or herself. Article 15, paragraph 4 states, "In all elections, the secrecy of the ballot shall not be violated. A voter shall not be answerable, publicly or privately, for the choice he has made." This principle is indispensable to guarantee a free election.

3. Equal Vote

391. Though the Constitution does not expressly so provide, there is no doubt that all voters are entitled to an equal vote in light of Article 14, paragraph 1 which guarantees equality under the law and Article 44 Proviso which prohibits discrimination in the qualification to vote. In order to carry out the spirit of the above provisions, the Public Office Election Act stipulates, "One person shall have only one vote per election" (section 36). Needless to say, a vote which a person has must be the same in value as that which another person has. This means that "one person, one vote" must be "one person, one equal vote." However, in reality, appropriate apportionment of seats in the Diet and assemblies of local public entities in proportion to their respective population has not been carried out, and imbalance in the value of a vote between cities and rural areas has been a serious constitutional issue in Japan (*supra* paragraph 159).

4. Direct Ballot

392. There are two kinds of elections: direct election and indirect election. The Constitution expressly requires that mayors and members of assemblies of local public entities be directly elected by the people (Article 93, paragraph 2). However, it has no express provision as to whether members of the Diet must be directly elected, though Article 43 states that both Houses shall consist of "elected members." Scholars are generally of the opinion that the so-called indirect election, a means by which those chosen by voters elect their representatives, is not permissible without an express constitutional provision. This position is based on the doctrine of people's sovereignty. In that regard, some scholars viewed the proportional representation in the House of Councillors as unconstitutional when it was first adopted in 1982. Under the existing system of proportional representation in both Houses, voters cast their votes for a list of candidates prepared by political parties, and seats are distributed among the parties in proportion to the votes acquired. Such a system is different in nature from an indirect election system under which those chosen by the electorate then elect representatives. Accordingly, the present system is not unconstitutional.

Chapter 3. Judicial Control of Administrative Action

by Prof. Hiroyuki Hata with updates by Prof. Takehisa Nakagawa

§1. General

393. Under the Meiji Constitution, the judicial courts did not have the power to decide administrative cases. Administrative cases, limited to certain categories of cases, could be referred to a separate one-instance Administrative Court which had been established in Tokyo, outside the judicial court system. Needless to say, those whose legal interests were damaged by governmental actions did not have a sufficient remedy.

Unlike its predecessor, Article 76, paragraph 2 of the Constitution of Japan stipulates, "No extraordinary tribunal shall be established, nor shall any organ or agency of the Executive be given final judicial power." This article explicitly prohibits the creation of special courts, such as the abovementioned Administrative Court. Other special courts, such as courts-martial, etc., are also prohibited. Thus, under the present Constitution, all people are guaranteed access to the judicial courts to seek relief for any unlawful governmental action or inaction.

394. To accommodate the new constitutional arrangements, a general law on judicial review of administrative action was quickly enacted in 1947. Being fairly a concise statute, the Special Act on Administrative Case Litigation of 1947 left several important questions unanswered. The result was that judicial opinions and academic views varied on essential issues. With a bold intent to resolve the confusion, a new general law was prepared, and the Diet passed the ACL Act in 1962.

The ACL Act was then amended in 2004 (hereinafter referred to as "the 2004 revision") under the auspices of the Judicial Reform Council, which, set up in 1999 by the Koizumi Cabinet, became a driving force for various judicial reforms in the early 2000s, including the introduction of the jury system in penal cases.

The 2004 revision did not intend to introduce drastic changes to the ACL Act of 1962. The Act's classification of administrative lawsuits (*see* paragraphs 364–370), for example, was maintained untouched. However, the amendment turned out to trigger a large-scale change in court opinions and academic views about judicial review of administrative action. The initiative of the Supreme Court drove this change. A kind of formalistic thinking characteristically found in the case law under the ACL Act of 1962 has been largely swept away since the 2004 revision.

§2. Categories of Administrative Litigation

395. According to the ACL Act, there are four categories of administrative litigation. First, a *Kokoku* suit (a suit filed by someone with a legally protected interest against the governmental agency in relation to the exercise of governmental power); second, a *Tojisha* suit (a suit between parties concerning the infringement of rights in relation to public law); third, a *Kikan* suit (a suit over a conflict of jurisdiction between governmental agencies), and fourth, a *Minshu* suit (a suit filed by any citizen someone in his or her capacity as a resident). The details of the abovementioned four types of suits are as follows.

I. *Kokoku* Suit

396. This is a category of suit which involves a complaint against the exercise of governmental power. The ACL Act provides for actions seeking: (1) reversal of an administrative disposition; (2) reversal of an administrative adjudication made on appeal; (3) affirmation of the invalidity of an administrative disposition; and (4) affirmation of the illegality of governmental inaction (section 3 of the ACL Act). There are about 1,000 administrative cases (939 cases in 1991, 877 in 1992, 1,047 in 1993, 1,150 in 1994, 1,018 in 1995, 1,235 in 1996, 1,337 in 1997, 1,318 in 1998, and 1,313 in 1999) brought in the district courts in Japan annually, and of these, most fall within the first category mentioned above: reversal actions. Because the ACL Act enumerates only these four kinds of *Kokoku* suits, there has been a controversy over whether a suit other than those four, such as a suit seeking a mandamus, or requiring a governmental agency to do a certain act, is possible. Unlike the majority of administrative law scholars, the courts have been reluctant to recognize a right to bring other such cases.

397. It must be noted that the time limit to file a suit to seek reversal of administrative dispositions or adjudications made on appeal is much shorter than in ordinary civil cases (section 14, paragraphs 1–3 of the ACL Act) and that the execution of administrative dispositions cannot as a principle be suspended, in light of their nature, unless deemed by a court to be urgently necessary to avoid an irreparable injury (section 25, paragraphs 1–3 of the ACL Act).

398. In the limited sense that is the subject of *Kokoku* suits, the exercise of governmental power is abbreviated as "administrative disposition" in the ACL Act (section 3). The Supreme Court defines the concept as an action authorized by statutes (or local ordinances) for an agency directly to create, change, or extinguish a right or a legal status of a specific private entity (9 *Minshu* 617, Sup. Ct., February 24, 1955). It ranges from drivers' licenses, business permissions, construction permits, revocation of such permits and approvals, denial of permit applications, restraining orders, and administrative penalty orders. It even includes statutorily authorized physical coercion by government agencies, such as involuntary hospitalization and deportation.

The 2004 revision did not address the concept of administrative disposition, but it did provide for new statutory categories of *Kokoku* suits. They are: (5) an action requiring the agency to make an affirmative administrative disposition on permit/license application; (6) a lawsuit requiring the agency to issue an administrative disposition, such as revocation, removal, or penalty orders; (7) an action to enjoin the agency from issuing administrative dispositions. The 2004 amendment also provides for an extended limitation period of six months for filing reversal actions, (which used to be sixty days from the date of the plaintiff's awareness of administrative dispositions). The defendant of *Kokoku* suits is now basically the government itself (national or local), rather than agencies, such as Ministers, prefectural governors, or mayors.

The Supreme Court decided in 2012 an action to enjoin the Tokyo Metropolitan Government from issuing disciplinary actions against high school teachers (66 *Minshu* 183, Sup. Ct., February 9, 2012). The opinion carefully made full use of the newly added category of *Kokoku* suits and showed a rather lenient standard of justiciability for such actions. It provides a good contrast to the Court's precedents on similar issues before the 2004 revision.

II. *Tojisha* Suit

399. *Tojisha* means parties. A *Tojisha* suit is an action filed for the purpose of determining a legal relationship between parties where public law is involved. There are two kinds of *Tojisha* suits (section 4).

400. One type is filed in accordance with an enabling statute in order to settle a legal dispute which has arisen as a result of an administrative disposition or adjudication made by a governmental agency (hereinafter referred to as "the first type"). For example, under the Land Expropriation Act, an action may be brought by either an entrepreneur who plans to expropriate land (whether the government or a private company) or a land owner by one against the other to determine title to the land or to determine how much the owner should be compensated for the land. This does not differ in nature from an ordinary civil case, except that the dispute has arisen as a result of an administrative disposition or adjudication made on appeal by a governmental agency. For example, under the Land Expropriation Act, an entrepreneur (whether the government or a private company) and a land owner must consult with each other about the price of land which is being expropriated for public use. If they are not able to reach an agreement, the Land Expropriation Commission (an agency of the prefectural government) makes a decision on their behalf. If they are not satisfied with the decision, the entrepreneur is required to file a suit against the owner (or the owner against the entrepreneur), not against the commission which has made the decision (section 133 of the Land Expropriation Act). Such a suit between private parties challenges a governmental administrative action.

The other type of *Tojisha* suit is one that seeks to determine the legal relations between parties based on public law (hereinafter referred to as "the second type"). An illustration would be a suit filed by a civil servant seeking affirmation of his or her status (and/or an award of back pay) brought against the national or local government.

401. In sum, a *Tojisha* suit seeks to resolve a legal dispute between parties who are put on equal footing. It does not differ in substance from an ordinary civil suit. Therefore, a *Tojisha* suit is basically decided in accordance with the Code of Civil Procedure. section 7 of the ACL Act stipulates, "All matters related to administrative case litigation shall follow standard civil procedure unless otherwise stipulated in this Act." However, since it is closely related to the exercise of administrative authority, the Act specifically requires that provisions concerning a *Kokoku* suit, such as section 23 authorizing the court to permit a third party (like a governmental agency) to participate in the suit and section 24 empowering the court to examine evidence upon request from either party or of its own will, be applied to the proceedings in a *Tojisha* suit (section 41). When a *Tojisha* suit concerning an administrative disposition or adjudication made upon appeal has been filed, the court must notify the governmental agency which made the disposition or adjudication (section 39). Except for these points, there is not much difference between a *Tojisha* suit and an ordinary civil suit.

402. The 2004 amendments unintentionally contributed to a significant resurgence of the second type of *Tojisha* suits. Until then, the second type's importance and potential (paragraph 394) were long neglected in judicial opinions and academia.

In the legislative process of the 2004 amendment, including the deliberative committee, there were discussions on what type of actions should be brought for disputes concerning governmental acts that do not constitute "administrative dispositions." Since no unanimous conclusion was reached, the deliberative committee proposed a compromise plan to add several words to section 4 of the ACL Act, which defines the concept of *Tojisha* suits. It was simply to confirm that the court can utilize a declaratory judgment as one form of *Tojisha* suit.

Far beyond what was envisaged by the drafters, the Supreme Court immediately discovered the usefulness of the amendment and has made extensive use of declaratory judgments in *Tojisha* suits.

The Supreme Court ruled that the Public Offices Election Act's failure to allow Japanese nationals abroad to vote was unconstitutional and declared in a *Tojisha* suit that the plaintiffs had legal status to vote from abroad in the next general election (59 *Minshu* 2087, Sup. Ct., G. B. September 14, 2005). In 2012, in answering the plaintiffs' petition for declaratory judgment in a *Tojisha* suit, the Court decided whether it was illegal for plaintiff's public school teachers not to sing the national anthem in school ceremonies (66 *Minshu* 183, Sup. Ct., February 9, 2012).

In 2011, the Supreme Court decided whether the prohibition of so-called mixed medical treatment was lawful by declaring, in a *Tojisha* suit, whether the plaintiff was eligible to receive mixed treatment under the Health Insurance Act (65 *Minshu* 2923, October 25, 2011). In 2013, after holding that the Ministerial regulation that prohibited the sale of specific categories of medicines on the Internet violated the Pharmaceutical Affairs Act, the Court declared in a *Tojisha* suit that the plaintiff was entitled to sell those medicines on the internet (67 *Minshu* 1, Sup. Ct., January 11, 2013).

In this context, some academic theorists have come to doubt the distinction between *Kokoku* suits and *Tojisha* suits, which dichotomy had been introduced by the ACL Act of 1962 but left untouched by the 2004 revision.

III. *Kikan* Suit

403. This is a suit over a conflict of jurisdiction between agencies of the national or local government (section 6). Usually, agencies of the national or the local government cannot be a plaintiff or a defendant. In addition, the conflict of jurisdiction between agencies of the government can and should be resolved within its own organization. In this respect, section 7 of the Cabinet Act provides that a "controversy over the conflict of jurisdiction between agencies of the national Government shall be ultimately resolved by the Prime Minister before the Cabinet Council." However, there are rare cases in which it is difficult to properly resolve the conflict in such a way. These cases are referred to a court for adjudication. For example, a case involving a controversy between the head of a local public entity and its assembly can ultimately be referred to the court (section 176, paragraph 7 of the Local Autonomy Act). Also, a minister of the national government can, after following certain specified procedures, file a suit against a prefectural governor seeking a ruling that the governor's failure to perform functions mandated by law is illegal (section 245-8, paragraph 3 of the Local Autonomy Act).

IV. *Minshu* Suit

404. There is a unique type of suit called a "resident's suit" (section 5 of the ACL Act) modeled after a taxpayer's suit in the United States. This suit is intended to prevent or correct an illegal expenditure of public money, or an illegal handling of financial affairs, by an agency or employee of a local public entity—not to protect an individual's legal right or interest (section 242-2 of the Local Autonomy Act). Accordingly, any citizen, so long as he or she is a registered resident of a prefecture, city, town or village involved, may file a suit seeking the local government's chief or other officials to bring actions for the return of illegally expended money or seeking the correction of mishandled financial affairs. In other words, a citizen can initiate a legal proceeding without proving that his or her concrete legal right has been infringed. The suite is limited only by the requirement that it follows an audit of the accounts in question by an auditor of the local government involved at the request of the citizen (section 242 of the Local Autonomy Act). Between 1983 and 1987, the number of resident suits filed at the prefectural level was 42, and 250 were filed at the city, town, and village levels. These figures have been steadily growing. For example, the number of cases filed between 1995 and 1999 was 261 at the prefectural level and 567 at the city, town and village level.

405. There is another type of suit, similar in nature to the abovementioned resident's suit, which is related to the validity of an election. According to the Public Offices Election Act, any voter can file a suit to challenge the validity of an election to public office which the plaintiff considers was illegally administered. To file such a suit, the voter need not have been a candidate in the challenged election (sections 203, 204, 207, 208, and 211). Such a suit is not designed to provide a direct remedy to the individual who has filed it and thus is not based on such a person's individual legal rights. Rather, the purpose of enabling a voter to sue is to ensure that an election to public office is lawfully and properly administered. All of the apportionment cases which have been decided by the Supreme Court of Japan fall into this category of action.

§3. Standing

406. Most of the administrative cases in Japan are *Kokoku* suits, and of these, most seek reversal of an administrative disposition. As section 9 of the ACL Act shows, the plaintiff of *Kokoku* suits must demonstrate standing to sue, arguing that a right, legal status, or legally protected individual interests are in danger because of the administrative dispositions which plaintiff attacks. In *Tojisha* suits, the plaintiff must also show a right to sue by asserting that the defendant's conduct endangers the plaintiff's rights or legally protected interests.

Both *Kikan* and *Minshu* suits are the types of proceedings in which the standing to sue is defined by specific statutes. The plaintiff must therefore show standing to sue under the relevant law.

407. It has often been the case that a person other than the addressee of the administrative disposition files a *Kokoku* suit. To what extent such a third party is allowed to be a plaintiff has been an important issue.

The Supreme Court has affirmed the standing of third parties as plaintiffs in cases where administrative dispositions endanger their legally protected interests. For example, the Supreme Court affirmed the plaintiffs' standing to sue as long as there was a risk of actual damage to nearby residents who claimed that the permission to construct nuclear reactors was illegal (46 *Minshu* 571, Sup. Ct., September 22, 1992). The Court also held that nearby residents had standing to sue, who claimed that the license for scheduled air routes was illegal because the airport noise was too severe (43 *Minshu* 56, Sup. Ct., February 17, 1989).

In the case of the plaintiffs who lived near the development permission area under the Forest Act, the Supreme Court affirmed the plaintiffs' standing to sue for the revocation of the permission as long as the plaintiffs had a risk of being harmed by the development activity (55 *Minshu* 283, Sup. Ct., March 13, 2001). Using the same logic, the Court affirmed the plaintiff's standing to sue for setting aside permits obtained by the owner of a high-rise building (56 *Minshu* 46, Sup. Ct., January 22, 2002).

The 2004 revision added a new provision to section 9 of the ACL Act, which summarizes the essence of the abovementioned Supreme Court opinions. The Court continues to use the same logic to determine the plaintiffs' standing to sue. In a case in which the residents near the railway brought a *Kokoku* suit to set aside the project approval for the multilevel crossing of the railway based on the City Planning Act, the Supreme Court affirmed the residents' standing to sue (59 *Minshu* 2645, Sup. Ct., December 7, 2005).

408. It must be noted that the time limit within which a *Kokoku* suit must be filed is much shorter than that for any other suit. A plaintiff must initiate the proceedings within the shorter of:

(1) six months from the day he or she acquires knowledge that the disposition challenged was made unless there is a just reason to excuse the delay (section 14, paragraph 1 of the ACL Act); or
(2) one year from the day when the disposition or adjudication was made, regardless of lack of knowledge, unless there is a just reason to excuse the delay.

Furthermore, some statutes, such as the National Civil Service Act, the Local Civil Service Act and the Building Standards Act, make filing a formal complaint with a designated administrative organ a prerequisite to bringing an action to the court. In such cases, a suit that has been filed without first resorting to the administrative proceedings must be dismissed.

§4. PROVISIONAL REMEDIES

409. It usually takes a long time before a decision in a suit is rendered. Moreover, even if a plaintiff wins the case, there is a strong possibility that it may be difficult or impossible for the plaintiff to exercise the right for which he or she has filed a suit. The Civil Preservation Act provides for a temporary remedy called the provisional disposition (section 23), which is designed to enable a plaintiff to exercise his or her right before winning the case.

410. Under the ACL Act, however, the provisional disposition as provided for in the Civil Preservation Act is not applicable to dispositions of governmental agencies nor does it apply to other acts involving the exercise of governmental authority (section 44). In addition, the initiation of a suit seeking reversal of an administrative disposition or adjudication upon appeal does not automatically suspend the validity of the disposition or adjudication challenged (section 25, paragraph 1). (This is to prevent the governmental administration from being disrupted by the filing of many administrative cases.) Instead, the ACL Act permits the court, in certain cases, to order the temporary suspension of a disposition (section 25, paragraphs 2 and 3). According to section 25, paragraph 2 of the Act, when a suit to seek reversal of a disposition has been filed, the court can in whole or in part suspend the validity or the execution of a disposition. In addition, the court may suspend the continuation of a proceeding if there is an urgent necessity to do so in order to prevent an irreparable injury stemming from the procedure or disposition. The validity of a disposition cannot be suspended if the threatened irreparable injury can be prevented by suspending the execution of an administrative disposition or the continuation of the proceeding (Proviso of section 25, paragraph 2). Section 25 of the ACL Act which provides for such temporary suspension is also applicable to a *Kokoku* suit seeking affirmation of the invalidity of a disposition (section 38).

411. The court may not grant temporary suspension when there is a fear that such suspension may seriously adversely affect the public welfare or when there is no basis on which to support the merit of the suit (section 25, paragraph 3). This limitation is attributed to the public nature of an administrative disposition.

§5. Prime Minister's Objection to the Temporary Suspension

412. There is a unique and controversial system called the "Prime Minister's objection," which has rarely been used by the Executive to restrain the court's power to suspend the validity of an administrative disposition. When an interested party has applied to the court for a provisional remedy, the Prime Minister may raise an objection to such provisional remedy stating the reasons why and showing the circumstances under which the public welfare might be seriously affected if the remedy is granted (section 27, paragraphs 1, 2 and 3). In that case, the court cannot issue a provisional remedy or, if one has already been issued, the court must cancel such provisional remedy (section 27, paragraph 4). Such a system which empowers the head of the executive branch to thwart a provisional remedy issued by the judicial branch is apparently extraordinary and unprecedented in the experience of other democracies. When this system was adopted in the old Special Act for Administrative Case Litigation of 1947, there was much criticism voiced against it on the grounds that (1) such a system impedes judicial power, infringing on the people's right of access to the court (Article 32 of the Constitution); (2) it confers absolute power on one side in a case, which contradicts the principle that parties to a suit must be basically on an equal footing; and (3) it constitutes an impairment of judicial independence (Article 76, paragraph 2 of the Constitution) by the executive branch, thus violating the constitutional doctrine of separation of powers. The government's view is that because a provisional remedy is a temporary measure taken before the court decides on the merits of a suit, the grant of provisional relief is executive in nature, rather than judicial, and accordingly, the restraint on the court's power to give provisional relief by the Prime Minister's objection does not violate any constitutional provisions.

413. Although the majority of constitutional and administrative law scholars in Japan were skeptical as to the constitutionality of this system, it was retained in the ACL Act which superseded the Special Act for Administrative Case Litigation in 1962. In order to prevent an abuse of power, the new law obligates the Prime Minister who has raised an objection to show the reasons for the objection (section 27, paragraph 6). This reporting is designed to make the Prime Minister who has unjustly used the objection politically accountable.

The Diet justified the adoption of such a problematic system out of fear of the allegedly frequent misuse of their provisional remedy power by lower courts. The Prime Minister's objection was resorted to on grounds of public safety six times during a period of two and half years from 1967 when the Prime Minister overrode a provisional remedy granted by a lower court (18 *Gyoshu* 737, Tokyo Dist. Ct., July 9 and 10, 1967) for the first time under the existing law. However, there has not been a single case in which the objection was raised following this period.

§6. Public Interest and Circumstance Decision

414. There is also a very unique system for resolving an administrative case in Japan. Section 31, paragraph 1 of the ACL Act provides that even if an administrative disposition is found defective, the court may choose not to reverse and invalidate such disposition in a case where it is deemed gravely harmful to the public to order invalidation. Such determination may be made in the light of such elements as "the degree of damage a plaintiff suffers, the method of reparations to be taken, prevention of further damage, and all other circumstances." While refusing invalidation, the court must instead declare in the text of the judgment that the administrative disposition at issue is illegal, so that the plaintiff may later file a separate suit and win monetary damages rather than invalidation of the disposition. Such a decision is called a "circumstance decision," and its constitutionality was affirmed by the Supreme Court (12 *Minshu* 1847, Sup. Ct., July 25, 1958).

415. The Supreme Court also used this technique in two reapportionment cases: *Kurokawa v. Chiba Prefecture Election Commission* (30 *Minshu* 223, Sup. Ct., G.B., April 14, 1976) and *Kanao v. Hiroshima Prefecture Election Commission* (39 *Minshu* 1100, Sup. Ct., G.B., July 17, 1985). The Court held in these cases that although the election at issue was based on unconstitutional apportionment rules and was therefore invalid, the petition for invalidation of the election could not be granted in light of the general principles of law found in section 31 of the ACL Act which authorizes the court to preserve defective administrative acts as valid if it finds that grave harm to the public interest would result if the act were invalidated (*supra* paragraph 159).

§7. Administrative Guidance and Judicial Control

416. It is widely known that government agencies in Japan, whether following the law or acting without a legal basis, frequently resort to so-called administrative guidance to achieve a governmental purpose. There are various kinds of administrative guidance, such as advice on agricultural planting, business consultation, counsel for children's health, tax consultation, and so on. In the early 1960s, government agencies, though they had no statutory basis for doing so, often tried to regulate business activities employing administrative guidance. Administrative guidance, which includes advice, counsel and persuasion by a government official, does not have legally binding force. Therefore, it is considered not to fall within the term "disposition," and thus is not subject to judicial control. This means that even if a person or entity has suffered a loss due to administrative guidance, there is no judicial remedy available. Nonetheless, courts occasionally give damages for a loss that has been brought on as a result of having followed erroneous or improper administrative guidance. For example, the Morioka District Court ordered the national government to pay damages to a group of farmers who had suffered a loss because they followed the advice of the director of a taxation office (6 *Kaminshu* 1993, Morioka Dist. Ct., September 13, 1955).

417. As administrative guidance is not binding, no one is legally bound to follow it. However, in a country like Japan where the executive branch has traditionally been powerful, it is psychologically difficult for ordinary citizens to refuse to obey administrative guidance, especially when it is reasonable and supported by public opinion. The *Shinagawa Building Permit Withholding* case (39 *Minshu* 989, Sup. Ct., July 16, 1985), is the best-known case here, one in which the Supreme Court gave damages to a construction company for a loss caused by compliance, after objection, with administrative guidance.

A construction company in Shinagawa, Tokyo, applied to the Director of Buildings of the Metropolitan Government for a permit to build an apartment. People living in the neighborhood strongly protested the construction on the ground that the planned building would impede sunlight and cause the wind to increase. As a result, even though the plan satisfied the requirements of the Building Standard Act, the city authorities withheld the issuance of the permit and persuaded both sides to consult together and reach a settlement. Eventually, a settlement was concluded, and the building permit was granted. However, as a result of the so-called oil shock, the price of construction materials had increased sharply during the period of delay caused by the refusal to issue the permit, and the construction company suffered a heavy economic loss. The company filed suit in the District Court against the Metropolitan Government claiming damages for the loss caused by the Director of Buildings' inaction.

The District Court ruled against the company on the grounds that the officials of the government had been performing their duties in good faith and the loss which the company suffered had been caused by socioeconomic factors beyond the officials' control. The case was appealed to the High Court, which upheld the company's claim, holding that unless there was a special reason for warranting it, administrative guidance was in principle impermissible and therefore illegal after the company had expressed its will to decline to comply with the officials' guidance. Sustained by the Supreme Court, this view has been the case law as to administrative guidance.

418. In order to prevent government agencies from using administrative guidance illegally or improperly, the Administrative Procedure Act (enacted in 1993 and enforced in 1994) contains several provisions regulating the use of administrative guidance. First, the Act provides that those who engage in administrative guidance must take care that their actions do not exceed the limit of their authority, and, assures that the purpose of the administrative guidance is realized by the truly voluntary cooperation of the parties concerned. The Act requires that those giving guidance must not adversely treat parties who refuse to comply with the guidance (section 32, paragraph 1). Second, the Act prohibits governmental agencies responsible for granting governmental licenses or permits from forcing applicants to obey its guidance by intentionally suggesting to those who apply for such license or permit that they have the power to limit such license or permit (section 34). And, third, the Act obligates those who engage in administrative guidance to clearly show to the parties concerned the gist and contents of the administrative guidance and to name the person in charge of such guidance, and to do so in writing if so demanded, unless such writing causes a special hindrance in the administration of the law (section 35, paragraphs 1 and 2).

Chapter 4. Legal Positions of Aliens

by Prof. Hiroyuki Hata with updates by Prof. Takehisa Nakagawa

§1. Constitutional Protection

419. Though the Constitution of Japan does not have any express provisions to guarantee rights and freedoms to foreigners, leading scholarly opinions and judicial precedents take the view that constitutional rights are, in principle, guaranteed to foreigners as well as to Japanese nationals. This view is taken in the light of the pre-State nature of human rights as well as the wording of paragraph 2 of the Preamble of the Japanese Constitution which states, "We recognize that all peoples of the world have the right to live in peace, free from fear and want." An example of this thinking is found in the Supreme Court's declaration in the *McLean* case (1978): "It should be understood that all rights and liberties guaranteed by the provisions of Chapter III of the Constitution, except for those deemed to be guaranteed only to Japanese nationals from the nature of the right, are equally applied to aliens staying in our country." (32 *Minshu* 1223, Sup. Ct., G.B., October 4, 1978.).

420. Those rights and freedoms which have been traditionally considered not available to foreign nationals include the right to vote, the right to civil service and such socioeconomic and property rights as the right to live a decent life, the right to free education, the right to work, the right to property, the right to engage in air and maritime shipping, and so on. However, this traditional interpretation has been changing as a result of the ratification of various international conventions granting such rights, such as the ICESCR and the ICCPR. (As to the details of this problem, *see supra* paragraphs 190–197 and 208–212.)

§2. Statutory Provisions Concerning the Settlement of Aliens

I. Act Concerning Immigration Control and the Recognition of Refugees

421. After the end of World War II, immigration control was placed under the direction of the Occupation authorities. In the early Occupation period, immigration work was mainly concerned with the homecoming of Japanese evacuees from abroad and the repatriation of Koreans and Chinese living in Japan to their respective countries. From around the spring of 1946, however, illegal entry into Japan from the Korean Peninsula began to increase rapidly in inverse proportion to the sharp decline in the number of those returning to Korea. In order to cope with this situation, and following a directive issued by the SCAP on May 2, 1947, an imperial order entitled "Alien Registration Order" was enacted. This order required aliens resident in Japan to regularly register with the immigration office and imposed criminal penalties on and eventual deportation of those who failed to comply with the requirement. On October 5, 1951, on the advice of the SCAP, a cabinet order entitled "Immigration Control Order," which is the predecessor of the Act on

Immigration Control and the Recognition of Refugees (AICRR) (1985), was enacted as the uniform legal basis for exercising immigration control.

422. On April 28, 1952, when the San Francisco Peace Treaty went into effect, both the Alien Registration Order and the Immigration Control Order were given the validity of statute law. Also, on the same day, a law entitled "Act Concerning the Measures for Orders Related to the Ministry of Foreign Affairs Based on Cases Concerning Orders Issued Following the Acceptance of the Potsdam Declaration" took effect. This Act provides for the legal status of those persons residing in Japan who were divested of Japanese nationality as a result of the conclusion of the San Francisco Peace Treaty. Japan's immigration control in the post-Occupation period has basically been exercised under these three statutes.

423. In 1965, however, as a result of the conclusion of the Agreement between Japan and the Republic of Korea on the Status and Treatment of Koreans Residing in Japan, a special statute to implement Japan's obligation under the treaty was enacted. Under this statute, citizens of the Republic of Korea who had been living in Japan since before the end of World War II were accorded permanent resident status. In 1991, this law was superseded by the Special Act on Immigration Control of Those Divested of Japanese Nationality Based on the Conclusion of the Peace Treaty with Japan (SAICTDJN) which accorded the special status as Special Permanent Resident to those Koreans and Taiwanese who came to Japan before the end of World War II. This special status was also granted to descendants born before the San Francisco Peace Treaty went into effect in 1952 (section 3). Under this law, Special Permanent Residents enjoy certain privileges in matters concerning deportation and reentry not available to resident aliens (sections 9 and 10).

424. In 1985, as a result of Japan's ratification of the Convention on the Status of Refugees and of the Protocol on the Status of Refugees, the AICRR came into being as the revised act on immigration control. This Act has provisions governing the entry into, residence in and deportation from Japan of aliens, including refugees. In this section, however, refugees will not be dealt with, for the admittance of refugees is a special case not dealt with as part of ordinary immigration control.

A. Entry into and Residence in Japanese Territory

425. Though aliens have no freedom of entry into Japan (*supra* paragraph 214), an alien who has met the following conditions is granted access to Japanese territory:

(1) possession of required documents, including a valid passport (section 3 of the AICRR);
(2) freedom from various physical or mental diseases designated by law;
(3) adequate means of support;
(4) lack of conviction of a crime (political crimes excepted) punishable by imprisonment of one year or more;

(5) not to have been found guilty of violating laws controlling narcotics, marijuana, stimulants and the like;
(6) not to possess a pipe to inhale opium;
(7) not to have engaged in businesses related to prostitution;
(8) not to illegally possess guns, swords or firepower;
(9) not to have been refused entry into or deported from Japan under certain provisions of the AICRR;
(10) not to plot or advocate to overthrow by force the Constitution of Japan or a government organized under it, or to organize or join an organization which plots or advocates such things;
(11) not to organize or join, or have close relation with, a political party or other organization which advocates to assassinate or use violence against public servants; destroy or damage public facilities; incite resort to strike or sabotage with the intent to obstruct the normal operation of safety facilities in factories;
(12) not to plot to make, distribute or display publications, films or other literature designed to propagate the aims of organizations mentioned in the preceding two items;
(13) not to be reasonably suspected, in the judgment of the Minister of Justice, of activities prejudicial to national interest or public order, etc. (section 5 of the AICRR).[36]

426. Unless otherwise stipulated in the AICRR and other statutes (section 2-2, paragraph 1), all aliens, except for Special Permanent Residents, personnel of the U.S. armed forces stationed in Japan, and such like, must, in order to reside in Japan, obtain from the Minister of Justice one of the statuses of residence provided for in Schedules I & II of the AICRR. Activities of nonnationals are restricted according to the respective status of residence obtained. The length of residence allowed to aliens (other than those for diplomats, designated government officials and Special Permanent Residents) cannot exceed five years (section 2-2, paragraph 3).

Nonnationals residing in Japan are required to always carry their passports or other designated documents and are required to show them at any time when asked by the competent officer so that the legality of their stay or activities can be immediately ascertained (section 23).

B. Deportation from Japanese Territory

427. The following foreigners are subject to deportation from Japanese territory (section 24):

36. Section 5 of the AICRR enumerates items 2 through 13. As of 2021, it also provides that the following persons shall not be admitted to Japan: a person who commits or assists human trafficking; a person who is likely to obstruct the smooth operation of an international competition to be held in Japan; and a person who has been sentenced to imprisonment for a crime in specific provisions of the Penal Code of Japan or other laws during his/her stay in Japan, who subsequently left Japan, whose sentence became final and binding when he or she was outside of Japan and for whom five years have not yet elapsed from the date when the conviction became final and binding.

(1) one who entered Japan without a valid passport or other required documents;
(2) one who engaged in gainful business or other remunerative activities without obtaining the required status;
(3) one who stays in Japan without having his/her period of stay renewed or changed;
(4) one who committed or assisted human trafficking or who was sentenced for the designated crimes;
(5) one who was found guilty of violating criminal and other laws controlling narcotics, marijuana, stimulants and the like;
(6) one who aside from the above items was convicted of a crime punishable by imprisonment of one year or more (suspended sentence excluded);
(7) one who engaged in businesses directly related to prostitution;
(8) one who incited, abetted or aided an alien to illegally enter Japan;
(9) one who plots or advocates the overthrow by force of the Constitution of Japan or a government organized under it, or who has organized or joined a political party or other organization which plots or advocates such activity;
(10) one who has organized or joined, or has a close relation with, a political party or other organization which advocates assassination or use of violence against public servants; destruction or damage to public facilities; or incites to resort to strike or sabotage with the intent to obstruct the normal operation of safety facilities in factories;
(11) one who has made, distributed or displayed publications, films or other literature designed to achieve the aims of organizations mentioned in the preceding two items;
(12) one who, in the judgment of the Minister of Justice, has engaged in activities prejudicial to national interest or public order, etc. (section 24).

428. Koreans and Taiwanese who have been living in Japan since before the end of World War II and their descendants enjoy special treatment in matters of deportation and reentry. Initially, under the old Special Act on Immigration Control Following the Enforcement of the Agreement Concluded between Japan and the Republic of Korea on the Status and Treatment of Koreans Residing in Japan, which was enacted in 1965, Korean residents could not be deported unless convicted of:

(1) a crime related to rebellion, foreign invasion and diplomatic relations punishable by imprisonment (section 6, paragraphs 1 and 2);
(2) a crime against foreign heads of State, foreign envoys or foreign diplomatic missions, the commission of which, in the judgment of the Minister of Justice, has impaired an important diplomatic interest of Japan (section 6, paragraph 3);
(3) a crime related to narcotics punishable by imprisonment of three years or more (section 6, paragraphs 4 and 5); or
(4) a crime (other than those mentioned above) punishable by imprisonment of seven years or more (suspended sentences excluded) (section 6, paragraph 6). (Other aliens were subject to deportation if convicted of a crime punishable by imprisonment of one year or more.).

429. The current statute on this issue is the SAICTDJN, which was enacted in 1991. It accords "persons who have lost Japanese nationality under the Treaty of Peace with Japan" and their children, as defined in section 1 of SAICTDJN, with a Special Permanent Resident status which entails more favorable treatment than other aliens in deportation and reentry matters (sections 20–23). For example, in the case that such Special Permanent Residents have been sentenced to lifetime imprisonment, imprisonment for more than seven years or more, or imprisonment without work for seven years or more, they can only be deported after the Minister of Justice has judged that their activities have impaired an important national interest of Japan (section 22).

430. Special Permanent Residents are also given preferential treatment in reentry (section 23). While the Minister of Justice sets the date of reentry for ordinary aliens within the five-year limit (section 26, paragraph 3 of the AICRR), he or she does so within a period of six years in the case of Special Permanent Residents (section 23 of the SAICTDJN). Also, in the case of ordinary aliens who, for an unavoidable reason, cannot reenter Japan by the designated date, the Minister of Justice can extend the date of reentry for a period not exceeding one year and within six years from the effective date of the permission (section 26, paragraph 5 of the AICRR). However, in a similar case involving a Special Permanent Resident, the Minister can extend the date of reentry for a period not exceeding one year and within seven years from the effective date of the permission (section 23 of the SAICTDJN).

II. Alien Registration Act

431. Under the Alien Registration Act, enacted in 1952 and repealed in 2012, all nonnationals who reside in Japan (except for refugees who enter with a refugee travel certificate) must, within ninety days from the date of entry, submit an alien registration application, a passport and two photographs to the heads of local self-governing bodies (cities, towns, etc.) where they reside (section 3). However, children who were born to foreign parents in Japan and aliens who lost Japanese nationality owing to the conclusion of the San Francisco Peace Treaty or for some other reasons are obligated to make such submission within sixty days from the date of their birth or from the date of having become an alien without entry procedures. Those heads of local governments who have accepted the abovementioned items from aliens must register the following matters in the original register of alien registration:

(1) registration number;
(2) date and year of registration;
(3) name;
(4) date and year of birth;
(5) gender;
(6) nationality;
(7) domicile or place of residence in home country;
(8) place of birth;

(9) occupation;
(10) passport number;
(11) date and year of issuance of passport;
(12) date and year of entry permission;
(13) status of residence;
(14) period of residence;
(15) place of residence;
(16) name of the head of household;
(17) family relationship with the head of household;
(18) (when the registering alien is head of the household) name, date and year of birth, nationality and family relationship with the head of a household of those who constitute the household;
(19) (when the registering alien is head of the household) name, date and year of birth and nationality of his/her parents and spouse residing in Japan; and
(20) name and address of office or place of employment (section 3, paragraph 1).

The original register of alien registration must be kept in the offices of local self-governing bodies.

After alien registration has been made in accordance with section 3, paragraph 1 of the Alien Registration Act, heads of local governments must issue an alien registration certificate describing the abovementioned items to aliens who apply for it (section 5, paragraph 1).

432. Under the Aliens Registration Act, nonnationals had their fingerprints taken until 2000. All aliens over 16 years of age (except for permanent residents, Special Permanent Residents, etc.) who are to reside in Japan for a year or longer must have a fingerprint taken at the time of registration (section 14, paragraph 1). The taking of fingerprints became a focus of controversy as many Japanese as well as aliens criticized it as an inhuman and degrading practice. There are some cases in which aliens refused to have their fingerprints taken and as a result application for a reentry permit was rejected. In these cases, the validity of fingerprinting was challenged on the basis of (1) Article 13 of the Constitution and Article 17, paragraph 1 of the ICCPR, which guarantees the right of privacy; (2) Article 14 of the Constitution and Article 2, paragraph 1 and Article 26 of the ICCPR, which provides for the principle of equality under the law; and (3) Article 7 of the ICCPR which prohibits inhuman and degrading treatment of human beings. The Japanese courts, however, rejected the contention that the taking of fingerprints was unconstitutional and violative of the provisions of the ICCPR. The courts held that, at the moment, there were no more objective and reasonable means to identify an individual and that such identification was indispensable for the registration system provided for in the Alien Registration Act.

433. In 1993, the amendment of the Alien Registration Act (section 14, paragraph 1) exempted Special Permanent Residents from the obligation to make an alien registration. Also, though other alien residents over 16 years of age who reside in Japan for more than a year must still register once with the head of a city or town where they reside, they are only required to have an index finger of their left hand fingerprinted with transparent ink (previously they had all their fingerprints taken with black ink).

434. The 1999 amendment to the Alien Registration Act finally abolished the whole fingerprinting system. However, following the terrorist attacks on the United States of America in September 2001, the AICRR was further amended in 2006 (which came into force in 2007). The amendment was to make it compulsory for foreign nationals entering Japan to provide fingerprints and a facial photograph except for Special Permanent Residents, those under the age of 16, and those invited by the government.

435. In 2009, the Diet decided to abolish the Alien Registration Act. It was part of the legislation to revise relevant statutes, including the AICRR, the SAICTDJN, and the Basic Resident Registration Act. In recent years, the number of foreign nationals residing in Japan has steadily increased. The need to improve convenience for foreign residents and streamline the administration of municipalities and other authorities has also increased, which was the background to revising the law.

The 2009 amendment introduced into the AICRR several new measures: (1) the "residence card" for foreign residents (effective from 2012); (2) the "special permanent resident certificate" for Special Permanent Residents (effective from 2012); and (3) the improved training and technical internship system (effective from 2010).

The abolition of the Alien Registration Act and the amendment of the Basic Resident Registration Act made foreign residents subject to the Basic Resident Registration System the same way as Japanese nationals. Except for short-term visitors such as tourists, foreign nationals who stay for more than three months and have a permanent address, such as mid-to-long-term residents (those eligible to receive residence cards) and Special Permanent Residents, are now subject to the Basic Resident Registration Act.

Before the amendment, foreign nationals and Japanese nationals that constituted the same household were not treated as such under the Alien Registration Act and the Basic Resident Registration Act. Thus the administrative services were provided separately. The new residence control system intends to overcome these inefficiencies.

III. Fugitive Extradition Act

436. According to the Fugitive Extradition Act, the extradition of criminal offenders to a foreign country must be based on the principle of reciprocity. The Minister of Foreign Affairs must forward all required documents to the Minister of Justice when the request for extradition has been made: (1) if it conforms to an extradition treaty which Japan has concluded with a requesting State; or (2) if there is an assurance by a requesting State to the effect that it will comply with Japan's request of the same kind (section 3).

There are some restrictions on the authority of the government to extradite a fugitive (section 2). The government is prohibited, unless otherwise provided for in an extradition treaty concluded with a foreign country, from extraditing an offender if:

(1) an extradition crime is a political offense;
(2) the request for extradition is found to have been made with a view to trying or executing a sentence given against a political offense;
(3) an extradition crime is not one punishable by death penalty or imprisonment of three years or more under the laws of the requesting State;
(4) an act which was committed in Japan and for which the request for extradition has been made is not one punishable by death penalty or imprisonment of three years or more under Japanese laws;
(5) an act for which the request for extradition has been made is found to be one which could not be penalized if it had been committed in Japan and tried in a Japanese court;
(6) there is no sufficient cause to suspect that an extradition offender has committed a crime for which the request of extradition has been made, except when the offender has already been convicted in a court of the requesting State;
(7) a case involving an extradition crime is pending, or has been finally decided, in a Japanese court;
(8) a case involving a crime other than an extradition offense which an extradition offender has committed is pending in a Japanese court, or the offender has been convicted of the crime and has not finished serving his or her time; or
(9) an extradition offender is a Japanese national.

437. The decision of extradition shall be made by the Tokyo High Court (section 10, paragraph 1). The Minister of Justice must order the chief public prosecutor of the Tokyo High Prosecution Office to transmit all required documents to the Tokyo High Court for decision unless there is a clear basis for refusal of extradition. Except in cases where there is no reason to fear that the offender may flee, the chief public prosecutor must then order an extradition offender detained under a warrant issued by a judge of the Tokyo High Court (section 4). The High Court must speedily review and decide whether to allow extradition. However, if the offender is detained with a warrant, the High Court must decide the matter within two months from the date of issuance of the warrant (section 9, paragraph 1). In extradition proceedings, the offender has the right to counsel and the High Court must also provide the offender with the opportunity to express his or her opinion (section 9, paragraphs 2 and 3).

Part V. Specific Problems

Chapter 1. War, Treaty, and Foreign Affairs Powers

by Prof. Hiroyuki Hata with updates by Prof. Takehisa Nakagawa

§1. National Defense

I. General

438. As stated in the Introduction (*supra* paragraphs 13–16), the Constitution of Japan specifically renounces both war and armed forces. Article 9 of the Constitution stipulates, "Aspiring sincerely to an international peace based on justice and order, the Japanese people forever renounce war as a sovereign right of the nation and the threat or use of force as means of settling international disputes" (paragraph 1) and "In order to accomplish the aim of the preceding paragraph, land, sea, and air forces, as well as other war potential, will never be maintained. The right of belligerency of the State will not be recognized" (paragraph 2). When the Constitution went into effect, it was considered that Article 9, paragraph 2 forever abandoned all armaments and war potential, whether for aggression or for self-defense. In fact, the Constitution of Japan does not contain any provisions for war powers such as are usually written into the constitutions of other countries.

439. In 1950, however, following the outbreak of the Korean War, the Japanese government, in accordance with the directive issued by General Douglas MacArthur, SCAP, established an armed force called the Police Reserve composed of 70,000 officers and men. Though a petition to challenge the constitutionality of laws and executive orders establishing the Police Reserve was immediately filed, it was rejected by the Supreme Court based on lack of standing (*supra* paragraph 155). The Police Reserve was later renamed and reorganized as Security Forces (Security Forces Act of 1952) and then as Self-Defense Forces (Self-Defense Forces Act and Defense Agency Establishment Act) as it grew in scale.

II. Self-Defense Forces

440. The Self-Defense Forces, established in June 1954 in place of the Security Forces, consists of ground, maritime and air forces. According to the "Defense of

Japan 2021," a white paper on Japan's national defense published by the Ministry of Defense, the ground force has approximately 151,000 authorized personnel, the maritime force 45,500, and the air force 47,00, as of July 13, 2021 (section 6 of the Defense Ministry Establishment Act).

Its main mission was to defend the country from direct and indirect aggression (section 3 of the Self-Defense Forces Act). Its activities include:

(1) defense mobilization (section 76);
(2) mobilization for the maintenance of public peace (section 78);
(3) operation for sea guard (section 82);
(4) action against the violation of territorial air space (section 84);
(5) mobilization for rescue and other activities in time of the earthquake and other natural disasters (section 83 & section 83-2), etc.

When mobilized for defense, the Self-Defense Forces can use necessary weapons to defend the country (section 88).

441. The constitutionality of the Self-Defense Forces was frequently challenged, but the courts either evaded considering it by narrowly construing a term used in the involved law (*Eniwa*, 9 *Kakeishu* 356, Sapporo Dist. Ct., March 29, 1967) or dismissed the suit resorting to the doctrine of political question (*Naganuma*, 27 *Gyoshu* 1175, Sapporo High Ct., August 5, 1976; *Hyakuri Base*, 842 *Hanji* 22, Mito Dist. Ct., February 17, 1977).

The government has taken the position that the Self-Defense Forces is constitutional on the grounds that it is subjectively organized for self-defense only and that objectively the scope of its activity is confined to the minimum necessary actions for self-defense. Accordingly, it was considered that sending units of the Self-Defense Forces overseas was prohibited because it exceeded the mission of the Self-Defense Forces which was limited to the defense of the country. In fact, when two defense laws (the Defense Agency Establishment Act and Self Defense Forces Act) were enacted in 1954, the House of Councillors passed a resolution against the dispatch of the Self-Defense Forces overseas, which virtually became Japan's national policy, restraining the Self-Defense Forces from being sent abroad.

442. In June 1992, however, a law entitled "Act concerning the Cooperation for United Nations Peace Keeping Operation, etc."(PKO Cooperation Act) was enacted so that Japan might make an international contribution to peacekeeping. This law opened the way for the government to send units of the Self-Defense Forces abroad for noncombat peacekeeping operations when asked by the United Nations. However, as there was strong opposition to the sending of the Self-Defense Forces overseas, the government inserted into the PKO Cooperation Act limiting provisions such as section 2, paragraph 2, which prohibits the peacekeeping activities of the Self-Defense Forces from becoming either a threat to use or the actual use of force, and section 24, which limits the use of weapons by individual members of the Self-Defense Forces engaged in peacekeeping operations strictly for self-defense only.

443. Discussion on national security legislation had long been a political taboo for many Diet members. Except for the Self-Defense Forces Act, there had been no such legislation for decades. This was so even though the Supreme Court held in 1959 that Article 9 of the Constitution "renounces war and prohibits the maintenance of so-called war power, which, however, obviously does not negate our inherent right of self-defense as a sovereign nation" (*Sunagawa*, 13 *Keishu* 3225, Sup. Ct., G.B., December 16, 1959).

However, after the end of the Cold War, the situation changed.

In the early 1990s, the tensions in East Asia (North Korea's shift to a nuclear armament policy and the threat of a military conflict in the Taiwan Strait) led the Japanese and U.S. governments to redefine the U.S.-Japan Security Treaty. They agreed to redefine the U.S.-Japan Security Treaty as a treaty not only for the defense of Japanese territory but also for maintaining peace in the Asia-Pacific region. As a result, in 1999, the Surrounding-Area Situations Act was enacted based on a bill introduced by the Obuchi Cabinet.

In 2003, the Koizumi Cabinet took the lead in having the Armed Attack Situations Act enacted, which stipulated the measures to be taken by the Self-Defense Forces in the event of an armed attack on Japanese territory, along with the Act Concerning the Protection of the People.

In 2007, the Defense Agency was elevated to the Ministry of Defense. The Diet amended its establishment act in response to a call from the first Abe Cabinet.

Furthermore, in 2015, the third Abe Cabinet pursued comprehensive security legislation by amending the relevant laws and enacting new laws as follows.

First, the Armed Attack Situations Act (originally enacted in 2003) was replaced by the Armed Attack Situations and Survival-Threatening Situations Act of 2015. The amendment created a new category of emergencies, called Survival-Threatening Situations.

An "Armed Attack Situation" is a situation in which Japan may constitutionally use force as an exercise of the so-called individual self-defense right, which the Japanese government has traditionally affirmed in its interpretation of Article 9 of the Constitution. However, a "Survival-Threatening Situation" is a situation in which Japan should use force as an exercise of "collective" self-defense right, which the previous official interpretation of the Japanese government had treated as constitutionally prohibited. In this regard, the Abe Cabinet changed the government's long-held Article 9 interpretation, which caused a very fierce debate inside and outside the Diet.

Second, the Surrounding-Area Situations Act (1999) was replaced by the Important Influence Situations Act. Section 1 of the new act defines an Important Influence Situation as "a situation which, if left unchecked, is likely to lead to a direct armed attack on Japan or other situation which has an important influence on the peace and security of Japan." These are situations in which armed force may not be used, but only logistical support by the Self-Defense Forces can be provided. The term "Surrounding-Area" refers to East Asia, such as the Korean Peninsula. The reason for changing "Surrounding-Area" to "Important Influence" is to remove geographical restrictions on the situations to be covered. Also, the scope of the logistical support is expanded to include other countries' forces other than the U.S. forces.

Third, until then, the Japanese government had allowed the Self-Defense Forces to provide logistical support to foreign troops on a case-by-case basis (such as the Special Measures Act for Iraqi Conflict Assistance during the Iraq War). The International Peace Support Act was introduced as a permanent law to change this practice. Section 1 of the Act defines a Joint International Peace Response Situation as "a situation that threatens the peace and security of the international community, in which the international community engages in joint activities following the objectives of the Charter of the United Nations to eliminate the threat, and to which Japan, as a member of the international community, must make a proactive and positive contribution."

Fourth, the 1992 International Peacekeeping Operations Act, which provides for cooperation in UN peacekeeping operations, was amended to expand the missions of the Self-Defense Forces.

In addition, the Self-Defense Forces Act was also amended to provide for measures to protect Japanese nationals overseas.

444. The Prime Minister, representing the Cabinet, has the highest command power over the Self-Defense Forces. The Minister of Defense superintends all units of the Self-Defense Force under the command of the Prime Minister. However, orders from the Minister of Defense to units of the Self-Defense Forces are issued to and carried out by the Chief of Staff of the ground force, maritime force or air force. Furthermore, the Minister's orders to units mobilized for defense or the maintenance of public peace, which are composed of two or more of the ground, maritime and air forces, are issued to and carried out by the chairperson of the Joint Chiefs of Staff.

III. Civilian Control

445. The idea of civilian control is to keep the military under the control of the civilian government. It is not too much to say that all Western democracies have adopted this system. Under the Meiji Constitution, however, the supreme commander of the Imperial Army and Navy was the Emperor, and both the Army and Navy were constitutionally under the direct command of the Emperor and, as far as their operation was concerned (Article 11) not subject to the control of the civilian government. In addition, the Minister of the Army was either a general or lieutenant general, while the Minister of the Navy was either an admiral or vice admiral. Both these Cabinet officers were military or naval officers on active duty (Ministerial Orders of Army and Navy). Accordingly, without the cooperation of the military, it was impossible to form a Cabinet. In addition, as they controlled the appointment of the Ministers, the military could act to bind the government. As a consequence, insofar as the movement and activity of the armed forces were concerned, the civilian government was powerless to act.

446. Unlike the Meiji Constitution, the present Constitution has no provisions whatsoever concerning the armed forces. On the contrary, Article 9, paragraph 2 of the Constitution expressly prohibits Japan from maintaining armed forces ("land, sea, and air forces, as well as other war potential"). Strangely enough, however, Article 66, paragraph 2 of the Constitution of Japan stipulates that "The Prime Minister and other Ministers of State shall be civilian." Views on the interpretation of this later provision are divided. The late ex-Prime Minister Hitoshi Ashida insisted that this provision had been placed in the Constitution in the expectation that armed forces for self-defense might be created in the future. The majority of scholars took the position that the provision was intended to bar all professional military and naval officers who had engaged in the prosecution of World War II from any portfolio in the Cabinet. In 1954, Prime Minister Ichiro Hatoyama of the Democratic Party (predecessor of the LDP) failed to appoint Kichisaburo Nomura (an ex-admiral of the Japanese Imperial Navy and Ambassador to the United States at the time of the Japanese attack on Pearl Harbor) as a Minister of State (concurrently Chief of the Defense Agency) because of Socialist and Communist Party opposition based on Article 66, paragraph 2. However, the significance of such an interpretation of the clause has almost disappeared as a result of the passage of time, for those officers who served in the Japanese Imperial Army or Navy have gradually aged and faded from the political scene.

447. In spite of Article 9, paragraph 2, Japan has a self-defense force which has grown out of the Police Reserve created in accordance with General MacArthur's directive issued in 1950 when the Korean War broke out. Although a considerable number of people still insist that the existence of the Self-Defense Forces is unconstitutional, the government takes the position that they are indeed constitutional insofar as those units remain a minimum necessary force for self-defense. The constitutionality of the Self-Defense Forces has never been squarely reviewed by the Supreme Court. However, now that the Self-Defense Forces exists based on such laws as the Defense Agency (now the Ministry of Defense) Establishment Act and Self-Defense Forces Act, the civilian requirement clause may well have significant meaning.

448. The basic mechanism of civilian control over defense matters under the Japanese legal system is as follows:

(a) The Prime Minister who is head of the Cabinet is also the supreme commander of the Self-Defense Forces and must be a civilian (Article 66, paragraph 2 of the Constitution). The Prime Minister is chosen by the elected members of the Diet, representatives of the people (Article 67), and the Cabinet which the Prime Minister heads is collectively responsible to the Diet (Article 66, paragraph 3) and must resign en bloc when the House of Representatives passes a vote of no-confidence against the government (Article 69).
(b) The Minister of Defense must be a civilian (Article 66, paragraph 2 of the Constitution; section 3 of the Defense Agency Establishment Act).
(c) The Chiefs of Staff and other officers in certain responsible posts of land, sea and air forces (in uniform) are subject to the control and command of the Prime Minister and the then Minister of Defense, both of whom are civilians (sections 7 and 8 of the Self-Defense Forces Act).

(d) The Prime Minister must consult with the National Security Council in deciding the basic policy of national defense, the outline of defense plans and other important matters concerning national defense (section 2 of the National Security Council Establishment Act).
(e) The personnel, organization, budget, etc., of the Self-Defense Forces cannot be determined without the consent of the Diet. Also, the mobilization of the Self-Defense Forces for defense or maintenance of internal order needs the prior or, depending on circumstances, subsequent consent of the Diet (sections 76 & 78 of the Self-Defense Forces Act).
(f) Members of the Self-Defense Forces who have their rights infringed are entitled to a trial by an ordinary court. Article 76, paragraph 2 of the Constitution prohibits the establishment of special tribunals such as the courts-martial of prewar days.

§2. Foreign Affairs

I. General

449. Under the Constitution of Japan, the management of foreign affairs is in the hands of the Cabinet (Article 73, No. 2). Generally, relations with foreign countries are dealt with in the form of concluding treaties and executive agreements. A treaty is a documented contract between nations, and a mere political declaration or a contract based on private law is not included in treaties. Also, an executive agreement is an international arrangement between heads of nations to carry out a treaty or is made under the mandate of a treaty. The details concerning treaties and executive agreements are as follows.

II. Conclusion of a Treaty

450. The Constitution vests the power to conclude a treaty in the Cabinet (Article 73, No. 3). However, since a treaty not only binds the State but also directly or indirectly imposes obligations on its people or restricts their rights, the approval of the Diet is required for its conclusion. The proviso of Article 73, No. 3 of the Constitution states, "it shall obtain prior or, depending on circumstances, subsequent approval of the Diet." This provision is intended to place the conclusion of a treaty, one of the most important executive functions, under the control of the Diet. This is in striking contrast with the Meiji Constitution under which the conclusion of a treaty was among the Emperor's prerogatives (Article 13) and therefore out of the Diet's control.

The process of concluding a treaty consists of negotiation and ratification. While negotiation is an act by which the plenipotentiary of a country confers with the representative of another country to determine the contents of a treaty which both countries are going to conclude, ratification is an act to confirm the will of a State to accept a treaty which has been signed and sealed by its plenipotentiary. It is ratification that constitutionally needs to be approved by the Diet.

III. Validity of a Treaty

451. Though the Constitution requires that a treaty be approved by the Diet, scholars are divided as to whether a treaty which has been ratified by the Cabinet but has failed to obtain the Diet's approval is valid. One theory insists that a treaty which has been ratified by the Cabinet lawfully takes effect even if it has not obtained the Diet's approval. According to this theory, the Diet's rejection of a treaty does not influence the validity of the treaty but only calls the Cabinet to account for its failure to obtain the approval. On the contrary, the other theory takes the stand that a treaty, the ratification of which has been rejected by the Diet, is invalid.

According to the former, a treaty which has been signed and sealed comes into being once ratified by the Cabinet, even if it has not obtained the Diet's approval. If this view is followed, there is the possibility that an absurd case, such as that in which the Cabinet ratifies a treaty rejected by the Diet, may arise. But such a case is inconsistent with the constitutional requirement that a treaty, in principle, obtains the prior approval of the Diet. Though Article 98, paragraph 2 of the Constitution requires that treaties concluded by Japan be faithfully observed, it is unthinkable that this provision seeks the observance of a treaty rejected by the Diet. Needless to say, the "treaties concluded by Japan" must be those concluded by the Cabinet with the approval of the Diet. In this sense, the latter theory which insists that a treaty rejected by the Diet is invalid is persuasive, and the majority of scholars in Japan take this view.

452. Of the treaties concluded by Japan, some directly impose obligations on people or restrict their rights, as domestic law. Such treaties take effect as domestic law when they are promulgated by the Emperor (Article 7, No. 1).

Finally, there is the problem of whether the Diet can modify the contents of a treaty submitted for approval. Unlike a law or a budget, a treaty is concluded in consultation with another country. Judging from the nature of a treaty, even if the Diet modified a treaty, such modification does not have an effect other than to obligate the Cabinet to renegotiate with the other party along the modified lines. In this sense, the Diet's decision should be rendered either in the form of approval or rejection, and modification by the Diet has the same effect as the rejection of the treaty.

IV. Conclusion of an Executive Agreement

453. As mentioned above (*supra* paragraph 444), an executive agreement is not a treaty and therefore does not need the Diet's approval. However, an agreement, the contents of which are so comprehensive as to allow the government to arbitrarily restrict people's rights because of the blanket mandate of authority by a treaty, is no longer an executive agreement but is considered a treaty which needs to be approved by the Diet.

When the old Japan-U.S. Security Treaty was concluded following the end of the United States occupation of Japan, the Japanese government concluded an executive agreement on areas, facilities and the status of U.S. troops based on section 3 of the treaty. The provision stipulated, "A treaty to govern the deployment of United

States forces in Japan and its vicinity shall be decided by an executive agreement between both Governments." The opposition parties asserted that the executive agreement had to be approved by the Diet on the grounds that this mandate by the treaty was a blanket delegation of authority to the Cabinet. However, the Diet subsequently sanctioned the Cabinet's attitude which was that the conclusion of the agreement was a legitimate exercise of Cabinet authority under the mandate of the treaty.

The present executive agreement, which was concluded based on section 6 of the Japan-U.S. Security Treaty of 1960, was referred to the Diet for approval. This was because there was strong criticism among the Japanese people that the agreement was, in light of its contents, a treaty in substance.

Chapter 2. Emergency Laws

by Prof. Hiroyuki Hata with updates by Prof. Takehisa Nakagawa

§1. Government Emergency Power

454. The Meiji Constitution had two provisions concerning government emergency powers, namely, Article 8 (executive emergency legislation) and Article 14 (state of siege). Under these articles, the Emperor (the government) was empowered:

(1) to enact ordinances with the force of law if necessary to preserve public safety and order when a national crisis occurred while the Diet was closed; and
(2) to declare a state of siege to suspend all or part of civil rights and liberties if deemed necessary.

The Meiji Constitution further stipulated that the provisions guaranteeing constitutional rights and liberties in no way prevented the Emperor from exercising its prerogatives in times of war or national exigency (Article 31).

455. Unlike the Meiji Constitution, the present Constitution does not have such provisions. There has been a controversy as to the reason why the Constitution lacks emergency provisions. Some scholars insist that the lack of emergency provisions is one of the defects of the Constitution and that such provisions should be added to the Constitution so that the government can cope with national emergencies. On the contrary, the majority of scholars take the stand that the makers of the Constitution intentionally deleted emergency provisions lest they should be abused as in prewar days. There is also a scholarly dispute with respect to whether, under the present Constitution, the government can take necessary measures to deal with a national crisis arising while the Diet is closed. Scholars' views on this point are sharply divided. However, the number of scholars who take the pragmatic view that the present Constitution allows the government to take minimum necessary steps to protect life, body and property from impending danger without statutory basis, subject to parliamentary and judicial control, has been increasing.

§2. Measures to Cope with Grave National Emergencies

456. There are some statutes concerning how to deal with national security emergencies which threaten the independence, safety and public order of the State. The National Security Council is established in the Cabinet as a body to deliberate on important matters concerning the security of the country. Armed attack situations and surrounding-area situations (paragraph 438) are among the topics to be deliberated by the Council. The Council is chaired by the Prime Minister and consists of other Ministers, including the Foreign Minister, Finance Minister, Defense Minister, and Cabinet Secretary-General (sections 1–5 of the National Security Council Establishment Act).

457. Section 76, paragraph 1 of the Self-Defense Forces Act stipulates that the Prime Minister, who is Supreme Commander of the Self-Defense Forces (section 7 of the Act), can mobilize all or part of the forces when deemed necessary to defend the country against armed attacks from abroad, with the consent of the Diet according to the Armed Attack Situations and Survival-Threatening Situations Act of 2015 (paragraph 438).

458. The Self-Defense Forces Act also provides for procedures to dispatch the Self-Defense Forces to disaster sites. First, section 83 of the Act provides that, in the event of a natural disaster or other calamities, the prefectural governor may request the Minister of Defense to send the Self-Defense forces when the governor considers it necessary for the protection of human life or property. Second, the Act authorizes in section 83-2 the Minister of Defense to dispatch the Self-Defense Forces to provide support when requested by the head of the Earthquake Disaster Warning Headquarters as prescribed in the Act on Special Measures Concerning Large-Scale Earthquake Countermeasures. The third category is a nuclear disaster. Section 83-3 of the Act provides that the Minister of Defense may provide the Self-Defense Forces' support to the disaster site when the Minister receives a request from the Director-General of the Nuclear Emergency Response Headquarters under the Act on Special Measures Concerning Nuclear Emergency Preparedness.

459. As mentioned above, although the Self-Defense Forces are empowered to take necessary measures to carry out its mission in case of emergencies, its powers must, in principle, be exercised within the limits of existing laws, such as the Gunpowder Control Act, Aviation Act, Shipping Act, Electric Wave Act, Road Transportation Act, Firearms and Swords Act, etc. Conservative politicians, as well as some businesspeople, scholars, etc., assert that it is necessary to enact a special law that makes it possible for the Self-Defense Forces to more effectively fulfill duties to repel foreign aggression or suppress internal disorder. However, there is strong popular sentiment against according more powers to the Self-Defense Forces.

Chapter 3. Taxing Power and Spending Power

by Prof. Hiroyuki Hata with updates by Prof. Takehisa Nakagawa

§1. DEMOCRATIC CONTROL OF PUBLIC FINANCE

460. There is no denying that the principle of "No representation, no taxation," which was derived from the Magna Carta of 1215 and was established by De Tallagio non Concendo (1295), the Petition of Right (1628), the Bill of Rights (1689), etc., occupies a central position among all principles of modern constitutionalism. This principle, which requires the consent of the people through their elected representatives in Parliament before taxes may be taken from the people, is a most important constitutional rule not only in the area of taxation but also in the whole field of public finance. In Japan, this concept is usually called the "public finance democracy" or "public finance constitutionalism."

461. The Meiji Constitution provided for the control of public finance by the Diet. This control was based on such articles as Article 62 (stipulating the requirement of the legality of taxation), Article 64 (vesting the Diet with the power to deliberate on a budget), Article 72 (vesting the Diet with the power to deliberate on a settlement of accounts), etc. However, the Diet's control was not absolute as there were some exceptions, such as Article 66 (stipulating the financial autonomy of the Imperial Household), Article 67 (prohibiting the Diet from rejecting or reducing certain expenditures without the concurrence of the government), Article 70 (authorizing the government to take necessary financial measures in time of national crisis when the Diet cannot be convened), Article 71 (permitting the government to carry out the budget of the preceding year when a new budget had not been brought into existence), etc.

462. Unlike the Meiji Constitution, the present Constitution of Japan (which is based on the theory of popular sovereignty) does not contain the undemocratic clauses mentioned above. Instead, the present Constitution takes a thoroughly democratic stance as to the operation of the State's public finance. In this regard, the Constitution of Japan stipulates, "The power to administer national finances shall be exercised as the Diet shall determine" (Article 83). "National finance" may be defined as a national act to acquire, manage and/or utilize funds which the State or a local public entity needs to carry out its functions. Since such an act may have a great impact on the people's economic life, the Constitution requires that the operation of public finance be subjected to the control of the Diet.

§2. TAXING POWER

I. General

463. Needless to say, no government, whether national or local, can exist without the power to raise money. The Constitution of Japan authorizes the State and local public entities to raise money based on the law or under such conditions as the law may stipulate. The taxing power, as well as the power to spend, is governed by constitutional and statutory rules.

In Japan, a tax is defined as money that a State or local public entity forcibly collects from the people without compensation and which is appropriated for its general expenses. Although there are various kinds of revenue which may be raised by a State or local public entity, the main revenue source is taxes.

When viewed in terms of the authority to tax, there are two kinds of taxes in Japan:

(1) national taxes imposed by the national government which are based on individual laws; and
(2) local taxes by prefectural and municipal governments, which are based on the Local Tax Act (the term "municipal governments" used here means governments of a city, town or village).

The national taxes consist of approximately twenty different taxes while there are approximately thirty different forms of local taxes.

464. The most important taxes presently imposed in Japan at the national level are individual income tax (Income Tax Act), corporation tax (Corporation Tax Act) and consumption tax (Consumption Tax Act enacted in 1988). At the prefectural level, the most significant taxes are a business tax and a prefectural inhabitant tax. A municipal inhabitant tax and property tax are the most significant taxes at the municipal level. This present tax system of Japan retains the essential elements of the Shoup Report, a report on Japanese taxation submitted in September 1949 by a mission headed by Dr. Carl S. Shoup, which recommended: (a) the reduction of indirect taxes and the increase of the percentage of direct taxes, especially an income tax, as the core of Japan's taxes, to secure a more equitable financial burden for citizens; and (b) the creation of an independent tax for local governments in order to strengthen their financial capability.

Table 1 Percentage of National & Local Tax Revenues Raised by Main Categories of National, Prefectural & Municipal Taxes[1]

		1950	*1965*	*1995*	*2000*
National Taxes (100%)	Income Tax	38.6%	29.6%	37.6%	36.9%
	Corporation Tax	14.7%	28.3%	24.2%	19.6%
	Consumption Tax	0%	0%	13.2%	19.5%

		1950	*1965*	*1995*	*2000*
	(adopted in 1989)				
Prefectural Taxes (100%)	Prefectural Inhabitant Tax (adopted in 1954)	0%	22.5%	36.1%	28.1%
	Business Tax	54.7%	42.2%	34.8%	25.5%
Municipal Taxes (100%)	Municipal Inhabitant Tax	39.2%	39.7%	44.4%	40.0%
	Property Tax	40.1%	36.1%	42.7%	45.9%

1. Quoted from the 1975, 1995 and 2000 editions of the *Zeisei Sanko Shiryo* (Reference Materials of Tax System) published by the *Nihon Sozei Kyokai* (Japan Tax Research Society).

II. Imposition of Taxes

465. In prewar days, national taxes were, in principle, imposed by the taxation office without any taxpayers' declaration. At present, however, such taxes are usually assessed following a taxpayers' report (namely, by the self-assessment system), unless otherwise stipulated. Individuals who have received an income must, in principle, file their income tax returns with a taxation office between February 16 and March 15 of the following year (section 120, paragraph 1 of the Income Tax Act). Domestic corporations must similarly declare their income earned during an accounting period with a taxation office within two months from the day following the end of the period (section 74, paragraph 1 of the Corporation Tax Act). However, if the accounting period exceeds six months, corporations must make a mid-period declaration within two months from the day following the passage of six months after the start of the accounting period (section 71).

Local taxes such as individual business tax, property tax, individual inhabitant tax, real property acquisition tax, etc., are generally imposed by the tax authorities without a taxpayer's declaration, although there are some exceptions to this general rule.

III. Constitutional and Statutory Principles

A. Principle of Legality

466. The Constitution of Japan has two provisions concerning taxation. Article 30 of the Constitution stipulates, "The people shall be liable to taxation as provided by law." Article 84 states, "No new taxes shall be imposed or existing ones modified except by law or under such conditions as law may describe." These provisions, the Japanese version of the English maxim of "No representation, no taxation" derived from the Magna Carta, are intended to express a principle that the imposition of taxes must be based upon a law enacted by the Diet. Although the Constitution does not have express provisions directly vesting the government with the power to tax, in light of those provisions there is no dispute that the national government has the power to tax. The problem is whether the local governments can constitutionally levy a tax without a statutory basis. Many scholars insist that the concept of "local autonomy" includes the local government's authority to tax. In any event, a statute entitled the Local Tax Act confers on local governments the power to tax within stipulated limits. Accordingly, there is no practical need to discuss the question of whether the power of local governments to tax is implied by "local autonomy."

The abovementioned constitutional requirement of the legality of taxation (which requires that the subject of taxation, tax rate, tax base, method of taxation, way to collect taxes, etc., be stipulated by law) is designed to provide predictability and thus guarantee the security of property.

467. A problem exists as to the scope of the term "tax" which must be stipulated by law. Article 62 of the Meiji Constitution provided, "The imposition of a new tax or the modification of the rates (of an existing one) shall be determined by law" (paragraph 1). However, it also stipulated, that "all administrative fees or other revenue having the nature of compensation should not fall within the category of the above clause" (paragraph 2). Thus, the term "tax" was construed narrowly, excepting administrative fees and other revenues. Although the Constitution of Japan does not have any provisions construing the term "tax," the Public Finance Act stipulates that a surcharge which has the same nature as a tax, the price of a government monopoly and a rate for service provided by a public enterprise must be determined by law or by a resolution of the Diet (section 3).

Although the Constitution states that the imposition of a new tax and the modification of an existing one must be determined by "law" or under such conditions as "law" may describe (Article 84), does this "law" have to be literally a statute enacted by the Diet? For example, section 3, paragraph 1 of the Local Tax Act allows for the determination of such matters as the items of local tax, the objects of taxation, the basis of assessment, tax rates, etc., by a prefectural or municipal ordinance. This is deemed not to violate the constitutional requirement of legality because of the doctrine of delegation. Action by local ordinance comes within the sphere of the law that contains general standards premised on the principle of local autonomy.

468. Also, although section 3 of the Customs Act stipulates that imported goods must be taxed based on law, there is an exception for customs duties prescribed in a treaty. It is understood that this exception does not violate the constitutional requirement of legality because a treaty is concluded with the consent of the Diet and also because customs duties have a special nature as compared to other kinds of taxes. In addition, the Customs Tariff Act delegates the increase and decrease of duties and certain other matters to a government order. This, too, is deemed constitutional because of the special nature of customs duties, although the general delegation of such matters to a government order is not constitutionally admissible.

B. Principle of Equality

469. The equality under the law provided for in Article 14 of the Constitution is applied to taxation. Differential treatment in taxation of those situated in the same position from the standpoint of taxation violates the principle of equality under the law. There are several Supreme Court decisions concerning the principle of equality in taxation. For example, in a case where an employer alleged that section 38 of the old Income Tax Act, which obligates employers to withhold at the source part of a wage earner's income as an income tax, violated the requirement of equality in taxation because business owners were not subject to a similar withholding plan, the Supreme Court held that:

(1) now that all taxes should be collected by the most efficient and rational means, it is natural that the most appropriate way of collecting taxes, time for paying them, etc., should be determined, respectively, depending upon the kind and form of each income, and it cannot be deemed to violate Article 14 of the Constitution even if a wage earner is differentially treated in tax collection from a business proprietor because of the system of withholding a tax at the source; and that
(2) although the Income Tax Act designates a wage payer (employer) as an income tax collector at the source, imposing on him or her a special obligation different from that which ordinary people have, in light of the facts that the wage payer has a specially close relationship with those who receive a wage and that he or she is in a particularly convenient position able to efficiently collect an income tax, it cannot be said to violate Article 14 of the Constitution now that this obligation derives from the constitutional provision, meets with the demand of public welfare, and is based on a reasonable ground (16 *Keishu* 213, Sup. Ct., G.B., February 28, 1962).

C. Principle of a Standing Tax

470. Taxes are divided into two categories, depending on whether they need the legislature's approval every year. These classes are annual taxes and perpetual taxes. The former cannot be levied unless the legislature decides to do so each year, while the latter can be repeatedly levied year after year based on a single approval of the legislature. The Meiji Constitution had expressly adopted the principle of a standing tax by stating, "The taxes levied at present shall, in so far as they are not remodeled by a new law, be collected according to the old system" (Article 63). The Constitution of Japan is also construed to have adopted the principle of a standing tax, although there is no express provision to this effect. However, it is constitutionally possible to adopt an annual tax system in order to strengthen parliamentary control over the State's finances.

§3. Spending Power

I. Principle of Legality

471. Article 85 of the Constitution stipulates, "No money shall be expended, nor shall the State obligate itself, except as authorized by the Diet." To "obligate" itself means to undertake an obligation to pay money. Accordingly, this provision is intended to require that the State have the consent of the Diet when it expends money or acknowledges an obligation. Article 85 does not specify the form which the authorization by the Diet must take. However, it is clear in light of Article 86, that the Diet's authorization of the State's expenditure of money is to be rendered in the form of a budget. However, the Diet's authorization of the State's acknowledgment of an obligation may take two forms: one is a budget and the other is a special law (section 15 and section 22 of the Public Finance Act). For example, an obligation that falls due in a future fiscal year need not be authorized in the form of a budget, which typically applies to the current year. Such obligation is usually in the form of a law passed before the year in which payment is to be made (section 15, paragraph 1). However, a State's debt that becomes due within a fiscal year, such as a temporary loan, is approved within a budget authorized by the Diet. Once included in the budget further approval by the Diet is not required (section 7). The State's acknowledgment of an obligation that cannot be covered within a budget, such as a contract to employ foreigners, a loan to finance the recovery of losses caused by calamities, etc., needs special approval of the Diet in the form of a budget (section 15).

II. Drafting and Decision on a Budget

472. Article 86 of the Constitution states, "The Cabinet shall prepare and submit to the Diet for its consideration and decision a budget for each fiscal year." A budget is an estimate of the State's revenue and expenditure within a fiscal year and is binding on all governmental organs as the working rules of the State. A State can perform its functions only when there is budgetary support. In that sense, a budget, together with the law, comprises an important basis for the governmental activities of the State. It is natural that the Diet, as representative of the people, should have the power to decide on a budget that is the basis for such State activities. Unlike the Meiji Constitution, the Constitution of Japan has strengthened democratic control over public finance based on the principle of popular sovereignty. The Constitution denies the government financial emergency power as stipulated in Article 70 of the Meiji Constitution, places the economy of the Imperial Household under the control of the Diet (Article 88), and eliminates such undemocratic provisions as Article 67 and Article 71 of the Meiji Constitution (*see* §1 of this chapter). Also, although the Meiji Constitution had a provision (Article 68) authorizing the continued expenditure of expenses for a particular project for two or more years (Article 68), the Constitution of Japan does not have a similar provision. However, as the necessity of continued expenditure cannot be denied, the Public Finance Act authorizes continued expenditure within a five-year limit (section 14-2).

473. A budget is drafted by the Cabinet and submitted for Diet consideration and decision by the Prime Minister (Article 73, No. 5, Article 86, Article 72). As mentioned above, a budget is an estimate of the revenue and expenditure for a fiscal year (from April 1 to March 31 of the following year) (section 11 of the Public Finance Act), but in cases where a budget has not been approved before the fiscal year begins, the Cabinet drafts and submits to the Diet a provisional budget for a portion of the fiscal year (section 30, paragraph 1). The provisional budget's effectiveness is lost when the budget for the entire fiscal year has been enacted. However, expenditures and acknowledgment of obligations based on the provisional budget are regarded as effective and are considered made in accordance with the fiscal year budget (section 30, paragraph 1). The Cabinet can also submit a supplementary budget to the Diet. Such supplementary budget may revise, subtract from and/or add to the budget. Usually, supplementary budgets are based on circumstances that arise after the original budget is decided upon (section 29).

474. The power to draft a budget resides in the Cabinet. The Constitution contains no provisions specifying whether the Diet has the power to revise the budget by either increasing or reducing the amount of money requested. However, in light of the fact that the Japanese Constitution does not have a provision such as Article 40 of the Constitution of the Fifth Republic of France (which expressly prohibits the amendment of a budget so as to cause a decrease in revenue and/or an increase in expenditure) and considering that the Public Finance Act contains a provision (section 19) authorizing the Diet to revise (with a condition attached) a budget drafted and submitted by the Cabinet, the majority of scholars in Japan think it proper to interpret the Constitution to allow the Diet to revise the budget. Such a revision must not be so drastic that it obliterates the identity of the budget drafted by the Cabinet. It is considered a better policy for the Diet to reject the whole budget rather than revise it drastically.

III. Budget and Law

475. A budget is approved by the Diet, as is a law. It binds the Cabinet and other governmental organs as the working rules of the State. Therefore, no one can deny that it has the nature of a type of law. There are, however, some differences between budgets and statutes. For example, the maxim "A subsequent law abrogates a prior law" does not apply to budgets.

Accordingly, an approved budget cannot be abolished by a later enacted statute. Also, while a statute is general and abstract and establishes rules to be applied repeatedly, a budget is specific and concrete and applied only once. If both budgets and statutes are considered legal in nature, then they must be reconciled so that they do not contradict each other. For this reason, the United States, Germany and France have adopted a system whereby a budget is enacted in the form of statutes (Article I, section 9, paragraph 7 of the United States Constitution; Article 110, paragraph 2 of the Basic Law of Germany; and Article 47 of the Constitution of the Fifth Republic of France). In Japan, however, the fact that a budget is a type of law has been overlooked, and the approval of the budget is regarded as an executive function. Therefore, the procedures whereby a budget and a statute are adopted are different and have been different ever since the Meiji Constitution was enacted.

IV. Approval of the Expenditure of Reserve Fund

476. Article 87 of the Constitution stipulates, "In order to provide for unforeseen deficiencies in the budget, a reserve fund may be authorized by the Diet to be expended upon the responsibility of the Cabinet" (paragraph 1) and "The Cabinet must get subsequent approval of the Diet for all payments from the reserve fund" (paragraph 2). Although the Meiji Constitution provided for a reserve fund (Article 69), it did not have a provision for the Diet's control over the expenditure of the reserve fund.

The reserve fund system, which is an exception to Article 86 of the Constitution, is designed to provide for the urgent expenditure of relatively small sums of money. Therefore, the Cabinet should draft and submit to the Diet a supplementary or revised budget whenever deficiencies in the budget are relatively large and there is time to proceed with the supplement.

The Public Finance Act provides the procedure for the Diet's subsequent approval of the expenditure of a reserve fund as follows: "The Cabinet must submit to the Diet in ordinary sessions for approval of the general accounts and the accounts of all ministries and administrative bodies paid by a reserve fund" (section 36, paragraph 3). This approval provides a means whereby the Diet may judge the propriety of the expenditures from the reserve fund. Even if the Cabinet cannot obtain such "after-the-fact" Diet approval, the expenditure made from the reserve fund will not lose effect. Needless to say, however, the Cabinet which made the expenditure is politically called to account.

V. Auditing and Examination of Final Accounts

477. Article 90, paragraph 1 of the Constitution stipulates, "Final accounts of the expenditures and revenues of the State shall be audited annually by a Board of Audit and submitted by the Cabinet to the Diet, together with the statement of audit during the fiscal year immediately following the period covered." While a budget is an estimate of expected expenditures and revenues in a fiscal year and is legally binding, final accounts of the expenditures and revenues are general accounts of expenditures and revenues actually executed in a fiscal year and an official statement of accounts which will be the basis for judging whether the State's organs have properly executed the budget. Article 90, paragraph 1 of the Constitution requires that final accounts of the State be audited by the Board of Audit, a special administrative organ of the State, and examined by the Diet.

478. Final accounts are prepared by the Minister of Finance (section 38, paragraph 1 of the Public Finance Act) and sent to the Board of Audit by the Cabinet by November 30 of the following year (section 39). The Board of Audit confirms expenditures and revenues of the State, investigates whether there are illegal or improper expenditures and revenues, and other matters, and reports to the Cabinet in writing (section 29 of the Board of Audit Act). The Cabinet submits final accounts which have undergone examination by the Board of Audit to the Diet in the ordinary session to be convened in the year following the expenditures (section 40 of the Public Finance Act).

The Diet, which has received final accounts of the expenditures and revenues of the State, must clarify whether they are lawful and proper. The purpose of the Diet's examination is to oversee (and, where appropriate, criticize) the Cabinet in charge of (and thus responsible for) the expenditures and revenues of the State. Accordingly, even if the Diet has not approved final accounts of the expenditures and revenues, this does not affect the legal validity of such expenditures and revenues. Rather, such Diet action relates to the Cabinet's political responsibility.

Selected Bibliography

H. Abe, M. Shindo & S. Kawato, *The Government and Politics of Japan* (Translated by J.W. White; University of Tokyo, Tokyo 1994).

L.J. Adams, *Theory, Law and Policy of Contemporary Japanese Treaties* (Oceana Publications Inc., 1974).

H.H. Baerwald, *Japan's Parliament: An Introduction* (Cambridge University Press, London 1974).

G.M. Beckmann, *The Making of the Meiji Constitution: The Oligarchs and the Constitutional Development of Japan, 1868–1891* (Greenwood Press, Westport, Connecticut 1957).

L.W. Beer (ed.), *Constitutionalism in Asia: Asian View of the American Influence* (University of California Press, Berkeley 1979).

L.W. Beer, "Freedom of Expression in Japan with Comparative Reference to the United States," in R.P. Claude (ed.), *Comparative Human Rights* (John Hopkins University Press, Baltimore, Maryland 1976).

L.W. Beer & H. Itoh, *The Constitutional Case Law of Japan, 1970 through 1990* (University of Washington Press, Seattle 1996).

G.L. Curtis, *The Japanese Way of Politics* (Columbia University Press, New York 1988).

J.E. de Becker, *Elements of Japanese Law* (Council of the Asiatic Society of Japan, Yokohama 1916; reprinted University Publications of America, Inc., Washington, D.C. 1979).

G. De Vos & H. Wagatsuma, *Japan's Invisible Race: Caste in Culture and Personality* (University of California, Berkeley 1966).

M. Dean, *Japanese Legal System: Text and Materials* (Cavendish Publishing Limited, London 1997).

S. Fujii, *The Constitution of Japan: A Historical Survey* (Kokushikan University, Tokyo 1965).

K. Fujikura, *Japanese Law and Legal Theory* (New York University Press, 1996).

C.F. Goodman, *The Rule of Law in Japan: A Comparative Analysis* (Kluwer Law International, 2003).

J. Gresser, K. Fujikura & A. Morishima, *Environmental Law in Japan* (The MIT Press, Cambridge, Massachusetts 1981).

J.O. Haley, *Authority Without Power: Law and the Japanese Paradox* (Oxford University Press, New York 1991).

J.O. Haley, *The Spirit of Japanese Law* (University of Georgia Press, 2006).

K. Hayao, *The Japanese Prime Minister and Public Policy* (University of Pittsburgh Press, 1993).
L. Hayes, *Introduction to Japanese Politics*, 6th edn (Routledge, 2017).
G.D. Hook & G. McCormack, *Japan's Contested Constitution: Documents and Analysis* (Routledge, 2001).
IIAS Tokyo Round Table Organizing Committee, *Public Administration in Japan* (International Institute of Administrative Sciences, 1982).
K. Inoue, *MacArthur's Japanese Constitution: A Linguistic and Cultural Study of Its Making* (The University of Chicago Press, Chicago 1991).
H. Ito, *Commentaries on the Constitution of the Empire of Japan* (Translated by M. Ito; Chuo-Daigaku, Tokyo 1906; reprinted Greenwood Press, Westport, Connecticut 1978).
H. Itoh, *The Japanese Supreme Court: Constitutional Policies* (Markus Wiener Publishing Inc., New York 1989).
H. Itoh & L.W. Beer (eds), *The Constitutional Case Law of Japan: Selected Supreme Court Decisions, 1961–70* (University of Washington Press, Seattle 1978).
C.P.A. Jones & F.S. Ravitch, *The Japanese Legal System* (West Academic Publishing, 2018).
C.P.A. Jones & F.S. Ravitch, *The Japanese Legal System in a Nutshell* (West Academic Publishing, 2020).
Local Autonomy College, *Local Government in Japan* (Jichi Kenshu Kyoukai, Tokyo 1981).
P.R. Luney Jr. & K. Takahashi (eds), *Japanese Constitutional Law* (University of Tokyo Press, Tokyo 1993).
J.M. Maki (ed.), *Court and Constitution in Japan: Selected Supreme Court Decisions—1948–60* (University of Washington Press, Seattle 1964).
T. Masujima & M. O'uchi, *The Management and Reform of Japanese Government* (Institute of Administrative Management, 1993).
A.T. von Mehren, *Law in Japan: The Legal Order in a Changing Society* (Harvard University Press, 1963).
C.J. Milhaupt, J.M. Ramseyer & M.D. West, *The Japanese Legal System*, 2nd edn (Foundation Press, 2006).
C.J. Milhaupt, J.M. Ramseyer & M.K. Young, *Japanese Law in Context: Readings in Society, the Economy, and Politics* (Harvard University Press, 2001).
O. Nishi, *Ten Days Inside General Headquarters (GHQ): How the original draft of the Japanese Constitution was written in 1946* (Seibundo Publishing Co. Ltd., Tokyo 1989).
Y. Noda, *Introduction to Japanese Law* (Translated and edited by A.H. Angelo; University of Tokyo Press, Tokyo 1976).
H. Oda, *Japanese Law*, 4th edn (Butterworth, London 2021).
A.C. Oppler, *Legal Reform in Occupied Japan: A Participant Looks Back* (Princeton University Press, Princeton 1976).
L. Pedriza, *Lectures on Japanese Law from a Comparative Perspective* (Osaka University Press, 2017).
K.L. Port, G.P. McAlinn & S. Mehra, *Comparative Law: Law and the Legal Process in Japan*, 3rd edn (Carolina Academic Press, Durham, North Carolina 2015).

J.M. Ramseyer, *Japanese Law: Readings in the Political Economy of Japanese Law* (Ashgate Pub Ltd., 2001).

W. Rohl, *History of Law in Japan Since 1868* (Brill, 2005).

S. Sugai & I. Sonobe, *Administrative Law in Japan* (Gyosei, 1999).

Supreme Commander for the Allied Powers, Government Section, *Political Reorientation of Japan, September 1945 to September 1948*, Vols. I & II (Greenwood Press Publishers, Westport, Conn. 1970; Reprint of United States Government Printing Office, Washington, D.C. 1949).

Supreme Court of Japan, *Series of Prominent Judgments of the Supreme Court upon Questions of Constitutionality*, No. 1–No. 25, (General Secretariat, Supreme Court of Japan, Tokyo 1954–1991).

H. Tanaka (ed.), *The Japanese Legal System: Introductory Cases and Materials* (Translated by M.H. Smith; University of Tokyo Press, Tokyo 1976).

F.E. Upham, *Law and Social Change in Postwar Japan* (Harvard University Press, Cambridge, Massachusetts 1987).

D. Vanoverbeke, et al., *The Changing Role of Law in Japan: Empirical Studies in Culture, Society and Policy Making* (Edward Elgar Publishing, Cheltenham 2014).

R.E. Ward, "The Origins of the Present Constitution," in *American Political Science Review*, Vol. 50 No. 4, pp. 980–1010 (1956).

R.E. Ward (ed.), *Political Development in Modern Japan* (Princeton University Press, Princeton 1968).

R.E. Ward & Y. Sakamoto (eds), *Democratizing Japan: The Allied Occupation* (University of Hawaii Press, Honolulu 1987).

J. Williams Sr., "Making the Japanese Constitution: A Further Look," in *American Political Science Review*, Vol. 59 No. 3, pp. 665–679 (1965).

Y. Yanagida, et al., *Law and Investment in Japan: Cases and Materials*, 2nd edn (Harvard University Press, 2000).

Y. Zhang, *Comparative Studies on the Judicial Review System in East and Southeast Asia* (Kluwer Law International, 1997).

Y. Zhang, *Comparative Studies on Governmental Liability in East and Southeast Asia* (Kluwer Law International, 1999).

Index

The numbers here refer to paragraph numbers.

www.ingramcontent.com/pod-product-compliance
Lightning Source LLC
Chambersburg PA
CBHW071440230926
51846CB00001B/297
9789403546087